# BABY

## *Bargains*

### SECRETS

**to saving 20% to 50% on baby furniture, equipment, clothes, toys, maternity wear and much, much more!**

*Denise and Alan Fields*
**WINDSOR PEAK PRESS**

*The Credits*
Saxophone, lead guitar and breastfeeding by Denise Fields
Drums, diaper funk and general widespread panic by Alan Fields
Grandparents played by Max & Helen Coopwood, Howard & Patti Fields
Babysitting and harmony vocals by Margot Voorhies and Katy McDougall
Pre-natal care and screaming guitar solo by Dr. Peter Ewing
Bagels by Moe's Broadway Bagel (we deserve a free t-shirt for this plug).
High-octane latté by Bean's of Boulder

Another incredibly creative cover design by Hugh Anderson of Archetype
Copy editing and maternal insight by Lisa Fleck
Cute smile by Meg Hardick
Icon management and wah-wah sounds by Karen Groves
Printer rep and barbecue appreciation by Steve Brandenberg
Marketing karma and expert funk by Mark Ouimet

Inspirational Songs
"Tennessee Plates" by John Hiatt
"Last Dance with Mary Jane" by Tom Petty & The Heartbreakers
Anything by Ric Ocasek and/or the Cars—here's hoping for a reunion.
God Bless the Bare Naked Ladies.

Special Thanks to our experts panel of juvenile products retailers—your
insights were invaluable.

More Special Thanks to Barb Koster, John Stehr and Deborah Copaken. We
greatly appreciate your support.

Distributed to the book trade and Jupiter by Publisher's Group West, 4065 Hollis St., Emeryville, CA 94608. 1-800-788-3123. Thanks to the entire staff of PGW for their support.

To order this book, call 1-800-888-0385. Or send $11.95 plus $3 shipping to Windsor Peak Press, 1223 Peakview Circle, Boulder, CO 80302. Questions or comments? Please call the authors at (303) 442-8792. Or fax them a note at (303) 442-3744. Or write to them at the above address in Boulder, CO.

Library Cataloging in Publication Data

Fields, Denise 1964-
Fields, Alan 1965-
    Baby Bargains: Secrets to saving 20% to 50% on baby furniture, equipment, clothes, toys maternity wear and much, much more/ Denise & Alan Fields
    256 pages.
    Includes index.
    ISBN 0-9626556-4-3
    1. Child Care—Handbooks, manuals, etc. 2. Infants' supplies—
Purchasing—United States, Directories. 3. Children's paraphernalia—
Purchasing—Handbooks, manuals. 4. Product Safety—Handbooks, manuals. 5. Consumer education.
    649'.122'0296—dc20.          1995.

# Contents

## Chapter 3

### Baby Bedding

## Chapter 4

### The Reality Layette: Little Clothes for Little Prices

## Chapter 5

### Maternity/Nursing Clothes & Breastfeeding

# Chapter 6

## Around the House: Baby Monitors, Toys, Bath, Foods, High Chairs, and Swings

# Chapter 7

## Places to Go! Car Seats, Strollers, Carriers & More

## Chapter 8

### Affordable Baby Proofing

## Chapter 9

### The Best Gifts for Baby

## Chapter 10

### The Best Books for Baby & You

## Chapter 11

### Do it By Mail: The Best Mail-order Catalogs for Clothes, Baby Products, and More

# Chapter 12

## Conclusion: What Does It All Mean?

# The Icons and What They Mean

 Sources

 The Name Game

 When do We Need this Stuff

 Do it by Mail

 What Are You Buying?

 Safe and Sound

Wastes of Money

 Smart Shopper Tips

 Money Saving Tips

 Spotlight on Best Buys

 Bottom Line

 Factoids

# Chapter 1

## "It's Going to Change Your Life"

That had to be the silliest comment we heard while we were pregnant with our first baby. Believe it or not, we even heard this refrain more often than "Do you want a boy or a girl?" and "I'm sorry. Your insurance doesn't cover that." For the friends and relatives of first-time parents out there, we'd really like to point out that this a pretty stupid thing to say. Of course, we knew that a baby was going to change our lives. What we didn't realize was how much a baby was going to change our pocketbook.

Oh sure, we knew that we'd have to buy triple our weight in diapers and be subjected to dangerously high levels of Barney. What we didn't expect was the endless pitches for cribs, bedding, toys, clothing, and other items parents are required to purchase by FEDERAL BABY LAW.

We quickly learned that having a baby is like popping on the Juvenile Amusement Park Ride from Consumer Hell. Once that egg is fertilized, you're whisked off to the Pirates of the Crib ride. Then it's off to marvel at the little elves in StrollerLand, imploring you to buy brands with names you can't pronounce. Finally, you take a trip to Magic Car Seat Mountain, where the salespeople are so real, it's scary.

Consider us your tour guides—the Yogi Bear to your Boo Boo Bear, the Fred to your Ethyl, the . . . well, you get the idea. Before we enter BabyLand, let's take a look at the Four Truths That No One Tells You About Buying Stuff For Baby.

### The Four Truths That No One Tells You About Buying Stuff for Baby

1 BABIES DON'T CARE IF THEY'RE WEARING DESIGNER CLOTHES OR SLEEPING ON DESIGNER SHEETS. Let's be realistic. Babies just want to be comfortable. They can't even distinguish between the liberals and conservatives on CNN's "Crossfire," so how would they ever be able to tell the difference between Laura Ashley crib bedding and another less famous brand that's just as comfortable, but 50% less expensive? Our focus is on making your baby happy—at a price that won't break the bank.

2 Your baby's safety is more important than your convenience. Here are the scary facts: 70,000 babies per year are injured by juvenile products, according to government estimates. Each chapter of this book has a section called "Safe & Sound," which arms you with in-depth advice on keeping your baby out of trouble. We'll tell you which products we think are dangerous and how to safely use other potentially hazardous products.

3 Murphy's Law of Baby Toys says your baby's happiness with a toy is inversely related to the toy's price. Buy a $200 shiny new wagon with anti-lock brakes, and odds are baby just wants to play with your keys. In recognition of this reality, we've included "wastes of money" in each chapter that will steer you away from the money pits.

4 It's going to cost more than you think. Whatever amount of money you budget for your baby, get ready to spend more. Here's a breakdown of the average costs of bringing a baby into the world today:

---

## *The Average Cost of Having a Baby*

*(based on industry estimates for
a child from birth to age one)*

| | |
|---|---|
| Crib, dresser, changing table, rocker | $1500 |
| Bedding | $ 250 |
| Baby Clothes | $ 500 |
| Disposable Diapers | $ 800 |
| Maternity/Nursing Clothes | $1300 |
| Nursery items, high chair, toys | $ 400 |
| Baby Food | $ 300 |
| Stroller, Car Seat, Carrier | $ 200 |
| Miscellaneous | $ 500 |
| **TOTAL** | **$5750** |

*Note: The above figures are based on buying name brand products at regular retail prices. The numbers above don't include prenatal care, the medical bills from the actual delivery, or day-care expenses—sorry, that's all extra. Baby food is based on an assumption that you'd breastfeed the baby for six months and then feed solid foods until age one. If you plan to use formula instead of breastfeeding, add $500 to the baby food figure.*

---

## Reality Check: Does it Really Cost that Much to Have a Baby?

 No, you can spend less. And that's what this book is all about: how to save money and still buy the best for your baby.

Follow all the tips in this book, and we estimate the above items will cost you $3625. Yes, that's a savings of over $2000!

Now, at this point, you might be saying "No way! I suppose you'll recommend buying all the cheap stuff, from polyester clothes to no-name cribs." On the contrary, we'll show you how to get the same quality name brands at discount prices. For example, we've got outlets and catalogs that sell all-cotton clothing at 20% to 40% off retail. You'll discover a mail-order company that discounts brand new, designer-brand bedding by 20% to 25%. You'll even learn how to get a name-brand car seat at its wholesale cost. And much more. Yes, we've got the maximum number of bargains allowed by federal law.

## What? There's no advertising in this book?

Yes, it's true. This book contains zero percent advertising. We have never taken any money to recommend a product or company and never will. We make our sole living off the sales of this and other books. (So, when your friend asks to borrow this copy, have them buy their own book!) Our publisher, Windsor Peak Press, also derives its sole income from the sale of this book and our other publications. No company recommended in this book paid any consideration or was charged any fee to be mentioned in it. As consumer advocates, we believe this ensures our objectivity. The opinions in the book are just that—our opinions and the opinions of the parents we interviewed.

Please note that the prices quoted in this book were accurate as of the date of publication. While the publisher makes every effort to ensure their accuracy, errors and omissions may exist. That's why we've established a phone line where you can talk directly to us: call (303) 442-8792 to ask a question, report a mistake, or just give us your thoughts. You can also write to us—here's our address: Denise & Alan Fields, "Baby Bargains," 1223 Peakview Circle, Suite 700, Boulder, CO 80302.

Of course, the prices quoted in this book may change at any time. Inflation and other factors may affect the actual prices you discover in shopping for your baby.

## So, who are you guys?

First off, we should tell you we're no Martha Stewart. This book does not contain instructions on how to hand-build a crib from twigs and tree branches.

Nope, we're just average folks like you. Our first book was BRIDAL BARGAINS, which was inspired by our experience planning our own wedding. One day we had a revelation that young couples like us had better things to do with their money than waste it on weddings costing the equivalent of the Federal Deficit. (This revelation came at the same time we realized that our job prospects upon graduating from college were somewhere between "Slim" and "None." And "Slim" had just left town.)

So we wrote a book. And then one day a producer from the "Oprah Winfrey" show called us. "Would you like to be on the Oprah Show?" Shazam! Suddenly, the book was a best-seller, with more than 100,000 copies sold in just three years. And, just as quick, we were now "bargain experts." This was a curious situation for us, for while we love to find bargains and save money, the only topic on which we would have truly considered ourselves experts at the time was which flavor of Ben & Jerry's ice cream had the most chocolate chunks. Of course, we quickly learned that being book authors beats having to find a real job.

So, here we are. Our first baby, Benjamin, was born October 1, 1993. And about the same time, we got a lesson in Modern Health Care Economics. Since we're self-employed, we quickly learned we were going to be saddled with BIG bills from Ben's prenatal care and delivery. Our health insurance company, No Cross and No Shield, has a special plan for book authors: they pay 2%, we pay 98% As quick as you could say "co-payment deductible," we were facing prenatal and delivery bills that topped $5000. As you can see, hunting for bargains for our baby was more than just a passing interest.

This book is more than just our experience shopping for cribs, clothing, and the like.We interviewed over 100 new parents—and learned about their experiences with products, which items were a waste of time, and how to save money. Finally, we consulted with veteran retailers of baby products and furniture. We discovered which brands are the most reliable and why certain products fly off the shelf.

Add all these ingredients together, throw in some wisdom from new moms and dads, bake for several months, and voila! You've got a book. We hope you enjoy it.

## *Let's go shopping!*

 Now that all the formal introductions are done, let's move on to the good stuff. As your tour guides to BabyLand, we'd like to remind you of a few park rules before you go:

1 NO FEEDING THE SALESPEOPLE. Remember, the juvenile products industry is a $3.5 BILLION DOLLAR business. While all those baby stores may want to help you, they are first and foremost in business to make a profit. As a consumer, you should arm yourself with the knowledge necessary to make smart decisions. If you do, you won't be taken for a ride.

2 KEEP YOUR PERSPECTIVE INSIDE THE CAR AT ALL TIMES. With all the hormones coursing through the veins of the average pregnant woman, now is not the time to lose it. As you visit baby stores, don't get caught in the hype of the latest doo-dad that converts a car seat to a toaster.

3 HAVE A GOOD TIME. Oh sure, sifting through all those catalogs of crib bedding and convertible strollers will frazzle your mind. Just remember the goal is to have a healthy baby—so, take care of yourself first and foremost.

How will you know you're at the end of the ride? When you see your baby smile for the first time.

# Chapter 2

## Nursery Necessities: Cribs, Dressers and More

How can you save 20% to 50% off cribs, dressers, and other furniture for your baby's room? In this chapter, you'll learn how, plus you'll discover the seven smart shopper tips to getting the most for your money. Then, you'll learn which juvenile furniture has safety problems and a toll-free number you can call to get the latest recall info. Next, we'll rate and review the thirteen top brands for cribs and spotlight two baby store chains that offer unbelievably low prices. Finally, you'll learn which crib mattress is best, how to get a deal on a dresser, and five more items you'll want for your baby's room.

### Getting Started: When Do You Need This Stuff?

So, you want to buy a crib for Junior? And, what the heck, why not some other furniture, like a dresser to store all those baby gifts and a changing table for, well, you know. Just pop down to the store, pick out the colors, and set a delivery date, right?

Not so fast, o' new parental one. Once you get to that baby store, you'll discover that most stores don't have all those nice cribs and furniture in stock. No, that would be too easy, wouldn't it? You quickly learn that you get to *special order* all that booty. (Baby trivia note: What's the difference between an order and a *special* order? A special order takes twice as long and costs three times more than a regular order.)

Most baby specialty stores told us it takes four to six weeks to order most brands. And here's the shocker: some imported cribs can take 12 to 16 weeks. It's hard to believe that it takes this long for companies to ship a simple crib or dresser—we're not talking space shuttle parts here. The way it's going, you'll soon have to order the crib before you conceive.

Obviously, this policy is more for the benefit of the retailer than the consumer. Most baby stores are small operations and they tell us that stocking up on cribs, dressers, and the like means an expensive investment in inventory and storage space. Frankly, we could care less. Why you can't get a crib in a week or less is one of the mysteries of modern retailing that will have to be left to future generations to solve. What if you don't have that much time? There are a couple of solutions: some stores sell floor models and others actually keep a limited number of styles in stock. Discounters (Target, Toys R Us, and others) stock cribs—the only downside is that while the price is low, often so is the quality.

An idea given to us by one new mother: don't buy the crib until after the baby is born. The infant can sleep in a bassinet or cradle for the first few weeks or even months, and you can get the furniture later. (This may be an option for the superstitious who don't want to buy all this stuff until the baby is actually born.) The downside to waiting? The last thing you'll want to do with your newborn infant is go furniture shopping. There'll be many other activities (such as sleep deprivation experiments) to occupy your time.

So, when should you make a decision on the crib and other furniture for the baby's room? We recommend you place your order in the sixth or seventh month of your pregnancy. By that time, you're pretty darned sure you're having a baby, and the order will arrive several weeks before the birth. (The exception: if your heart is set on an imported crib, you may have to order in your fourth or fifth month to ensure arrival before Junior is born).

## Cribs

### Sources: Where to Shop

There are four basic sources for finding a crib, each with its own advantages and drawbacks:

1 BABY SPECIALITY STORES. Baby specialty stores are pretty self-explanatory—shops that specialize in the retailing of baby furniture, strollers, and accessories. Some also sell clothing, car seats, swings, and so on. While there are a few large chains (later in this chapter, we review one of the priciest, Bellini), most are small mom-and-pop operations. *Thumbs up*: specialty stores have a good selection of the best name brands. Generally, you get good service—most stores have knowledgeable staffers (usually the owner or manager) who can answer questions. We also like the extra services, like set-up and delivery. *Thumbs down*: You're gonna pay for that service with high prices—sky high in some cases. Later, we'll give you some money-saving tips if you want to go this route.

**2** DISCOUNTERS/DEPARTMENT STORES. Big stores like Target, Sears, and Toys R Us carry cribs, albeit with a very small selection. You'll see lower-end brands (like Cosco's metal cribs) and no-name imports. Prices are low, but so is the quality. Delivery and set-up? Forget it; you're often on your own. Another negative: the salespeople (if you can find any) often seem to have the IQ of a rutabaga.

**3** MAIL-ORDER CATALOGS. Yes, you can order a crib from mail-order catalogs. J.C. Penney (800-222-6161) has several catalogs with baby furniture, accessories, maternity wear, and more (check out the review of Penney's catalog in Chapter 11 for more information). The prices aren't that bad—we noticed a Child Craft "sculpted" crib in white maple with a single drop side for $229. Other brand names available include Welsh, Cosco, and Bassett. Of course, if you go mail order, you have to set up the crib yourself. Most mail-order prices are about the same as regular retail, making this more of an option for those who live in remote areas or in a town where the local baby stores are charging sky-high prices for name brands.

**4** BABY MEGA-STORES. In the past few years, a new breed of baby store has emerged as a very attractive alternative to specialty stores: the mega-store. With huge stores that top 30,000 square feet, mega-stores combine the best of both worlds: a good selection of the best brand names AND discount prices. And those prices are hard to beat—sometimes 20% to 40% below retail. We review two of the best mega-stores, LiL' Things and Baby Superstore, later in this section under "Best Buys." Service at the baby mega-stores is variable—some have knowledgeable staffers who can answer questions and others at least tag their cribs and furniture with information on features, accessories, and color options.

## *What Are You Buying?*

 While you'll see all kinds of fancy juvenile furniture at baby stores, focus on the items that you really need. First and foremost is a crib, of course. Mattresses are sold separately, as you might expect, so you'll need one of those. Another nice item is a dresser or chest to hold clothes, bibs, wash cloths, etc. A changing table is an optional accessory; some parents just use the crib for this (although that can get messy) or buy a combination dresser and changing table. Some dressers have a removable changing table on top, while others have a "flip top": a hinged shelf that folds up when not in use.

So, how much is this going to cost you? Crib prices start at $80 to $100 for an inexpensive metal crib. A crib made of wood by such popular manufacturers as Simmons and Child Craft (see reviews later in this chapter) start at about $150 and go up to $350. Super-expensive import brands can range from $400 to $600—Bellini (the chain of exclusive baby stores that sells its own cribs—see review later) has cribs that top out at $700!

Fortunately, mattresses for cribs aren't that expensive. Basic mattresses start at about $40 and go up to $100 for fancy varieties. Later in this chapter, we'll have a special section on mattresses that includes tips on what to buy and how to save money.

Dressers and changing tables (known in the baby business as case pieces) have prices that are all over the board. A basic four-drawer dresser from Child Craft is around $280, while Simmons prices this item at $330 to $350. If you want a "flip-top" dresser/changing table combination, expect to spend another $50 to $100. A separate changing table can start at $100 and go up to $300 for fancy models. With the expensive import brands, the sky is the limit on case pieces. We've seen five-drawer dressers by the Canadian manufacturer Ragazzi top out at $750! If you want to go all out, Ragazzi even has an armoire for baby at a whopping $1000.

So, you can see that your quest for a crib, mattress, dresser, and changing table could cost you as little as $300 or more than $1000.

## Smart Shopper Tips

 **Smart Shopper Tip #1**
SMART SHOPPER TIP #1
BEWARE OF "BABY BUYING FRENZY."

*"I went shopping with my friend at a baby store last week, and she just about lost it. She started buying all kinds of fancy accessories and items that didn't seem that necessary. First there was a $50 womb sound generator and finally the $75 Star Trek Diaper Changing Docking Station. There was no stopping her. The salespeople were egging her on—it was quite a sight. Should we have just taken her out back and hosed her down?"*

Yes, you probably should have. Your friend has come down with a severe case of what we call Baby Buying Frenzy—that overwhelming emotional tug to buy all kinds of stuff for Junior. And baby stores know all about this disease and do their darnedest to capitalize on it. Check out this quote from *Juvenile Merchandising* (October 1993) advising salespeople on how to sell to expectant parents: "It's surprising how someone who is making a purchase (for baby) sometimes can be led into a buying frenzy." No kidding. Some stores encourage their staff by giving them bonuses for every second item sold to a customer. Be wary of stores that try to do this, referred to in the trade as "building the ticket." Remember what you came to buy and don't get caught up in the hype.

## Smart Shopper Tip #2
GET IT DELIVERED AND SET-UP.

*"My wife and I thought we'd save some money buying an unassembled crib and putting it together ourselves. Big mistake. Five hours later, the crib wasn't set up, and we were missing a part that had to be special ordered from Tanzania."*

Yes, it costs extra to have a crib delivered and set up (about $25 to $50 in most cities). But the cost may be worth it. We've spoken to folks who actually deliver and set up cribs for a living, and they tell us stories of cribs that are often missing crucial parts. Even for name brands, you may discover a missing screw here or a defective part there. We'd prefer to let someone else deal with this hassle.

Of course, putting a crib together isn't exactly rocket science. And cribs from mail-order catalogs always come unassembled. If you don't live near a baby store or department store that delivers, mail-order may be the only option, and you'll have no choice but to set up the crib yourself.

Another side issue: sales taxes. If you live outside a city, the savings in sales tax may pay for the delivery and set-up. Why? When you purchase an item for delivery, you're only charged the sales tax rate where you live, not where the store is. For example, the nearest city to us has a 6.75% sales tax. Yet we live just outside the city in a county that has a 4.05% sales tax rate. On a $350 crib and a $300 dresser, you'd save about $20. That nearly covers the delivery and set-up fee at many baby stores. Mail-order purchases are even a better deal—in most states, purchase an item from a mail-order catalog and you don't have to pay any sales tax.

## Smart Shopper Tip #3
THE ART AND SCIENCE OF SELECTING THE RIGHT CRIB.

*"How do you evaluate a crib? They all look the same to me. What really makes one different from another?"*

Yes, selecting a good crib is more than just picking out the color and finish. You should look under the hood, so to speak. Here are our seven key points to look for when shopping for a crib:

♣ *Mattress Support.* Look underneath that mattress and see what is holding it up. You might be surprised. Some lower-end cribs use cheap vinyl straps. Others use metal bars. One crib we saw actually had a cardboard deck holding up the mattress—boy, that looked real comfortable for baby. The best option: a set of springs that provides both mattress support and a springy surface to stand on when Junior gets older. Remember, your infant won't just lay there for long. Soon, Junior will be standing up in the crib, jumping up and down, and causing general mayhem.

♣ *Ease of Release.* At least one side of the crib has a railing that lowers down so you can pick up your baby. How easily this locking mechanism release varies widely from crib to crib. Some just have a hand release, but most require you to lift up the side while depressing a foot bar. We suggest trying it out several times. Do you need more than one hand? Is the foot mechanism easy to use? One mother complained to us about how loud many crib locking mechanisms are. If you're putting a sleeping baby to bed, the last thing you need is a crib side that locks into place with a loud CLANK! Unfortunately, crib makers have yet to figure out how to make silent release mechanism for the side rail.

♣ *Mattress Height Adjustment.* Most cribs have several height levels for the mattress—you use the highest setting when the baby is a newborn. Once she starts pulling up, you adjust the mattress to the lowest level so she won't be able to punt herself over the railing. Cheaper cribs use a screw system—you adjust the mattress by loosening a screw on each of the four posts. The problem: the holes can become stripped, weakening the support system.

A better system is a series of hooked brackets—the mattress lays on top of springs, anchored to the crib frame by hooked brackets. Child Craft uses this system, and we believe it provides superior mattress support and safety—there's even a little catch to prevent a sibling from getting under the crib and pushing the mattress upward. While Simmons has a similar system, it's missing that little catch. As a result, you can accidently dislodge the mattress by pushing up from the bottom—a potential death trap if Junior's got (or will have) adventurous siblings.

♣ *How stable is the crib?* Go ahead and abuse that crib set up in the baby store. Push it and see if it wobbles. Wobbling is not good. Most cribs we recommend are quite stable. The cribs with a drawer under the mattress are the most stable. Unfortunately, all this extra stability comes at a price. Bellini's cribs have a drawer. . . and a price tag of $500 to $600.

♣ *Check those casters.* Metal are much better than plastic. We also prefer wide casters to those thin, disk-shaped wheels. You'll be wheeling this crib around more than you think—to change the sheets, to move away from a drafty part of the room, etc. One solution: if you find a good buy on a crib that has cheap casters, you can easily replace them. Hardware stores sell the good, thick, metal casters for $10 to $20—or less.

♣ *How easy is it to assemble?* Ask to see those instructions—most stores should have a copy lying around. Make sure it's not in Greek.

♣ *Compare the overall safety features of the crib.* In a section later in this book, we discuss crib safety in more detail.

## The Name Game: Reviews of Selected Manufacturers

 Here is a look at some of the best known brand names for cribs. As you might have guessed, there are over 100 companies in the U.S. that manufacture and/or import cribs. Because of space limitations, we can't review each one, so we decided to concentrate on the best and most common brand names. If you've discovered a brand that we didn't review, feel free to share your discovery by calling us at (303) 442-8792.

How did we evaluate the brands? First, we looked at samples of cribs at retail stores. With the help of veteran juvenile furniture retailers, we checked construction, release mechanisms, mattress support, and overall fit and finish.

Then we stood back and asked the question, "Would we put our baby in this crib?" We checked safety features and inquired about delivery schedules. Of course, we also evaluated the prices and how that compared to the competition. To supplement our own field research, we also interviewed dozens of new parents about their cribs. What did they like? Which cribs held up to real world baby abuse? Our highest ratings went to cribs that combined good quality with affordable prices.

We should note that the following ratings apply only to cribs. You'll see these same name brands on a myriad of other products, including "case goods" (dressers, changing tables, etc.), crib mattresses, high chairs, rockers, and much more. Of course, just because a company makes a great crib at an affordable price doesn't necessarily mean that their dressers or rockers are good deals. Later in this chapter, we'll take a look at crib mattresses and the "name game" for case goods.

# *The Ratings*

★★★★  EXCELLENT—*our top pick!*
  ★★★  GOOD—*above average quality, prices, and creativity.*
  ★★  FAIR—*could stand some improvement.*
  ★  POOR—*yuck! could stand some major improvement.*

*Bassett* .............................................................................★★
*Main Street, Bassett, VA 24055. ( 703) 629-6000.* Bassett cribs are sold to stores in large truckloads; hence, you're more likely to see them at chain stores like Sears and J.C. Penney. In fact, Penney's catalog features several Bassett models, including a white contemporary design with curved headboard for $180. And that's Bassett's key advantage—a pretty good crib at an affordable price. Some Bassett cribs can be had for as little as $150. *Consumer Reports* ranked Bassett third overall (based on convenience and durability factors) in their May 1993 report. The two top-ranked crib makers (Child Craft and Simmons) are generally higher in price. As for safety, we thought the Bassett cribs we saw were passable, but the mattress support bracket could use some beefing up. Another negative: it's also difficult to get replacement parts from the company.

*Bellini* ..........................................................................★★¹/₂
*2216 Agate Ct., Unit A, Simi Valley, CA 93065. (800) 332-BABY (2229) or (805) 520-0974.* Bellini's cribs are sold exclusively in Bellini stores. And that's a good thing, because when you consider the prices they're charging, it's doubtful they'd sell anywhere else. And just how expensive are these cribs? Well, prices *start* at $425 and range up to an astronomical $705. At that price, we expect the cribs to be works of art with side rails that are gilded in platinum or some other exotic metal. Sadly, they're just made out of wood. And the styling, surprisingly, is rather conservative—contemporary but hardly exciting. For example, the Fabio (no, not that Fabio) features an arched, oval headboard. That's it. Price: $620! At least, for that price you do get a drawer under the crib mattress (useful for storing silver spoons, we suppose). The drawer helps stabilize the crib, which offers greater safety.

An embarrassing glitch with one of Bellini's release mechanisms led *Consumer Reports* to "not recommend" the Bellini Alessandro (also known as the Alessio) crib in 1993, highly ironic considering their high prices and Bellini's brochures, which are splashed with verbiage touting their safety tips. (To be fair, Bellini claims to have fixed the problem and no longer makes that model crib). Bellini's brochures also claim that all their furniture is "European-crafted," but when pressed, a salesperson admitted to us that the products are only designed in Italy (the manufacturing actually occurs in North Carolina and Canada, which at last check were not part of Europe).

We realize we are being somewhat harsh, but for the price, we expect a lot. On the upside, fans of Bellini cite the stores' superior service as a good selling point. And, we discovered that the prices on other items in the Bellini store (strollers, for example) can be very competitively priced—depending on the market. In Los Angeles, the Bellini store was very price competitive with discounters. That was not true in Austin, Texas, where the Bellini store faces little competition and is priced accordingly. The lesson: shop carefully.

*Child Craft* .................................................................★★★★
*PO Box 444, Salem, IN 47167. (812) 883-3111.* This is our favorite brand for cribs—and after you shop the competition, we think you'll agree. We like Child Craft for three reasons—styling, safety, and price. The designs (all in wood) run the gamut from contemporary to traditional. For example, we liked the "Sculptures" line with a curved headboard ($229). The safety features are top notch—the mattress height adjustment/locking system is the best on the market. The simple release mechanism (with a foot bar) is easy to use. Best of all, you get a stylish and safe crib at a very reasonable price. Retail prices range from $230 to $400—but we've seen a single-drop side Child Craft for as low as $150 at LiL' Things (see review later in this chapter). Delivery takes 12 to 16 weeks on most orders. If we had one complaint about Child Craft, it would have to be that the company still markets Crib N Beds ($400 to $550), combination crib/youth beds with attached dressers. In our opinion, all these products should be withdrawn from the market for safety reasons (see the Safe & Sound section later in this chapter for more details). Nonetheless, we still like Child Craft and pick them as one of the best crib makers in the country.

*Cosco* .................................................................★★
*2525 State St., Columbus, IN 47201. (812) 372-0141.* Cosco's claim to fame is their very inexpensive metal cribs. In fact, we saw these cribs for as low as $78 at discount stores (retail prices are $100 to $200). But what do you get for that money? Not much, as it turns out. Like most metal cribs, the mattress doesn't rest on a set of springs but instead sits on a series of straps or metal bars, which is inadequate in our opinion. The welding of the joints looks sloppy, and the mattress height adjustment mechanism consists of a metal bar that screws into the side post. The problem? Those screws can strip

and the mattress could conceivably disconnect from the frame. Our advice: spend some extra money to get a basic wood crib with a spring mattress support and better safety features. Cosco does have an outlet store (with savings of up to 50%) that sells cribs as well as many of the other products they manufacture (see the section "Outlets" later in this chapter).

*Delta* .................................................................................★¹/₂
*175 Liberty Ave., Brooklyn, NY 11212. (718) 385-1000.*
Imported from Indonesia, Delta makes a crib that looks like a knock-off of Bellini's Fabio with an oval-shaped headboard. This double-drop side crib is made of "Ramin wood with a white finish" (we're not quite sure what Ramin wood is) and a hand-release side mechanism. Cost: $269. Our biggest complaint with Delta—the crib's mattress rests on a wood platform, instead of bed springs.

*Million Dollar Baby* ..................................................................★
*855 Washington Blvd., Montebell, CA. (800) 282-3886 or (213) 722-2288.* We just didn't like these cheap imported cribs. One Jenny Lind-style crib at a discount store was about $140. In our opinion, construction was just barely passable— we noted that the crib didn't seem very stable when we shook it. We recommend you pass on this brand.

*Morigeau.* .........................................................................★★ ¹/₂
*2625 Rossmoor Dr., Pittsburgh, PA 15241. (800) 326-2121 or (412) 942-3583.* Based in Quebec, Canada, this family-run juvenile furniture company has been in business for 50 years. Their pricey cribs are quite stylish, with a basic Shaker sensibility. Morigeau cribs run $400 to $500, while a five-drawer dresser topped $579. The cribs (which have just two mattress levels) have a weird locking mechanism that we found awkward. On the upside, Morigeau sells a wide assortment of accessories, including coordinating desks, armoirs, and even baby entertainment centers. As for the finishes, we thought the white looked the best (the whitewash was a loser). Morigeau is mainly available through baby specialty stores.

*Okla Homer Smith* ...............................................................★ ¹/₂
*416 S. 5th St., PO Box 1148, Ft. Smith, AR 72902. (501) 783-6191.* This mass market brand is available in many stores and through the J.C. Penney catalog. On the upside, the cribs come with optional under-mattress drawers, which make the cribs more stable. For example, the Nod-A-Way single-drop side crib sells for $199 in the Penney's catalog (the drawers are $80 extra). Frankly, we weren't very impressed by this

crib—it was made of pine, a soft wood that tends to scratch and nick easily (we prefer hard woods like maple and oak for cribs—they wear better). Also, the "Nod-A-Way" scored dead last in *Consumer Reports* recent crib survey, which cited "difficult to release drop-sides." We should note that in the same survey, a Okla Homer Smith crib made for Sears (model number 37017, $159 plus shipping) was rated much higher. The bottom line: you can find a higher-quality single-drop side crib made by Child Craft or Simmons for the same price at most discount stores.

*Pali* ..........................................................................★★★
*Imported by R. Levine Distributor, 107 E. Farnham, Wheaton, IL 60187. (708) 690-6143.* Italian-made Pali cribs enjoy a good reputation for two reasons: quality and delivery. The contemporary-styled cribs feature better than average construction and safety features. We saw a Pali crib at LiL' Things that featured an under-mattress drawer for $249. Shipping from their Illinois-based distributor takes only six weeks or so—not bad for a foreign-made crib.

*Ragazzi* ....................................................... ★★ $^1/_2$
*8965 Pascal Gagnon, St. Leonard, Quebec H1P 1Z4. (514) 324-7886.* This Canadian import features very adult-looking furniture at very-adult prices. Cribs run a whopping $469 to $510, while a five-drawer dresser will set you back an amazing $749. Ragazzi's claim to fame is their two-tone wood finishes in contemporary colors (forest green, a deep burgundy, etc.). The base of the dresser is a natural finish wood, with the knobs and top finished in color. While we liked the look, we wondered if it was a bit too faddish. As for the crib itself, the side-rail release mechanism was somewhat difficult to use. We also didn't like the mattress height adjustment system, which had metal straps that screwed to the side post (unusual for this price level). If you like the look but want to spend less money, we noted that the Baby Superstore (see below) sells knock-off versions of Ragazzi made by Lullabye and Norcrist (their five-drawer dressers with two-tone finishes ran $289 to $309).

*Simmons* ..................................................★★★ $^1/_2$
*613 E. Beacon Ave., New London, WI 54961. (414) 982-2140.* Another high-quality maker of cribs, Wisconsin-based Simmons makes an incredibly wide variety of styles and designs. In fact, we counted nearly 30 coordinating sets of cribs, dressers, and other furniture! One design that caught our eye was the Camden, a sleigh-style crib with Queen Anne,

turned spindles. Like many Simmons cribs, this is available in cherry, white, and aspen white finishes. The price: $389 at a discount store (Baby Superstore). If that's too much, simpler designs start at $180 and run to $300. The Matino, for example, features a "contemporary maple design with arced top and tapered spindles." A single-drop side version of this crib was just $179 at LiL' Things. The safety features of Simmons cribs are good, but we wish the mattress locked into place when the height is adjusted. Another gripe: the "spring release knob" mechanism on Simmons' Victoria, Chatham, Camden, and Salerno cribs is difficult to use and hard to find parts for (according to retailers we interviewed). On the upside, Simmons cribs are widely available, at both pricey specialty shops and discount stores. Delivery takes 12 to 16 weeks. One interesting trivia note: one of the original owners of the company was Thomas Alva Edison, of light bulb fame.

*Tracers* ........................................................................★★ ½
*30 Warren Place, Mt. Vernon, NY 10550. (914) 668-9372.* This crib brand was highly rated by *Consumer Reports*, but we think they're slightly wrong on this one. One style of Tracers cribs is made from plastic and molded wood, giving it a contemporary feel. Although the hardware is good, we've heard reports from retailers that the the cribs' finish cracks and chips. We also didn't like the metal straps that hold up the mattress and the side rails with no teething guards. Tracer's single-drop side crib is rather pricey, retailing for $350 to $375 (though we saw it on sale for as little as $200 in one store). On the upside, Tracers wood cribs are much better quality—similar to Bellini, but more affordable.

*Welsh* .............................................................................. ★★
*1535 S. 8th St., St. Louis, MO 63104. (314) 231-8822.* If you like traditional styling, you'll like Welsh. This St. Louis-based company churns out cribs with turned spindles and basic finishes like cherry and oak. A single-drop side crib runs $239— about middle of the road as far as pricing goes. Other models go for as little $100. We saw this brand more at department stores than at speciality shops.

## Safe & Sound: Safety Tips and Advice

 Here's a little fact to make you sleep better at night: cribs are associated with more children's deaths than any other juvenile product. That's right, number one. In the latest year for which statistics are available, over 13,000 injuries and 50 deaths were blamed on cribs.

Now, before you get all excited, let's point out that many

injuries were caused by old cribs. Surprisingly, these old cribs may not be as old as you think—some models from the 1970s and early 1980s have caused many injuries and deaths. Nearly all new cribs sold in the United States meet the current safety standards designed to prevent injuries. This brings us to our biggest safety tips on cribs:

♣ *Don't buy a used or old crib.* Let's put that into bold caps: **DON'T BUY A USED OR OLD CRIB.** And don't take a hand-me-down from a well-meaning friend or relative. Why? Because old cribs can be death traps—bars that are too far apart, cut-outs in the headboard, and other hazards that could entrap your baby's head. Decorative trim (like turned posts) that looks great on adult beds are a major no-no for cribs—they present a strangulation hazard. Other cribs have lead paint, an unpleasant appetizer for a teething baby.

It may seem somewhat ironic that a book on baby bargains would advise you to go out and spend your hard-earned money on a new crib. True, we find great bargains at consignment and second-hand stores. However, you have to draw the line at your baby's safety. Certain items are great deals at these stores—toys and clothes come to mind. However, cribs (and, as you'll read later, car seats) are no-no's, no matter how tempting the bargains. It's hard to tell whether an old crib is dangerous just by looking at it—the current standards are so specific (like the allowable width for side bars) that you just can't judge a crib's safety with a cursory examination. If the brand name is rubbed off, it will be hard to tell if the crib has been involved in a recall.

♣ *Combination crib/youth beds are a major safety hazard, in our opinion.* These beds convert from a crib to a "youth" bed, which is somewhat smaller and narrower than a twin-size bed. Some have attached dressers. All of this is supposed to constitute a major money savings. Child Craft's Crib N Bed is only about $400 in stores—not bad for a crib that converts into a youth bed and a dresser. However, we still think you should pass.

The first hitch in these great "deals" is that most children can go directly from a crib to a twin bed, making the "youth" bed an unnecessary item. Even worse, our research turned up cases of injuries related to these products. One problem area is the railing—in many of these designs, the railing is hinged so that it folds down. Children have been hurt hurling themselves out of the crib by using the folded down railing as a jumping point. Many of these beds have attached dressers, which may seem to be a plus but really could pose a hazard. One mother we interviewed was horrified to find her 10-

month-old infant sitting on top of a four-foot-high dresser one night—he had climbed out of the crib and onto the dresser. And that's the scary thing about these combo crib/youth beds: there's too much opportunity for the baby to climb out of the crib and into danger.

♣ *Metal beds.* Metal beds are cheap (under $100 retail), but they have safety problems. First, sloppy welding between parts of the crib can leave sharp edges. Clothing can snag and fingers can get cut. Remember that when your baby starts to stand, she will be all over the crib—pulling on the railings, handling the safety bars, and more. We've also noticed that inexpensive metal cribs tend to have inadequate mattress support. In many models, the mattress is held up with cheap vinyl straps. A series of springs provides better support and safety. Despite these problems, a new metal crib is still a better buy from a safety point of view than old cribs and combination crib/youth beds.

♣ *Forget about no-name cribs.* Many less-than-reputable baby stores import cheap cribs from some third world country whose standards for baby safety are light years behind the U.S. Why would stores do this? Bigger profits—cheap imports can be marked up big-time and still be sold to unsuspecting parents at prices below name-brand cribs.

Take the Baby Furniture Outlet of Marathon, Florida. These scam artists imported cribs and playpens that grossly failed to meet federal safety standards. From the construction to the hardware, the cribs were a disaster waiting to happen. As a result, 19 babies were injured, and the Consumer Products Safety Commission permanently banned the items in 1987. Sold under the "Small Wonders" brand name at the Baby Furniture Outlet (and other outlets nationwide), parents were undoubtedly suckered in by the "outlet" savings of these cheap cribs. Instead of recalling the cribs, the company declared bankruptcy and claimed it couldn't pay to fix the problem.

What's the lesson? Stick to brand names, like the ones we review later in this chapter. Also check to see if the crib has the Juvenile Products Manufacturers Association (JPMA) seal. In the next box, we explain exactly what that means.

## Recalls: Where to Find Information

The U.S. Consumer Product Safety Commission has a toll-free hotline at (800) 638-2772 for the latest recall information on cribs and other juvenile furniture. It's easy to use—the hotline is a series of recorded voice mail messages that you access by following the prompts. You can also report any potential hazard you've discovered or an injury to your child caused by a product. Write to the U.S. Consumer Products Safety Commission, Washington, D.C. 20207.

JUVENILE
PRODUCTS
MANUFACTURERS
ASSOCIATION

**CERTIFIED**

THIS MODEL TESTED BY AN
INDEPENDENT LABORATORY
FOR COMPLIANCE TO ASTM
SAFETY STANDARDS

### Certifications—Do they really matter?

As you shop for cribs and other products for your baby, you'll no doubt run into "JPMA-Certified" products sporting a special seal. But who is the JPMA and what does their certification mean?

The Juvenile Products Manufacturers Association (JPMA) is a group of over 225 companies that make juvenile products, both in the United States and Canada. Twenty years ago, in a stroke of marketing genius, the group started a testing program to help weed out unsafe products. Instead of turning this into a propaganda effort, they actually enlisted the support of the Consumer Products Safety Commission and the American Society of Testing and Materials to develop standards for products in several categories: carriages/strollers, cribs, play yards, high chairs, safety gates, portable hook-on chairs, and walkers (which we think are dangerous, but more on this later).

Manufacturers must have their product tested in an independent testing lab and, if it passes, they can use the JPMA seal. To the group's credit, the integrity of this process has been so good that the JPMA seal carries a good deal of credibility with many parents we interviewed. But does it really mean a product is safe? Well, yes and no. First, with any product, you must follow instructions for assembly and use very carefully. Second, the testing program (and standards) are voluntary and manufacturers aren't required to certify all the products in a line of merchandise. Hence, if a manufacturer wants to make a cheap version of a popular product that wouldn't meet the guidelines, they just don't have it certified. The result: confusion at the store level, where some products carry the JPMA seal and others don't, even though they're made by the same manufacturer.

To be fair, we should note that just because you don't see the JPMA seal on a product does not mean that it failed to meet the safety standards—the Consumer Products Safety Commission sets minimum requirements that all manufacturers have to meet. (The JPMA's voluntary standards are stricter versions of the CPSC rules). Nevertheless, to clear up this confusion and give the program some teeth, we'd like to see safety testing be a mandatory requirement for all JPMA members. As with all industries that pledge to police themselves, the JPMA certification does have its weaknesses—the fact that they can certify walkers as "safe" is a glaring example. Yet, despite the fact that the cynical side of us wonders whether the fox can ever watch the hen house, we have to give a hand to the JPMA for creating a successful certification program. With some fine-tuning, it might be a model for other juvenile-related industries as well. To contact the JPMA for a list of certified products, you can call (609) 985-2878 or write PO Box 955, Marlton, NJ 08053. A safety brochure (in both English and Spanish) is available—send a self-addressed stamped business size envelope to the above address.

Toys R Us also posts product recall information at the front of their stores. Although they don't sell much in the way of furniture, you will find recall information on a myriad of other products like high chairs, bath seats, and toys.

## Money Saving Secrets

1 GO FOR A SINGLE INSTEAD OF DOUBLE. Cribs that have a single-drop side are usually less expensive ($50 to $100 cheaper) than those with double-drop sides. Sure, double-drop side cribs are theoretically more versatile (you can take the baby out from either side), but ask yourself if your baby's room is big enough to take advantage of this feature. Most small rooms necessitate that the crib be placed against a wall—a double-drop side crib would then be a tad useless, wouldn't it?

2 FORGET THE DESIGNER BRANDS. What do you get for a $500 crib from such fancy names as Bellini or Regazzi? Safety features that rival the M-1 tank? Exotic wood from Bora Bora? Would it surprise you to learn that these cribs are no different than those that cost $200 to $300? Oh sure, "Italian-designed" Bellini throws in an under-crib drawer for storage and Canadian-imported Regazzi has designer colors like "persimmon." But take a good look at these cribs—we found them to be surprisingly deficient in some ways. For example, the release mechanism on the Regazzi crib is awkward and difficult to use.

3 CONSIDER MAIL-ORDER. Say you live in a town that has one baby shop. One baby shop that has sky-high prices. What's the antidote? Consider mail-order. J.C. Penney sells such famous (and quality) name brands as Child Craft and Bassett. Granted, they don't sell them at deep discount prices (you'll find them at regular retail). But this may be more preferable than the price-gouging local store that thinks it has a license from God to overcharge everyone on cribs and juvenile furniture. Another option: many baby mega-stores like LiL' Things offer mail-order service at their "every-day" low prices. You can order anything in the store (including cribs and strollers), charge it to a credit card, and get it delivered via United Parcel Service (UPS). The delivery fee is based on the UPS charge. For the store nearest you, call (817) 649-6100.

4 SHOP AROUND. We found the same crib priced $100 less at one store than at a competitor down the street. Take the time to visit the competition, and you might be pleasantly surprised to find that the effort will be rewarded.

**5** Go NAKED. Naked furniture, that is. We see an increasing number of stores that sell unfinished (or naked) furniture at great prices. Such places even sell the finishing supplies and give you directions (make sure to use a non-toxic finish). The prices are hard to beat. At a local unfinished furniture store, we found a three-drawer pine dresser (23" wide) for $90, while a four drawer (38" wide) was $160. Compare that to baby store prices, which can top $300 to $500 for a similar size dresser. While we haven't seen an unfinished crib at these places (yet), unfinished furniture stores at least offer affordable alternatives for dressers, bookcases, and more.

**6** SHOP AT REGULAR FURNITURE STORES FOR ROCKERS, DRESSERS, ETC. Think about it—most juvenile furniture looks very similar to regular adult furniture. Rockers, dressers, and bookcases are, well, just rockers, dressers, and bookcases. And don't you wonder if companies slap the word "baby" on an item just to raise the price 20%? To test this theory, we visited a local discount furniture store. The prices were incredibly low. A basic three-drawer dresser was $56. Even pine or oak three-drawer dressers were just $129 to $189. The same dresser at a baby store by a "juvenile" manufacturers would set you back at least $300, if not twice that. We even saw some cribs by such mainstream names as Bassett at decent prices.

What's the disadvantage to shopping there? Well, if you have to buy the crib and dresser at different places, the colors might not match exactly. But, considering the savings, it might be worth it. The baby can't tell.

## Best Buys

 *LiL' Things*
(To find the store nearest you, call 817-649-6100)

Wow! We've seen the future of baby stores, and its name is LiL' Things. If you're tired of stores with limited selection and sky-high prices, then you've got to go to this place.

We visited two LiL' Things locations in Texas and were impressed by their selection and the every-day low prices— among the best deals we've seen anywhere. When you first walk into the store, you see a computerized baby gift registry, complete with suggested gift items. Bright signs point you to the various departments inside this mega-baby store.

We first visited the clothing department, which features a wide selection of clothes, sized infant to age six. What about the brands? We were amazed to see such premium brands as Baby Guess and Esprit at rock-bottom prices. For example, we spotted a Baby Dior sleeper for $17.99—that's 30%

below the retail price you'd see in department stores. In fact, LiL' Things' price was the same as Carter's outlet store (Carter's makes the Baby Dior line).

The clothing selection includes a nice mix of everyday items (Carter's, Cotton Club) and fancier outfits (grandma bait, as its known in the trade). For example, we saw a Bonnie Baby dress with a strawberry pattern skirt, gingham-checked bloomers, and embroidered t-shirt for $20—and that included a hair bow. LiL' Things even carries shoes by Buster Brown, Street Hot, and LA Gear.

Next, we sashayed to the furniture department. We have to admit this was our favorite part of the store. And not just because we saw some of our favorite brands (Child Craft and Simmons) at drop-dead prices. Nope, what really impressed us were the little baby room "vignettes" that LiL' Things has set up to showcase cribs, bedding, and accessories. Instead of looking through catalogs or sample books, you can actually see what this bedding pattern looks like with that crib, and so on. Tags describing the cost of every item shown are conveniently displayed on the wall of each room.

Prices for cribs start at $80 for a metal Cosco crib. We saw a Child Craft crib (model number 14721) for $150, and Simmons cribs ran $179 to $334. Mattresses were similarly affordable. We thought the Simmons 160 coil was a best buy at $80. Foam mattresses were $59. Our only complaint about the furniture section was that the wallpaper center, which features about 50 samples, seemed cramped.

As for the bedding, we saw such familiar names as Lambs & Ivy and NoJo. While we weren't surprised to find budget brands like Red Calliope's Little Bedding, we were pleased to find high quality names like Patsy Aiken. A quilt from this top-notch line ran $99, sheets $22, bumpers $99, and a dust ruffle $59.

Next we checked out the rocker selection, which included the super-popular Dutailier glider line. Prices were about 10% to 20% below comparable retail—we noticed a basic Dutailier glider at $199 and ottoman at $130. You can go whole hog with a leather Dutailier for $419. If that's too much, LiL' Things had a variety of other brands of rockers and gliders from $170 to $400, with most in the $200 to $300 range.

Toward the back of the store, we found LiL' Things selection of car seats, strollers, and carriages. We found the Travel Safety inflatable car seat for the low price of $85 (compared to $100 to $120 elsewhere). If a more traditional car seat is on your list, we saw all the famous brand names like Century, Evenflo, Kolcraft, and more. Infant car seats were $39 to $59, while convertible car seats were $50 to $110.

LiL' Things' stroller selection was somewhat skimpy, but all the famous brands were in attendance. We saw at least one stroller each from such hot names as Aprica, Peg Perego, Combi, Century, Graco, and Kolcraft. Combi's Travelight Savvy stroller (one of our favorites) was $159—compare that to $225 retail. Missing from the stroller department were the pricey Emmaljunga carriages and a few other brands.

The toy department, however, didn't miss a beat. We spied the Evenflo's alternative to walkers, the Exersaucer for $49.99. Best of all, all the toys were arranged by age appropriateness, making easy to find a gift for a three year old or a book for a six month old. One thing you won't see are violent action figures like the "X-Men"—LiL' Things doesn't sell any toys that promote violence. This is a rather admirable stance, considering their competition doesn't have any misgivings about selling this stuff.

Perhaps it's the sheer selection of LiL' Things that's most impressive. Looking for a children's book? LiL' Things has one of the best children's book departments we've ever seen, all at a 10% discount. You can find the entire line of Safety 1st items, videos and video games, and even the ever-popular Diaper Genie ($24.99, refills $4.99). While you can't buy disposable diapers, you can buy wipes (an 84-count box of Freshette wipes runs $3). If that isn't enough, LiL' Things also has a hair salon, a photo studio, and a pretty decent gift shop that sells baby announcements. Bright signs point the way to various departments and inventive displays (our favorite was the bath tub full of—you guessed it—bath toys) make the experience more enjoyable. For older kids, a "LiL' Land" play center in the center of the store features slides, climbing ladders, and other distractions.

So, how's the service? We know what you're thinking—at other big discount stores, you can roll a bowling ball down the middle of the place and be guaranteed not to hit one salesperson. That's because they're all in the back on break. Well, we're happy to say that LiL' Things actually has salespeople. On the floor. What a concept.

We found the service most helpful in the furniture department. The staff seemed knowledgeable and went out of their way to explain the features of various items. If we had a question, there was usually an employee within arm's reach who was familiar with the products. Another plus: big ticket items like strollers are tagged with information on features, accessories, and the like.

In fact, if we had to criticize one thing about LiL' Things, it would have to be that there are just not enough of the darn stores. Founded in 1993 by the guru who started Bizmart in the '80s, as of this writing LiL' Things has just 13 stores in

Texas, Oklahoma, Arizona, and Colorado. (The lucky cities are Dallas/Ft. Worth, Austin, Denver, Phoenix, and Tulsa). Their goal is to have 75 to 100 stores open in just a few years. By the time you read this, however, they'll probably be in a town that's closer to you (call the number at the beginning of this article for the latest information).

Let's say you live in a town that's just not close to a LiL' Things. The good news is that you can still get these great deals because the company offers a mail-order service. (Since they don't have a catalog, you'll have to call for a price quote.) You can order any item they carry, pay by credit card, and get it shipped via United Parcel Service (UPS). The delivery fee is based on the UPS charge. To find the store nearest you to place an order, call (817) 649-6100.

What more can we say? LiL' Things combines the best of both worlds—a bright and cheerful store with a large selection of the best name brands. And prices that are hard to beat.

## Best Buy

### Baby Superstore
To find the store nearest you, call (803) 968-9292

Baby Superstore was among the first big baby stores to realize that new parents aren't automatic cash machines. The 50-store chain has locations in the Southeast, Mid-Atlantic, Southwest, and even parts of the Midwest (Kentucky and Indiana)—all with the theme that "prices are born here and raised elsewhere." Their no-frills warehouses combine name brands at unheard of low prices.

And we mean no-frills. We visited one of the newer Baby Superstores in Texas and were greeted by a giant stack of Diaper Genies that went to the ceiling. The price was unbelievably cheap—$19.95, which was $5 cheaper than LiL' Things. Refills were about the same price ($4.97). And that basically describes the Baby Superstore—huge piles of merchandise that are stacked to the ceiling. If you can get past the bare-bones warehouse style of merchandising, the deals are pretty good.

We were most excited by the Baby Superstore's clothing selection. The most impressive brands included Little Me, Alexis, and Good Lad of Philadelphia. There was even a smattering of Baby Dior thrown in for good measure. One outfit that caught our eye was an Alexis shorts outfit in a safari motif—khaki shorts with suspenders, an African print shirt, and a straw hat. Not bad for $24.97. Another great buy: a 100% cotton romper with hood by Fusen Baby for $14.97.

Less exciting was Baby Superstore's crib and furniture selection. Scattered about the store, cribs are grouped by color and loaded up and down each aisle. This made comparison shopping difficult. The brand names were also not as impressive, including such obscure ones as Lullabye and Norcrist. Both of these brands seem to be cheap copies of Regazzi, replicating the Canadian brand's two-tone finish. For bargain shoppers, you could get a metal Cosco crib for $78. On the upside, we did see some Simmons models—a cherry finish sleigh bed was $389.

The bedding selection included slightly better brand names, including NoJo, Lambs & Ivy, and Quiltex. A four-piece set (comforter, sheet, bumper, and dust ruffle) from Lambs & Ivy in the "Paradise" design was $199. We saw several six-piece sets for as low as $139. Overall, the linen department was hit or miss, with some good brands at great prices scattered among the regular offerings. The same holds true for the rockers and gliders at the Baby Superstore. While we did see Dutailier gliders starting at $280 (ottomans were $130), some of the 30 styles featured fabric choices that could best be described as "1970s hideous."

The Baby Superstore redeemed itself with a super selection of car seats and strollers. We saw Century car seats in a myriad of colors and styles. But the deals here were overshadowed by the great prices on strollers. We actually saw the Combi Travelight Stroller on sale for just $99. Yes, that was the same one as the one we saw for $225 in other stores. Other brands included Aprica (the CitiMini was $180) and the popular Peg Perego line, which ranged from $130 to $185. We were impressed with the sheer depth of offerings here—you could find the basics like Kolcraft, and Century and the exotic, such as Emmaljunga.

Once again, organization (or the lack thereof) was the undoing of the toy department, which had a variety of offerings crammed together at the back of the store. We were disgusted to see walkers still for sale here, despite the numerous reports of injuries from these products.

There is one product you'll find at the Baby Superstore that you won't find cheaper anywhere else: diapers. The store carries disposable diapers at prices discounted below anywhere else on the planet, as far was we can determine. Check out these prices: Huggies Step 1, 50 count, for just $7.09! The store brand ("Ultra Loving Touch") was even cheaper at $6.57 for 50 diapers. Wipes were also cheap, running just $2.97 for an 84-count box of Baby Fresh wipes.

Across from the diapers was an area that we call "The Wall of Gerber": practically every product and accessory these guys make is here. We also liked the well-stocked selection of baby monitors, including the Sony Baby Call for $39.

All in all, we had mixed feelings about the Baby Superstore. We sure liked the clothing department and the incredible selection of name brand strollers, car seats, and accessories. Yet, the store's organization and merchandising (especially the furniture) leaves a lot to be desired. The service was friendly—we found most salespeople to be knowledgeable and helpful.

Will there be more Baby Superstores in the future? The chain was tight-lipped about expansion plans, but it's a pretty good bet that they will continue to expand to other cities in the near future. To find the store nearest you, call (803) 968-9292.

## Outlets

Very few manufacturers of cribs and juvenile furniture have outlets. In fact, we only found one. If you discover an outlet that you'd like to share with our readers, call us at (303) 442-8792.

### Cosco
*2525 State St., Columbus, IN 47201. (812) 372-0141 x473.*

Located inside their factory in Columbus, Indiana, Cosco's outlet store sells cribs, high chairs, play pens, and more. In fact, the store sells nearly every product that bears the Cosco name. Prices are up to 50% off retail, and both new and second merchandise is on display. As we mentioned in the Name Game, we're not wild about Cosco's metal cribs, but their other products (most notably baby monitors, high chairs, and other accessories) are good buys. The store is only open weekdays, 10-6.

*Special thanks to the* Joy of Outlet Shopping *magazine for helping us track down the Cosco outlet. To order a copy of the magazine, call 1-800-344-6397.*

## Wastes of Money

1 "CONVERTIBLE" CRIBS. Convertible to what, you might ask? Manufacturers pitch these more expensive cribs as a money-saver since they are convertible to "youth beds," which are smaller and narrower than a twin bed. But, guess what? Most kids can go straight from a crib to a regular twin bed with no problem whatsoever. So, the youth bed business is really a joke.

2 BASSINET. Do you really need one? A newborn infant can sleep in a regular crib just as easily as a bassinet. The

advantage of a bassinet is that you can keep it in your room for the baby's first few weeks, making midnight (and 2 am and 4 am) feedings more convenient. Is it worth the extra money (bassinets cost $30 to $100)? It's up to you, but our baby slept in his crib from day one, and it worked out just fine. If the distance between your room and the baby's is too far and you'd like to give a bassinet a try, see if you can find one at a consignment or second-hand store.

**3** CRIBS WITH LOTS OF MATTRESS HEIGHTS. A big pitch from manufacturers is that their crib has multiple mattress levels, allegedly making it more convenient for you to take the baby out. At first, the mattress is set at the highest level. As the baby grows (and starts sitting up, pulling up, etc.), you are supposed to lower the mattress level by level until you reach the bottom point. The reality? Once your baby starts to pull up, you'll need to lower the mattress all the way to the lowest level—forget about these middle levels. The reason is the "in-between" levels are probably unsafe; a baby that pulls herself up on the railing when the mattress is set at a higher level can possibly climb out of the crib. So forget the pitch about the mattress levels and remember that all you need are two.

## Do it by Mail: The Best Mail-Order Sources for Cribs and Baby Furniture

### J.C. Penney.

*To Order Call:* (800) 222-6161. Ask for the following catalogs: "Baby and You," "For Baby," and "Starting Small."
*Shopping Hours:* 24 hours a day, seven days a week.
*Credit Cards Accepted:* MC, VISA, J.C. Penney, AMEX, Discover.

 J.C. Penney has been selling baby clothes, furniture, and more for over 90 years. Their popular mail-order catalog has three free "mini-catalogs" that should be of particular interest to parents-to-be.

"For Baby" is Penney's main furniture catalog, with over 51 pages of cribs, bedding, mattresses, safety items, car seats, strollers, swings, and even a few pages of baby clothes. The crib section features such famous brand names as Cosco, Welsh Bassett, and Child Craft. The best deal: A Child Craft "sculptured" crib in white maple with a single-drop side was $229. If you buy both the crib and mattress, Penney's offers discounts of $15 to $50 off the crib—a pretty good deal. Other crib offerings range from a Cosco metal crib for $139 to a Bassett shaker-style crib for $279. Penney's also sells Welsh, Delta Luv, and Stork Craft cribs.

Looking for a bassinet? Penney's sells a basic model with

hood for $34.99, plus a wide variety of accessories like liners, skirts, and hood covers. Crib mattresses run from $25 for a Kolcraft foam mattress (call 312-247-4494 to find a store near you) to $90 for a Sealy Baby Posturpedic.

The catalogs could be organized better—the furniture catalog mixes prices for cribs, linens, and other accessories on the same page, making price comparisons somewhat difficult. Nevertheless, if you live in a remote area or in a town with sky-high prices, the Penney's catalog offers a good deal—name brands at decent prices.

## LiL' Things

*For the store nearest you, call 817-649-6100.*

Were you salivating after reading about the great deals at LiL' Things, the baby mega-store chain with stores in Texas, Oklahoma, Colorado, and Arizona? Well, you don't have to have a LiL' Things in your town to enjoy the great prices on cribs and furniture (not to mention the bedding, strollers, car seats, and so on). LiL' Things will ship any item they sell in their stores. (They don't have a catalog; call for price quotes and availability.) The delivery charge is based on the United Parcel Service fee. Compare LiL' Things' price with what you can do at your local stores. You might be surprised to find that even after you pay for shipping, you still come out ahead. (Another plus: you typically don't have to pay sales tax, which on a $300 crib is no small amount).

---

 ## FACTOID

### WHO IS JENNY LIND?

You can't shop for cribs and not hear the name "Jenny Lind." Jenny Lind isn't a brand name; it refers to a particular style of crib. But how did it get this name? Jenny Lind was a popular Swedish soprano during the 19th century. During her triumphal U.S. tour, it was said that Lind slept in a "spool bed." Hence, cribs that feature turned spindles (which look like stacked spools of thread) became known as Jenny Lind cribs. All this begs the question—what if today we still named juvenile furniture after famous singers? Could we have Whitney Houston cribs and Mariah Carey dressers? Nah.

---

## Mattresses

Now that you've just spent several hundred dollars on a crib, you're done, right? Wrong. Despite price tags that can soar over $500, cribs don't come with mattresses. So, here's our guide to buying the best quality mattress for the lowest price.

## Smart Shopper Tips

### Smart Shopper Tip #1
FOAM OR COIL?

*"It seems the choice for a crib mattress comes down to foam or coil? Which is better? Does it matter?"*

Yes, it does matter. After researching this issue, we've come down on the foam side of the debate. Why? Foam mattresses are lighter than those with coils (or springs), making it easier to change the sheets in the middle of the night when Junior reenacts the Great Flood in his crib. Foam mattresses typically weigh less than five pounds, while coil mattress can top 20 pounds! Another plus: foam mattresses are less expensive, running $25 to $60. Coil mattresses can top $100.

### Smart Shopper Tip #2
BEWARE OF THE CHEAP FOAM MATTRESS

*"Okay, so foam mattresses are better. But, my friend bought a cheap foam mattress and had nothing but problems. All of them look alike—what's the difference?"*

We recommend you choose a foam mattress that is more dense—five-inch thick ones are better than four-inch options. For example, we thought the Simmons 5-inch foam mattress was a good buy at $59 at LiL' Things. We were less impressed with the Kolcraft brand foam mattresses, which weren't as dense. Most brands come with an "easy-cleaning" vinyl cover. Which reminds us that if the mattress doesn't have one, you need to buy a water-proof, flannel-back mattress cover that is not fitted (it's easier to change). This prevents "spills" from seeping into the foam.

### Smart Shopper Tip #3
COIL OVERKILL?

*"I'm still not convinced about foam mattresses. They just don't look very substantial. If we want to buy a coil innerspring crib mattress, what's the best advice?"*

Coil innerspring mattresses are priced based on how many coils they have. The cheapest ones have just 60 to 80 coils and cost $40 or so. Our advice: stay away from them. They won't last and will get lumpy, forcing you to buy another mattress if you have a second child. A better bet is a 150 to 160-coil mattress that provides enough support and durability at a decent price. For example, the Simmons 150-coil innerspring mattress retails for $110, although we saw it regularly discounted to $80 to $85.

What about those super deluxe crib mattress with over 200 coils? It's overkill. Your baby doesn't need that much support, and you're just wasting your money. These mattresses can cost $100 to $150. The best deal we saw on these was a Simmons 213-coil at LiL' Things for $99 (although J.C. Penney sells a 280-coil mattress from Kolcraft for $60).

## Safe & Sound

 Babies don't have the muscle strength to lift their head up when put face-down into soft or fluffy bedding—some have suffocated as a result. The best defense: buy a firm mattress (foam or coil) and don't place your baby face down in soft, thick quilts, wool blankets, pillows, or toys. Never put the baby down on a vinyl mattress without a cover or sheet since vinyl can also contribute to suffocation. In addition, you should know that one study into the causes of Sudden Infant Death Syndrome (SIDS) has found that a too-soft sleep surface (such as the items listed above) and environmental factors (a too-hot room, cigarette smoke) are related to crib death, though exactly how has yet to be determined. Experts therefore advise against letting infants sleep on a too-soft surface.

## Dressers & Changing Tables

The trade refers to dressers, changing tables, and the like as "case pieces" since they are essentially furniture made out of a large case (pretty inventive, huh?). Now that you've got a place for the baby sleep (and a mattress for the baby to sleep on), where are you going to put all those cute outfits that you'll get as gifts? And let's not forget that all too important activity that will occupy so many of your hours after the baby is born: changing diapers.

The other day we calculated that by our baby's eight-month birthday, we had changed over 3000 diapers! Wow! To first-time parents, that may seem like an unreal number, but babies actually do go through 70 to 100 diapers a week at this stage. That translates into 10 to 15 changes a day. Hence, the modern-day invention of the diaper changing station. In this section, we'll explore some money-saving tips in buying both dressers and changing tables.

## What are You Buying

**1** DRESSERS. As you shop for baby furniture, you'll note a wide variety of dressers—three drawer, four drawer, armoirs, combination dresser/changing tables, and more. No matter which type you choose, we do have two general tips for getting the most for your money. First, choose a dresser whose drawers roll out on roller bearings. Cheap dressers have drawers that simply sit on a track—no roller bearings. As a result, they don't roll out as smoothly and are prone to come off the track. Our second piece of advice: make sure the dresser top is laminated. If you're in a rush and put something wet on top, you want to make sure you don't damage the finish. Also, unlaminated tops are more prone to scratches and dings.

**2** CHANGING TABLE. Basically, you have two options here. You can buy a separate changing table or a combination dresser/changing table.

We thought the Right Start Catalog's changing table (#A031, to order call 1-800-548-8531) was a pretty good deal at $109.95 (plus about $20 shipping). Made from an aluminum alloy, the heavy, quilted-vinyl top provides a convenient changing area and is easy to clean. Our only complaint: the plastic-coated wire shelves that are supposed to "slide in and out for easy access" to diapers and supplies would occasionally come off their tracks—not any fun when you have a fussy baby who'd rather be doing something else than getting a diaper change. Other than that, we've been happy.

Another option is the combo package, a dresser and changing table all rolled into one. Called "flip-top dressers," they have a top unit that flips forward to provide a space to change the baby. Some of these models convert to regular dressers (the changing table top detaches and can be removed). For example, Child Craft flip-top dressers run $309 to $425.

So what should you buy? If you're short of space, a flip-top dresser is a good choice. Our only advice is to make sure you can get easy access to diapers and supplies. Some flip-tops make it difficult to reach the shelf with supplies when the top is flipped down—check this in the store to make sure it's practical.

If space isn't a big problem in the baby's room, then you might consider a separate diaper changing station. You'll have more room to store supplies such as rubbing alcohol (for umbilical cord care), lotion, sunscreen, diaper wipes, etc. (In Chapter 6, we discuss in more detail what supplies you'll need.) We bought a separate dresser and used the top for an attached bookshelf.

Let's say you're on a really tight budget. What should you do? Forget the diaper changing station altogether! Some mothers we interviewed just change their baby in the crib. Of course, there are a couple of disadvantages. First, there's not a convenient place for diapers and supplies. This could be solved by a rolling nursery cart (cost: about $25 in many catalogs). Another disadvange: if you have a boy, he could spray the crib sheets, bumper pads, and just about anything else in the crib with his little "water pistol." Hence, you might find yourself doing more laundry.

## Smart Shopper Tips

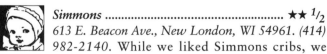

### Smart Shopper Tip #1
MASTERING THE HORIZONTAL HOLD
*"After three babies, I'm convinced that the best diaper changing table is one that let's you change the baby in a perpendicular instead of horizontal position."*

We agree. Having the baby lie on the changing table perpendicular to your body (that is, with his feet toward your stomach) is much easier on you and baby. The standard, horizontal position for a diaper change requires you, the parent, to be a contortionist to get the job done. Some furniture makers have realized this as well and now market flip-top dressers that enable the perpendicular diaper change.

If you are shopping for this type of changing table, make sure it is stable enough to support the full weight of a baby (and later toddler) without tipping over.

## The Name Game: Reviews of Selected Manufacturers

## The Ratings

★★★★ EXCELLENT—*our top pick!*
★★★ GOOD—*above average quality, prices, and creativity.*
★★ FAIR—*could stand some improvement.*
★ POOR—*yuck! could stand some major improvement.*

---

**Simmons** ..................................................... ★★ ¹/₂
*613 E. Beacon Ave., New London, WI 54961.* (414) 982-2140. While we liked Simmons cribs, we weren't as wild about their case pieces. Why? The prices are just too high. For example, a basic four-drawer dresser weighs in at a pricey $339. And that price is from one of the baby mega-store discounters. For your money you at least get

drawers with solid wood sides (cheaper dressers have pressed-board drawer sides). But this feature is really overkill when it comes to juvenile furniture. Another negative: the dressers we saw did not have laminated tops.

*Child Craft* .................................................................★★★
*PO Box 444, Salem, IN 47167. (812) 883-3111.* Child Craft is a better buy when it comes to dressers and other case pieces. A four-drawer dresser is about $280, while flip-top dressers/changing tables are in the $310 to $425 range. Child Craft uses roller bearings for their drawers, giving them a smoother pull. The only negative: the drawer sides are not solid wood. On the upside, however, the tops of the pieces are laminated.

*Rumble Tuff* .............................................................★★★★
*1186 North Industrial Park Dr., Orem, UT 84057. (800) 524-9607. (801) 226-2648.* Rumble Tuff is our pick as the best buy in juvenile furniture. A small manufacturer based in Utah, Rumble Tuff has won fans nationwide with their affordable and stylish dressers. Their strategy is to knock-off the big guys, making similar furniture styles in the exact same finishes as Child Craft and Simmons. And the prices are fantastic—we noticed that Rumble Tuff is often 10% to 25% less than the competition. For example, their popular "three-drawer" combo unit combines both a four-drawer dresser/changing table and a taller base cabinet and drawer. Simmons sells the same unit for $530, but the Rumble Tuff price is $415—that's a 20% savings. All in all, Rumble Tuff makes 30 different pieces, in both contemporary and traditional finishes.

All of Rumble Tuff's drawers feature roller bearings. Sorry, no solid wood drawer sides, and the tops (and sides) of the units are solid wood veneer, no laminate. Nevertheless, we bought a Rumble Tuff dresser and bookshelf unit and have been very happy—it matches our Child Craft crib exactly and we saved about $80. Rumble Tuff is available in stores nationwide (especially on the East and West Coasts), but they're somewhat underrepresented in the Southeast. As a side note, Rumble Tuff also makes pads for changing tables, washcloths, and even a "car seat support kit," which is a foam bar that's used to level infant car seats.

## Safe & Sound

 Just like the crib, you must also think about the safety aspects of the other pieces of furniture in your baby's room. Here are our tips:

♣ ***Anchor those shelves.*** A nice bookcase (whether on the floor or on top of the dresser) can become a tip-over hazard as the baby begins pulling up on objects. The best advice is to attach any shelves to a wall to provide stability.

♣ ***Baby proof the diaper station.*** If your diaper changing table has open shelves, you may have to baby proof the bottom shelves. As the baby begins to climb, you must remove any dangerous medicines or supplies from easily accessible shelves.

## Even More Stuff To Spend Money On

Just 'cause to this point you have spent an amount equivalent to the gross national product of Peru on baby furniture doesn't mean you're done, of course. Nope, we've got five more "must haves" for your baby's room:

1 ROCKER. We're not talking about the rocking chair you've seen at grandma's house. No, we're referring to the high-tech modern-day rockers that are so fancy they aren't mere rockers—they're "gliders-rockers." What's the difference? Market-leader Dutailier (298 Chaput, St-Pie, Quebec, Canada JOH 1WO; 800-363-9817 or 514-772-2403) says their glider-rockers have a "unique bearing system (tested to six million cycles) that ensures the best rocking sensation money can buy!" Wow! Sounds like the same system used on the Stealth bomber.

Basically, what all this hoo-hah means is gliders rock easier than rockers. We were somewhat skeptical about this before we bought our glider, but after doing a test drive we're convinced they're worth the extra money.

And how much money are we talking about here? A basic Dutailier (pronounced due-tal-yay) glider starts at $330, with some leather versions topping out at $500 or more. And you've got to get that cute ottoman that glides too—cost: another $150 to $180. How can you get a deal on a Dutailier? Well, you'll have to find a LiL' Things or Baby Superstore. We found gliders starting at $280 in such stores, with ottomen running $130.

We should note that there are dozens of other companies that make gliders, with entry-level prices at about $200. For example, Town Square's Baby Love Rocker by Lamaze (800-526-2732) has a more square and shaker style look than Dutailier offerings. Their "exclusive glider nursing ottoman" is quite unusual looking—low to the ground at a height that the manufacturer claims is "ideal for nursing." Price: $399.

## Who is Dutailier?

Dutailier, Inc., is the IBM of glider-rockers. But how did this company from Quebec come to dominate the glider-rocker market here in the United States?

First, consider the glider-rocker itself. It's really cool. Dutailier has an incredible selection of 45 models, 12 finishes, and 70 different fabrics. The result: over 37,000 possible combinations. All wood is solid maple or oak and features non-toxic finishes. You have to try real hard to avoid seeing a Dutailier—the company has an amazing 3500 retail dealers, from small specialty stores to major retail chains.

While Dutailier claims it delivers rockers in just five days, retailers tell us the process can take as long as several weeks. Another possible option for faster service: many dealers stock a wide number of sample models that you can buy right off the floor.

We do have a bone to pick with the company: check out some of their fabric choices. Dutailier (and other glider-rocker companies) must search the world to find the ugliest fabrics known to man. I mean, we're talking really hideous here. Oh sure, there are a few decent choices, but you would think that Dutailier would have phased out "Harvest Gold" and "Really Disgusting Brown" years ago.

To find a dealer near you, call (800) 363-9817 or (514) 772-2403.

**2** LAUNDRY BASKET. Here's a useful extravagence: the Speigal catalog (800-345-4500) features a nice laundry basket that has a cotton/polyester laundry bag in a folding hardwood frame. The cost: $29.90 and available colors include royal blue, forest green, black, and natural (order #N94 941 4671). We've seen similar laundry baskets in retail stores for about the same price.

**3** A STEREO. During those sleep deprivation experiments, it's sure nice to have some soothing music to make those hours just whiz by. Sure, you could put a cheap clock radio in the baby's room, but that assumes you have decent radio stations. And even the best radio station will be somewhat tiring to listen to for the many nights ahead. Our advice: buy (or get someone to get you as a gift) one of those new boom box radios. Models with a radio, cassette deck, and even a compact disc player are about $100 to $300 in most electronics stores. Another hint: get one with digital tuning, where you can hit preset buttons to find stations. We made the mistake of buying one with analog tuning—just try to tune in that fuzzy talk-radio station at 2 am with one hand in the dark, and you'll know why digital is the way to go.

**4** PLACE FOR DAD TO SIT. Yes, parenting in the '90s is supposed to be a shared experience. Translation: dad is supposed to be up at 4:30 am to assist mom with that sunrise diaper change. Or fussy baby. But while mom has one of those glider-rockers from the Starship Enterprise, where is dad suppose to sit? One possible solution: a twin-size futon that converts from a chair into a bed. Hand in Hand Professional catalog (800-872-3841) features just such a futon for $169.95 (in black, red, or royal blue—sorry, no pink). Speigel has a 3-position futon for $129.00 (800-345-4500— order #N94 941 6500 sleepover futon outfit in red, blue, or black)

Since our hometown has more futon stores than gas stations, we priced the local competition and found that a twin-size futon runs $150 to $218 for a frame and mattress. Look under furniture in the phone book for a futon place near you.

**5** DIAPER GENIE. Your parents had a diaper pail. Our generation has the Diaper Genie, the wonderful invention of a parent who apparently smelled one too many diaper pails. In Chapter 4, we'll explore the Eighth Wonder of the World: The Diaper Genie.

## THE BOTTOM LINE:
### A Wrap-Up of Our Best Buy Picks

For cribs, it's hard to beat the single-drop side crib by Child Craft (model 14721) for just $150 at LiL' Things (call the number earlier in the chapter for the store nearest you or to place an order). Of all the brands, Child Craft combines the best safety features and styling at the most reasonable of prices. Even if you have to order by mail and pay shipping, this is a great deal. Another good buy was the Matino by Simmons (also $179 at LiL' Things). A double-drop side crib will set you back more ($200 to $350), but it's a nice feature if you have the room to take advantage of it.

As far as stores go, we thought the baby mega-stores LiL' Things and Baby Superstore had incredible prices, although we liked LiL' Things furniture selection slightly better. For the best selection of cribs via mail order, it's hard to beat the brand names available from J.C. Penney.

The best and most convenient crib mattresses are made of foam. And they happen to be less expensive—a Simmons five-inch foam mattress costs about $60 at discount stores. Most coil mattresses are not only more difficult to use but also twice as expensive.

Dressers and other case pieces by Rumble Tuff were great deals—they exactly match the finishes of Child Craft and Simmons, but at prices 10% to 25% less than the competition. We liked their three-drawer combo unit that combines a changing table and a dresser for $415.

Finally, we recommend the Dutailier line of glider-rockers. At $330, the basic model isn't cheap but is better made than the competition. A matching ottoman runs $150 to $180. Once again, LiL' Things and Baby Superstore had the best prices when we checked, about 10% to 30% less than retail. For example, LiL' Things sells a basic Dutailier glider with matching ottoman for just $350.

## *Here's the Total Damage So Far:*

| | |
|---|---|
| Child Craft Crib | $150 |
| Rumble Tuff Changing Table/Dresser | $415 |
| Dutailier Glider-Rocker with ottoman | $350 |
| Miscellaneous | $195 |
| (Laundry basket, stereo, etc.) | |
| **TOTAL** | **$1110** |

*(Prices are from discount stores or other low-price sources.)*

By contrast, if you bought a Bellini crib ($500), a 200-coil mattress ($150), a flip-top dresser/changing table ($450), a glider-rocker ($510) and some of the miscellaneous items ($195) at full retail prices, you'd be out $1805 by this point.

Of course, you don't have any sheets for your baby's crib yet. Nor any clothes for Junior to wear. So, next we'll explore those topics and save more of your money.

 Questions or comments? Did you discover a nursery bargain you'd like to share with our readers? **Call the authors at (303) 442-8792!**

# Chapter 3

*Baby Bedding*

How can you find brand new, designer-label bedding for 25% off the retail price? We've got the answer in this chapter, plus you'll find nine smart shopper tips to getting the most for your money. Then, we'll share six important tips that will keep your baby safe and sound. Finally, we've got reviews of the best bedding designers and an interesting list of seven top money-wasters.

## Getting Started: When Do You Need This Stuff?

 Begin shopping for your baby's linen pattern in the sixth month of your pregnancy, if not earlier. Why? If you're purchasing these items from a baby specialty store, they usually must be special-ordered—allow at least four to six weeks for delivery. If you leave a few weeks for shopping, you can order the bedding in your seventh month and be assured it arrives before the baby does.

If you're buying bedding from a store or catalog that has your pattern in stock, you can wait until your eighth month. It still takes time to comparison shop, and some stores may only have certain pieces you need in stock, while other accessories (like wall hangings, etc.) may need to be ordered.

### Sources:

There are four basic sources for baby bedding:

1 BABY SPECIALTY STORES. These stores tend to have a limited selection of bedding in stock. Typically, you're expected to choose the bedding by seeing what you like on sample cribs or by looking through manufacturers' catalogs. Since the stores don't stock the bedding, you have to special-order your choices and wait six to eight weeks for arrival. And that's the main disadvantage to buying linens at a specialty stores: you can't always touch the merchandise. Plus, it's no fun having to wait so long. On the upside, specialty stores do carry high-quality brand names. On the downside, you'll pay through the nose for them.

2 DISCOUNTERS/DEPARTMENT STORES. Who are the discounters? Well, they include a range of chain stores, from K-Mart and Target to Marshalls and TJ Maxx. Even Toys R Us is selling bedding, clothes, and diapers.

Compared to specialty stores, discount stores like Toys R Us certainly carry more bedding items in stock, but the brand names are lesser-known and of lower quality. Prices are very affordable, but don't expect the items to last long—synthetic fabrics and cheaper construction means this bedding may not withstand repeated washings.

Meanwhile, the selection of baby bedding at department stores is all over the board. Some chains have great baby departments and others need help. For example, J.C. Penney carries linen sets by such companies as NoJo, while Foley's (part of the May Department Store chain) seems to only have a few blankets and sheets. Prices at department stores vary as widely as selection; however, you can be guaranteed that they will hold occasional sales, making them a better deal.

3 BABY MEGA-STORES. As we mentioned in the last chapter, the two major baby mega-stores, LiL' Things and Baby Superstore, are an incredible resource for name brands at low prices—especially for bedding. These stores stock a good selection of bedding sets by well-known brand names at up to 50% savings off retail. We even found such premium labels as Patsy Aiken at LiL' Things. The baby mega-stores also offer a special-order service similar to specialty stores. Mega-stores tend to stock designs that have broad appeal, so if you're looking for the unusual, you may need to special-order.

4 MAIL-ORDER. Some of the big catalogs like J.C. Penney carry a limited selection of linens, and they tend to be lower-end options. Other catalogs offer high-quality brand names, but expect to pay for the privilege of buying them. Later in this chapter, we spotlight one mail-order company that offers the best of both worlds: famous brand names at discounted prices.

## What are You Buying

 Walk into any baby store, announce you're having a baby, and stand back: the eager salespeople will probably pitch you on all types of bedding items that you "must buy." We call this the "Diaper Stacker Syndrome," named in honor of that useless (but expensive) linen item that allegedly provides a convenient place to store diapers. Most parents aren't about to spend the equivalent of the Federal Deficit on diaper stackers. So, here's our list of the absolute necessities for your baby's linen layette:

♣ *Fitted sheets—at least three to four.* We like cotton flannel sheets because we live in a cold climate, and flannel is less of a cold shock to our baby when we lay him down. In warmer climates, regular woven cotton sheets would be a good choice.

♣ *Bumper pads.* An important safety item. We should note all you need is a standard, four-sided bumper. Some designers sell bumpers with headboard designs—these feature a larger design at the head of the baby's bed.

✳ *Mattress cover/protector.* Baby mattress covers are similar to adult mattress covers, while mattress *protectors* have a rubber backing to protect against stains. Here's a piece of good advice from a seasoned parent: buy a non-fitted mattress cover or protector. The non-fitted versions are easier to remove for cleaning (which you'll be doing often).

♣ *Good blanket or quilt.* Obviously, a quilt is better in cold climates, while a nice cotton blanket will do in warmer regions. Of course, salespeople will still pitch that quilt to everyone, even if you live in steamy Florida, because they look so darn cute.

### Smart Shopper Tips
PILLOW TALK: LOOKING FOR MR. GOOD BEDDING

*"Barney or not Barney—that seemed to be basic choice in baby bedding at our local juvenile store. Since it all looks alike, is the pattern the only difference?"*

Of course there's more than that. And buying baby bedding isn't the same as purchasing linens for your own bed—you'll be washing these pieces much more frequently, so they must be made to hold up to extra abuse. Since it's more than just another set of sheets, here are nine points to keep in mind:

**1** RUFFLES SHOULD BE FOLDED OVER FOR DOUBLE THICKNESS—instead of a single thickness ruffle with hemmed edge. Double ruffles hold up better in the wash.

**2** COLORED DESIGNS ON THE BEDDING SHOULD BE PRINTED ONTO THE FABRIC (like you'd see with any calico print fabric), not stamped (like you'd see on a screen-printed t-shirt). Stamped designs on sheets will fade with only a few washings. The problem: the pieces you wash less frequently (like dust ruffles and bumpers) will fade at different rates, spoiling the coordinated look you paid big money for. In case you're wondering how to determine whether the design is printed rather than stamped, printed fabrics have color that goes through the fabric to the other side. Stamped patterns are merely painted onto the top of the fabric.

**3** MAKE SURE THE PIECES ARE SEWN WITH COTTON/POLY THREAD, NOT NYLON. Nylon threads will melt and break in the dryer, becoming a choking hazard. Another negative for nylon: the batting in bumpers and quilts bunches up when the thread is gone.

**4** CHECK FOR TIGHT AND SMOOTH STITCHING ON APPLIQUES (THOSE CUTE ANIMALS, DINOSAURS, ETC.). If you can see the edge of the fabric through the applique thread, the applique work is too skimpy. Poor quality applique work will probably unravel after only a few washings. We've seen some applique work actually fraying in the store—check it before you buy. As a side note, linens with thick applique stitching must have a high thread count, another plus.

**5** HIGH THREAD-COUNT SHEETS. Unlike adult linens, most packages of baby bedding do not list the thread count. But, if you can count the threads when you hold a sheet up to the light, you know the thread count is too low. Also, use the applique test mentioned above to help determine thread count. High thread-count sheets (200 threads per inch or more) are better since they are softer and smoother against baby's skin.

**6** FEEL THE FILLING IN THE BUMPER PADS. If the filling feels gritty, it's not the best quality. Look for bumpers that are very thick and soft to touch—bumpers that are too thin will collapse. Bumpers are more than a bedding item; they're also a safety device that cushions your baby from bumps against the side of the crib. Our advice: buy the best (Dacron-brand filling is a good bet).

**7** THE TIES THAT ATTACH THE BUMPER TO THE CRIB SHOULD BE AT LEAST FOUR INCHES IN LENGTH. Another tip: make sure the bumper has ties on both the top and bottom and are securely sewn.

**8** THE DUST RUFFLE PLATFORM SHOULD BE OF GOOD QUALITY FABRIC—OR ELSE IT WILL TEAR. Longer, full ruffles are more preferable to shorter.

**9** REMEMBER THAT CRIB SHEETS COME IN DIFFERENT SIZES— BASSINET/CRADLE, PORTABLE CRIB, AND FULL-SIZE CRIB. Always use the correct-size sheet.

## The Name Game: Reviews of Selected Manufacturers

 Here are reviews of some of the brand names you'll encounter on your shopping adventures for baby bedding. You'll notice that we include the phone numbers and addresses of each manufacturer—this is so you can find a local dealer near you (most do not sell directly to the public). We rated the companies on overall quality, price, and creativity factors, based on an evaluation of sample items we viewed at retail stores. We'd love to hear from you—tell us what you think about different brands and how they held up in the real world by calling us at (303) 442-8792.

## The Ratings

★★★★ EXCELLENT—*our top pick!*
★★★ GOOD— *above average quality, prices, and creativity.*
★★ FAIR—*could stand some improvement.*
★ POOR—*yuck! could stand some major improvement.*

***Glenna Jean*** .............................................................................★★
*230 N. Sycamore St., Petersburg, VA 23803. (800) 446-6018 or (804) 861-0687.* We liked Glenna Jean's designs—as long as you stick with non-appliqued patterns. (The quality and sewing construction of the appliques just wasn't very impressive). One nice, non-appliqued pattern is "Sweet Violet," a beautiful design featuring violets. The price for this pattern: $99 for a quilt and bumper, $20 for the sheet, and $60 for the dust ruffle—not bad for the quality and design.

***House of Hatten*** ............................................................. ★★★
*2200 Denton Dr., Suite 110, Austin, TX 78758. (800) 938-4467 or (512) 837-4467.* House of Hatten makes beautiful appliqued and embroidered quilts. For example, the wonderful "Farmyard Friends" quilt design features brightly colored farm animals like cows, chickens, ducks and rabbits. A bold black and red border on a white background sets off the characters—a nice look. Most quilts run $60 to $140.

House of Hatten's specialty is delicate embroidery on either white fabric or pastel patchwork designs. While the quilts get rave reviews, we heard mixed reviews on Hatten's other products: the bumper pads and dust ruffles get lower marks, thanks to cheaper construction and skimpy fabrics.

Our recommendation: buy a quilt from House of Hatten and forget the bumper pads and dust ruffle. You can buy coordinating sets from other manufacturers—in fact, Lollipops & Gumdrops (see the review later in this section) makes their bumper pads, sheets and dust ruffles in colors that specifically coordinate with House of Hatten's designs.

*Judi's* ............................................................................★ ¹/₂
*7733 East Gray Rd., Scottsdale, AZ 85260. (800) 421-9433 or (602) 991-5885.* Judi's offers quite a few designs with three-dimensional applique work. Unfortunately, in our opinion the applique construction is very skimpy—you can see the fabric through the stitching. As with any sloppy applique work, we worry about its ability to hold up after several washings. If you like Judi's bedding designs, consider sticking with non-appliqued styles. One popular design from this manufacturer is "Judi's Jungle," which is similar to Lambs & Ivy's popular "Paradise" pattern. The tropical theme is accented by bright colors.

We priced the 4-piece set with quilt, headboard bumper, dust ruffle, and sheet at $199.

*Lambs & Ivy*................................................................★★★
*5978 Bowcroft St., Los Angeles, CA 90016. (800) 345-2627 or (310) 839-5155.* This LA-based bedding company was founded in 1979 by Barbara Lainken and Cathy Ravdin. Their creative and affordable designs have generated legions of fans. Their hottest design today: the "Paradise" line. This bright, cheerful print with appliqued jungle animals runs $75 for quilt, $68 for bumper, $30 for ruffle, $16 for sheet. The tropical colors (purple, blue, and pink hues) are a nice contrast to traditional designs that either use black and white or some muted pastel. Lambs & Ivy recently launched "Bedtime Originals," a more affordable line of baby bedding available through "mass market" (read: discount) stores. All in all, we like Lambs & Ivy; the designs are well stitched and prices are reasonable.

*Laura Ashley* ................................................................★ ¹/₂
*To find a store near you, call (800) 223-6917.* Of the many Laura Ashley stores that dot the country, about 30 combination stores sell Ashley's baby bedding. We visited one in Denver and were not overly impressed. First, the colors are dull, mostly muted yellows and greens. The styling didn't overwhelm us either, with patterns that lacked pizazz. As you might expect, the prices are at the upper end. The comforter was somewhat affordable at $95, as was the bumper (also

$95), but the sheets weighed in at a hefty $26, and the dust ruffle was $75. Ordering regular merchandise (if not in stock) takes two to four weeks, while custom orders take eight weeks. Fabric is available by the yard, as are coordinating lamps and bibs. Laura Ashley bedding is an acquired taste, like zucchini—some like it, but some won't.

*Lollipops & Gumdrops* ................................................ ★★★★
*Available exclusively through Baby on a Budget; (800) 575-2224,* reviewed below in this chapter's Best Buy section. Lollipops & Gumdrops offers custom-quality bedding at very affordable prices. Using only high-quality, soft-finish fabrics with high thread count, the company offers quilts, bumpers, sheets, and dust ruffles in solid pastels or primary colors that are well designed and constructed. Good-quality thread is used and the stitching is permanent (no unraveling). You can choose from several fabric samples and add pipping and eyelet to your taste. If you prefer, they'll even use your own fabric.

And check out these prices: sheets for just $17.50 to $21, dust ruffles for $56 to $72, bumpers for $75 to $88, and pillows for $28 to $36. Quilt prices run only $90 to $110 and vary depending on the design (monogramming runs an extra $16 to $20). We had our baby's name monogrammed on a quilt we bought from Lollipops & Gumdrops—and it looks marvelous, darling. We couldn't be happier with the quilt; the quality of fabric and stitching is quite impressive.

*My Dog Spot* ................................................ ★★★
*PO Box 1711, Rancho Santa Fe, CA 92067. (619) 756-1614.* Looking for something different? Check out My Dog Spot, a hilarious and funky collection of baby bedding that is anything but boring. Seven designs include our favorite, "Spot Goes to Botswanna," with a 100% cotton quilt featuring the famous canine visiting a plaid elephant and striped palm trees. Accessories include a coordinating bumper, valance, pillow (in either elephant or Spot styles), and a flannel "blankie." They even sell fabric by the yard. Of course, you must pay for the privilege of visiting Botswana with Spot. The quilt is a whopping $300, while the bumper (with Spot's dog house headboard) is $146, the ruffle is $60, and the sheets are $32 each. Ouch!

Other designs include Spot Goes to Tonga (an island scene), This is Spot's House, Spot Goes Skating (yes, he's on roller skates), Spot Goes to Saturn (the dog rides a rocket to the ringed planet), Spot Goes to the Circus (he's riding a circus elephant), and Spot Goes Underwater (friendly fish accompany him). Colors are bright and flashy except for the Saturn quilt, which is black and white. Want to know who

Spot is? According to company literature, he was born in San Diego in the summer of 1990, loves adventure, and "hates split pea soup." Need we say more?

***Nava's Designs*** .................................................................★★ $^1/_2$
*16742 Stagg St. #106, Van Nuys, CA 91406. (818) 988-9050.* Want to spend a fortune on baby bedding? Check out Nava's Designs, a California-based bedding manufacturer that has sky-high prices. A typical example: a beautiful pattern like "Old Macdonald," which features various barnyard animals in a pastoral setting. The price? Are you sitting down? How about a whopping $760 for a seven-piece set (quilt, ruffle, pillow, bumper, diaper stacker, stuffed animal, and sheet). A major negative (besides the price): some designs don't wash well and may even have to be dry-cleaned (check the washing instructions carefully). On the upside, the fabrics are very heavy, high-quality cottons, and the stitching is excellent. Nava is sold at many upper-end baby stores like Bellini (see review of this chain in the last chapter).

***NoJo*** .....................................................................................★★
*22942 Arroyo Vista, Rancho Santa Margarita, CA 92688. (714) 858-9717.* Shirley Pepys founded NoJo in 1970 with just one product—a quilted infant seat cover. Since then, NoJo's expanded into a wide range of bedding and nursery products. The company has shown remarkable marketing timing—their "Bright Dino" line of bedding was introduced years before Barney and Jurassic Park made dinosaurs a hot commodity. Prices are moderate: a three-piece set (quilt, bumper, sheet) is $159. The matching dust ruffle is $44. While we liked the bright pink and blue dinosaurs design, we did notice the fabric was a 50/50 poly/cotton blend—we'd expect 100% cotton at these prices.

Another popular product by NoJo is their revolutionary Baby Sling carrier, which has become quite famous. It retails for about $40 (for more information on this and other carriers, see Chapter 7). An additional interesting note: NoJo actually has a factory outlet store, which is rare in this business (see review in the outlet section of this chapter). And the company is looking into establishing a chain of NoJo retail stores.

***Patsy Aiken*** .................................................................★★★★
*4812 Hargrove Rd., Raleigh, NC 27604. (800) 828-2351 or (919) 872-8789.* One of our favorite bedding designers is Patsy Aiken, whose patterns incorporate wonderful applique work and high-quality construction. One of Aiken's most popular designs is the "Moo Cow" pattern with its appliqued cartoon-type cow and farm scene. The cost for this pattern is

$98 for the quilt, $120 for the headboard bumper, $28 for the sheet, and $52 for the dust ruffle. As you can see, this isn't a cheap bedding line—but, considering the quality, we think it's worth the investment. (We should note that Patsy Aiken also makes a wonderful line of children's clothing as well—see our next chapter for details.)

### *Quiltcraft Kids* ............................................................★★★

*1233 Levee St., Dallas, TX 75207. (800) 462-2805 or (214) 741-1662.* Texas-based Quiltcraft Kids features good quality fabric, folded ruffles, and thick bumpers—at prices that are 15% to 20% less than comparable brands. We liked the American Gingham pattern the best; prices for this style ran $70 for a quilt, $70 for a bumper, $16 for sheets, and $35 for a dust ruffle.

### *Quiltex* ............................................................................★★

*100 W. 33rd St., New York, NY 10001. (800) 237-3636 or (212) 594-2205.* Quiltex is famous for their Peanuts-inspired patterns, including the popular Snoopy Collection. "Country Snoopy" has bright, primary colors, while "Rainbow Snoopy" features subdued pastels. Prices are moderate, with a quilt from this collection running $50 to $75 and sheets $18 to $20. Another popular Quiltex pattern is the Beatrix Potter collection. We saw a 5-piece set for $200 at LiL' Things; retail is $250 (the set includes headboard bumper, sheet, dust ruffle, diaper stacker, and quilt).

The quality of the Quiltex designs we viewed is middle-of-the-road: some applique work leaves a bit to be desired, while other designs are merely stamped on the fabric. Make sure you check the stitching before you buy.

### *Red Calliope*...........................................................★ ¹/₂

*13003 S. Figueroa St., Los Angeles, CA 90061. (800) 412-0526 or (310) 516-6100.* This manufacturer's bedding designs are widely available and priced affordably; however, the quality isn't much to shout about. Most of Red Calliope's designs have patterns that are stamped into the fabric—as you know, we aren't big fans of stamped designs. Fortunately, the line isn't all bad—a few designs, like the watercolor-inspired "Floral Fantasy," utilize higher quality fabric with shirred detailing. This line runs $60 for a quilt, $18 for the sheet, and $60 for a bumper.

---

"MAKE SURE YOU CHECK THE
STITCHING BEFORE YOU BUY."

We hope to expand our reviews in future editions to encompass more resources. In our research we came across three other brand names worth checking out:

- ♣ *Sweetpea*: PO Box 90756, Pasadena, CA 91109. (818) 578-0866.
- ♣ *Patchcraft:* 70 Outwater Ln., Garfield, NJ 07026. (201) 340-3300.
- ♣ *Carousel Designs:* 4519 Bankhead Hwy., Douglasville, GA 30134. (404) 949-2123.

## Safe & Sound

While you might think to cover your outlets and hide that can of Raid, you might not automatically consider safety when selecting sheets, comforters, and bumpers. Yet, your baby will be spending more time with these products than any other. Here are several points to remember to keep your baby safe and sound.

♣ *All linens should have a tag* indicating the manufacturer's name and address. That's the only way you would know if it's being recalled. You can also contact the manufacturer if you have a problem or question. While this is the law, some stores may sell discounted or imported linens that do not have tags.

♣ *Recent studies of Sudden Infant Death Syndrome* (SIDS, also known as crib death) have reported that there is an increased incidence of crib death occuring when infants sleep on fluffy bedding, lambskins, or pillows. A pocket can form around the baby's face if she is placed face down in fluffy bedding, and she can slowly suffocate while breathing in her own carbon dioxide. The best advice: prop your infant on her side when she sleeps. And forget the lambskins and pillows.

♣ *Beware of ribbons or long fringe.* These are a possible choking hazard if they are not attached properly.

♣ *Buy bumper pads with well-sewn ties at the top and bottom* (12 to 16 total). Ties should be between six and seven inches in length. Some bumpers just have top ties, enabling your baby to scoot under the bumper and get trapped.

♣ *Never use an electric blanket.* Babies can overheat, plus any moisture, such as urine, can cause electric shock.

♣*Avoid blankets that use nylon (or fish-line type) thread.* Nylon thread melts in the dryer and then breaks. These loose threads can wrap around your baby's neck or break off and become a choking hazard. Cotton thread is best and is a better bet in the dryer.

## Money Saving Secrets

**1** IF YOU'RE ON A TIGHT BUDGET, GO FOR GOOD BUMPER PADS AND A NICE SET OF HIGH THREAD-COUNT SHEETS. What does that cost? Bumpers are about $70, while a fitted sheet runs $15 to $20. Forget all the fancy items like pillow cases, window valances, and dust ruffles. After all, your baby won't care if she sleeps in a perfectly coordinated room.

**2** FORGET BUYING BEDDING SETS (IN MOST CASES). You'll probably notice many bedding items grouped into sets for your convenience. The problem? Bedding sets often include frivolous items you don't need or won't use. For example, even at a discount store, a four-piece set (sheet, quilt, bumper pad, dust ruffle) is about $140 to $200—but if you live in a warm climate, do you really need a quilt? Or dust ruffle? If you do buy a set, be sure it contains only those items you really want and will use.

**3** DON'T BUY A QUILT. Sure, they look pretty, but do you really need one? Go for a nice cotton blanket, instead—and save the $50 to $100. Better yet, hint to your friends that you'd like receiving blankets as shower gifts.

**4** INSTEAD OF EXPENSIVE WALL HANGINGS, MAKE YOUR OWN. Consider using stencils to give your baby's room a decorator border (craft stores like Michaels Arts & Crafts have all the supplies; call 214-580-8242 for a store near you). Or paint stars on the nursery ceiling, so baby will have an interesting view. If you're handy with a sewing machine (or have a friend or relative who is), make a small quilted wall hanging yourself. There are dozens of neat patterns available at fabric stores. Avoid expensive wallpaper and other decorator accents for now. You can always add them later if you like.

**5** INSTEAD OF BUYING A CURTAIN VALENCE, BUY AN EXTRA DUST RUFFLE AND SEW YOUR OWN CURTAIN VALENCE. This was a great money-saving tip from a mom we interviewed in Georgia—she saved $70. Another solution: buy an adult-size dust ruffle in coordinating fabric to make a curtain valence. All you need to do is remove the ruffle from the fabric platform and sew a pocket along one edge. I managed to do this simple procedure on my sewing machine without killing myself, so it's quite possible you could do it too.

**6** SHOP AT OUTLETS. Scattered across the country, we found a couple of outlets that discount baby linens. Among the better ones were House of Hatten and NoJo—see their reviews in the next section.

## Best Buys

### Baby on a Budget
#### 1-800-575-2224

Looking for top-quality baby bedding, but tired of seeing top-dollar price tags? We found a great solution: Baby on a Budget, a mail-order company that specializes in name brand designer baby bedding at fantastic discounts.

How does it work? Well, you first shop for the bedding, deciding on the brand, pattern style, and options. Then call Baby on a Budget for a price quote—and be prepared to be pleasantly surprised with the savings. Delivery takes four to six weeks, but expedited service may be possible. The company accepts both Mastercard and VISA credit cards. (We should note that Baby on a Budget does not have any bedding catalogs to send out—you have to shop local stores and the pick the pattern before you call).

The discounts are fantastic. We're talking brand-new, first-quality bedding at 20% discount off retail price. Order more than the basic four bedding items (bumper, sheet, dust ruffle, and comforter) at the same time, and you get a 25% discount on the additional items! Baby on a Budget sells wall borders, additional sheets, mobiles, canopies—nearly every accessory you see in those expensive specialty stores.

And that's just the beginning. Baby on a Budget also has lamps, accessories, and a complete line of silver-plated, pewter, and sterling silver engravable gift items.

We've searched the country and haven't found a more affordable source for bedding than Baby on a Budget—it's nearly impossible to get up to a 25% discount on brand-new linens from any other source, retail or mail-order! How do they do it? First, the owners have 10 years of experience in the baby bedding business, so they know the brands and how to spot quality. Second, they keep their overhead low by operating out of an unpretentious office in the nation's heartland. You're not paying for a fancy shop and all that overhead—Baby on a Budget can pass the savings on to you in lower prices.

What brands are available? Many of the famous labels you read about earlier in this chapter, plus some fancy brands seen in the most exclusive baby stores—call for a list of items available. Here's another plus: Baby on a Budget is the exclusive dealer for Lollipops & Gumdrops (see review earlier in this chapter in the Name Game). This line offers custom-made, quality bedding at unbelievably low prices. For example, Lollipops & Gumdrops' ultra-thick bumper pads cost just $75 to $88—you'd pay twice that for the same quality in a retail shop.

We can't say enough nice things about Baby on a Budget— if you don't call them for a quote before you buy your baby's bedding, you're probably spending too much.

## Outlets

### NoJo

*Location*: Rancho Santa Margarita, CA. (714) 858-9496. Fall in love with a NoJo pattern early in your pregnancy, only to discover later that it has been discontinued? Don't fret. Call the NoJo outlet store. This popular Orange County, California-based bedding manufacturer has a wonderful outlet that carries discontinued items and factory seconds—they even have items that are exclusively made for the outlet. Best of all, the savings is 20% to 60% off retail. They even discount their famous Baby Sling to $34.95. Another plus: they take phone orders (and major credit cards) and ship nationwide! You can find crib bedding, lamps, wall boarders, fabric, car seat covers, head rests, and more at the store.

### House of Hatten

*Location*: 3939 IH-35, Suite 725, San Marcos, TX. (512) 392-8161.

Perhaps the only thing more beautiful than a great quilt is a great quilt on sale. That's why we love House of Hatten's fantastic outlet store in San Marcos, Texas—the only one like it in the country. You can find their quilts, as well as headboards, mobiles, bumper pads, dust ruffles, and sheets at 30% off retail. The store also sells their clothing line, which features smocked outfits for girls and boys (starting at 3-6 month size). Look for their sales near holidays for additional savings. The outlet offers mail-order service and ships nationwide. All items are discontinued, and some are imperfect or flawed.

### Laura Ashley

*Locations*: Secaucus, New Jersey (201) 863-3066; Woodbridge, Virginia (703) 494-3124; Myrtle Beach, South Carolina (803) 236-4244; Freeport, Maine (207) 865-3300; and Orlando, Florida (407) 351-2785.

The famous British designer has five outlets that occasionally get in baby bedding and clothing. The savings range from 20% to 50% off retail. We urge you to call before you visit since the selection may vary widely.

Have you found an outlet store for baby bedding that's not listed above?  Call us at 303-442-8792.

## *Wastes of Money/Worthless Items*

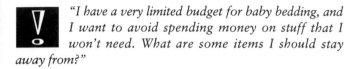

*"I have a very limited budget for baby bedding, and I want to avoid spending money on stuff that I won't need. What are some items I should stay away from?"*

It may be tempting to buy every new fad and matching accessory. To help you spend your money more wisely, here's our list of the worthless products to stay away from:

**1** DIAPER STACKER. This is basically a bag (in coordinating fabric, of course) used to store diapers—you hang it on the side of your crib or changing table. Apparently, bedding makers must think stacking diapers on the shelf of your changing table or storing them in a drawer is a major etiquette breach. Take my word for it: babies are not worried if their diapers are out in plain sight. Save the $30 to $50 that bedding makers charge for diaper stackers and stack your own.

**2** PILLOWS. We are constantly amazed at the number of bedding sets that include pillows or pillow cases. Are the bedding designers nuts, or what? Haven't they heard that it's dangerous to put your baby to sleep on a pillow? What a terrible safety hazard, not to mention a waste of your money. We don't even think a decorative pillow is a good idea. Forget the pillow and save $20 to $30.

**3** CANOPIES. We know how tempting it is to go for the whole "look" when you're shopping for your baby's bedding. Your local baby store also realizes how easy it is to sell you on items like canopies, especially when you have a daughter. The emphasis is on giving her "everything" and achieving a "feminine" look for your nursery. Don't buy into it. The whole set-up for a canopy is going to be more expensive (you'll need a special crib, etc.)—it'll set you back $75 to $175 in the end. And enclosing your baby's crib in a canopy won't do much for her visual stimulation or health (canopies are dust catchers).

**4** KNIT SHEETS. They cost $10 more than woven sheets and are softer—unfortunately, they also discolor more easily and don't wash well. A better alternative: flannel sheets.

**5** ALL-WHITE LINENS. If you think of babies as pristine and unspoiled, you've never had to change a poopy diaper or clean spit-up from the front of an outfit. I'm amazed that any-one would consider all-white bedding, since keeping it clean will probably be a full-time job. Stick with colors, preferably bright ones. If you buy all-white linens and then have to go back to buy colored ones, you'll be out another $100 to $200.

**6** SETS OF LINENS. Sets may include useless or underused items like diaper stackers, pillows or pillow cases, and window valances. Another problem: sets are often a mixed bag when it comes to quality. Some items are good, while others are lacking.

For example, we saw a bedding set by American Pacific called "Chicken Farm." Included in the set was a hand-pieced patchwork quilt, bumper, dust ruffle, and sheet. The quilt was well made with good stitching, but the bumper was incredibly flimsy and inadequate. The whole set was $170. We found the same quilt available separately in the Right Start catalog (800-548-8531). The quilt alone was priced at $39, the sheet at $19, and the ruffle at $29. You could buy a better-made coordinating bumper pad for about $70, making the total cost $160—that's still $10 less than the set with the cheap bumpers.

**7** TEETHING PADS FOR CRIB RAILS. Most new, name brand cribs will already have plastic teething guards on the side rails, so adding pads (cost: $20 extra) is redundant. One store owner pointed out that if your baby has nothing better to teeth on than the crib railing, the baby is spending too much time in the crib anyway.

## Do It By Mail

 Here's an overview of several catalogs that offer great deals on bedding and other layette items. For more information on these and other mail-order catalogs, see Chapter 11.

## The Company Store.

*To Order Call:* (800) 285-3696; (800) 289-8508; Fax (608) 784-2366.
*Shopping Hours:* 24 hours a day, seven days a week.
*Or write to:* 500 Company Store Rd., La Crosse, WI 54601.
*Credit Cards Accepted:* MC, VISA, AMEX, Discover.

The Company Store manufactures their own down products, including comforters and pillows—plus they sell brand name and in-house bedding. They also offer down comforters in crib sizes priced at $55. Available in four different sizes and colors, the comforters are covered in 232-thread-count cotton fabric—very high quality for the price. They also offer mattress pads, crib blankets, comforter covers, and sheets.

## Right Start Catalog.

*To Order Call:* (800) LITTLE-1 (800-548-8531);
Fax (800) 762-5501.
*Shopping Hours:* 24 hours a day, seven days a week.
*Or write to:* Right Start Inc., Right Start Plaza, 5334 Sterling Center Dr., Westlake Village, CA 91361.
*Credit Cards Accepted:* MC, VISA, AMEX, Discover.

Right Start doesn't carry a huge amount of baby bedding, but it does have the popular Lambs & Ivy "Paradise" design, as well as several popular patterns by Boynton and Beatrix Potter. Be careful to check the fabric content of the bedding, since some designs are 50/50 poly/cotton blends and others are 100% cotton.

All the options are available by the piece, rather than in sets, making it easier to buy what you really want and need. Most of the comforters range between $40 and $75—rather affordable. The most expensive bedding design, the "Paradise" pattern, features a quilt for $75, bumpers for $69, a dust ruffle for $32, and a sheet at $16. For comparison, we saw just the quilt at a baby specialty shop for $100!

## Lands' End.

*To Order Call:* (800) 356-4444; Fax (800) 332-0103.
*Shopping Hours:* 24 hours a day, seven days a week.
*Or write to:* Lands' End Inc., 1 Lands' End Ln., Dodgeville, WI 53595.
*Credit Cards Accepted:* MC, VISA, AMEX, Discover.
*Retail Outlets:* They also have 11 outlet stores in Iowa, Illinois, and Wisconsin—call the number above for the nearest location to you.

The Lands' End "Coming Home" catalog offers a few bedding options for infants. While they only carry two crib sets, the 200-thread-count sheets are a bargain, given the quality.

At only $13 for the sheet, $36 for the comforter, $38 for the bumpers, and $18 for the dust ruffle, you can't beat the price.

Of the two designs featured in their spring/summer catalog, we especially liked the Piglets pattern. The comforter is covered with line-drawn piggies, complete with brightly colored snouts on a white background. Matching pieces were black and white striped. The other design, "Glorious Garden," features pastel flowers on a white background.

Blankets are also available from Lands' End for $16.50 to $18. In the winter season, the catalog showcases flannels for the young set as well.

## J.C. Penney.

*To Order Call:* (800) 222-6161. Ask for the following catalogs: *Baby and You, For Baby,* and *Starting Small.*
*Shopping Hours:* 24 hours a day, seven days a week.
*Credit Cards Accepted:* MC, VISA, JC Penney, AMEX, Discover.

J.C. Penny carries quite a wide range of name brand baby bedding from manufacturers like Lambs & Ivy (yes, including that famous "Paradise" line), NoJo, Red Calliope, Glenna Jean, and Judi's Originals. While Penney's prices aren't always affordable (we compared some designs to other mail-order sources and found Penney's to be a few dollars higher), they do offer the most accessories we've ever found. For example, they carry every accessory available for the Boynton for Babies line. The catalog carries valances, wallpaper borders, mobiles, and wall hangings for this and other bedding designs. If you want a "complete look," give Penney's a call.

## One Step Ahead.

*To Order Call:* (800) 274-8440; (800) 950-5120; Fax (708) 615-2162.
*Shopping Hours:* 24 hours a day, seven days a week.
*Or write to:* One Step Ahead, 950 North Shore Dr., Lake Bluff, IL 60044.
*Credit Cards Accepted:* MC, VISA, AMEX, Discover, Optima.

One Step Ahead offers a limited number of baby linen options. Two sets, "Rock Along Bear" and "North Forty," were poly/cotton blends. Available either in separate pieces or as a four-piece set ($149 to $169), these patterns were both attractive and affordable.

Perhaps more impressive, however were the two quilts available from One Step Ahead—the "Contemporary Brights" patchwork pattern in bold colors and a more subdued "Dresden Plate," both of which cost $150 (for a four-piece set). While the quilts were nice, the bumper pads looked somewhat skimpy.

We also noticed that One Step Ahead sells 100% cotton sheets and receiving blankets. Sheets were priced at $12.95, and thermal blankets ranged in price from $9.95 to $14.95 depending on the size. What we liked best was One Step Ahead's wide variety of colors—from bright hues like purple and jade, to pastels like mint and periwinkle.

## Garnet Hill.

*To Order Call:* (800) 622-6216; Fax (603) 823-9578.
*Shopping Hours:* Monday-Friday 7:00 am-11:00 pm; Saturday and Sunday 10:00 am-6:00 pm Eastern Time.
*Or write to:* Garnet Hill, 262 Main St., Franconia, NH 03580.
*Credit Cards Accepted:* MC, VISA, AMEX, Discover.

If you want to spend the big bucks on bedding, check out Garnet Hill. This catalog makes a big deal out of its "natural fabric" offerings, and they do sell products we haven't seen elsewhere. They just offer them at a premium.

For example, the patterned crib sheet sets are a whopping $44 and include a fitted sheet, flat sheet, and pillow case. Since you'll probably only use the fitted sheet, this seems like overkill. And you can't purchase the patterned pieces separately. Nevertheless, the designs are attractive, especially the "Cloud and Stars" pattern.

If you'd rather keep it plain, cotton flannel fitted sheets (available separately) from Garnet Hill list at a hefty $17. The catalog's patchwork quilts are quite beautiful (especially the tumbling blocks design) and cost $90 to $195, depending on the pattern. Cotton crib blankets are $22.50. Overall, while the designs are unique and in many cases appealing, you may want to save your money and shop elsewhere.

## THE BOTTOM LINE:
### A Wrap-Up of Best Buy Picks

 For bedding, we thought the best brands were Lollipops & Gumdrops, Patsy Aiken, and Lambs & Ivy. For example, the popular "Paradise" bedding from Lambs & Ivy was $189 for a four-piece set. For quilts, it was hard to beat the beautiful handiwork of House of Hatten ($60 to $140).

No matter what brand you buy, we thought Baby on a Budget had the best prices. The premium brands and low prices from this mail-order source were hard to beat.

Let's take a look at the savings. We recommend the following pieces:

| | |
|---|---:|
| Sheet | $16 |
| Bumper | $68 |
| Dust ruffle | $30 |
| Blanket | $20 |
| **TOTAL** | **$134** |

*(The above prices are from the "Paradise" line and are quoted from discount sources and outlets).*

If you live in a place that gets cold in the winter, you might add a quilt to this list (an extra $60 to $150).

In contrast, if you go for a designer brand and buy all those silly extras like diaper stackers, you could be out as much as $750 on bedding alone. So, the total savings from following the tips in this chapter could be as much as $600.

Now that your baby's room is outfitted, what about the baby? Flip to the next chapter to get the lowdown on those little clothes.

Questions or comments? Did you discover a bedding bargain you'd like to share with our readers? **Call the authors at (303) 442-8792!**

# Chapter 4

## The Reality Layette: Little Clothes for Little Prices

What the heck is a "onesie"? How many clothes does your baby need? How come such little clothes have such big price tags? These and other mysteries are unraveled in this chapter as we take you on a guided tour of baby clothes land. We'll reveal our secret sources for finding name brand clothes at one-half to one-third off department store prices. Which brands are best? Check out our reviews and ratings of the best clothing brands for your baby and our 11 tips from smart shoppers on getting the best deals. Next, read about the many outlets for children's apparel that have been popping up all over the country. At the end of this chapter, we'll even show you how to save big bucks on diapers.

### Getting Started: When Do You Need This Stuff?

♣ BABY CLOTHING: You'll need basic baby clothing like t-shirts and sleepers as soon as you're ready to leave the hospital. Depending on the weather, you may need a bunting at that time as well.

You'll probably want to start stocking up on baby clothing around the seventh month of your pregnancy. It's important to have some basic items on hand (like sleepers or strechies)in case you deliver early; however, you may want to wait to do major baby clothes shopping until after any baby showers to see what clothing your friends and family give as gifts.

Be sure to keep a running list of your acquisitions so you won't buy too much of one item. Thanks to gifts and our own buying, we had about two thousand teeny, side-snap shirts by the time our baby was born. In the end, he didn't wear the shirts much (he grew out of the newborn sizes quickly and wasn't really wild about them anyway), and we ended up wasting the $20 we spent.

♣ DIAPERS: How many diapers do you need for starters? Are you sitting down? If you're going with disposables, we recommend 600. Yes, that's six packages of 100 diapers each (purchase them in your eighth month of pregnancy, just in case Junior arrives early). You may think this is a lot, but believe us, we bought that much and we still had to do another diaper run by the time our son was a month old. Newborns go through many more diapers than older infants. Also, remember that as a new parent, you'll find yourself taking off diapers that turn out to be dry; then you can't really reuse them because the tabs don't stick as well. Or worse, you may change a diaper three times in a row because Junior wasn't really finished.

If you plan to use a diaper service to supply cloth diapers, sign up in your eighth month. Some diaper services will give you an initial batch of diapers (so you're not without diapers when the baby comes home) and then await your call to start-up regular service. If you plan to wash your own cloth diapers, buy two to five dozen diapers about two months before your due date. You'll also probably want to buy diaper covers (6 to 10) at that time.

## Sources:

There are six basic sources for baby clothing and diapers:

1 BABY SPECIALTY STORES. Specialty stores typically carry 100% cotton, high-quality clothes, but you won't find them affordably priced. While you may find attractive dressy clothes, playclothes are usually a better deal elsewhere. Because the stores themselves are usually small, selection is often limited.

As for diapers, most specialty shops don't carry disposables. If they do at all, it seems to be the new eco diapers (Tushies is one brand). These are as much as twice as expensive as the major name brands. However, specialty shops do often carry a good selection of cloth diapers and diaper wraps.

2 DISCOUNTERS/DEPARTMENT STORES. When it comes to basic sleepwear, your best bet may be discount chains like Toys R Us. T-shirts, booties, and such from brands like Carter's are just fine for the short time your baby will be wearing them. As for playclothes, which will get much more wear, we were less impressed with the polyester-blend clothes available from discounters like K-Mart and Target. Department stores are more likely to carry playclothes in the higher-quality, all-cotton brands we will recommend later in this chapter—and with frequent sales, department store prices can be relatively affordable.

While we had mixed feelings about discounters for baby clothes, they do have great buys on disposable diapers. You'll see later in this chapter that stores like Toys R Us are incredibly affordable compared to the place most folks buy diapers (grocery stores, of course). The discounters may even have promotional specials from time to time, and, to save even more money, you can utilize the many coupons you'll be getting in the mail. As far as cloth diaper supplies go, discounters don't have as much of a selection.

**3** BABY MEGA-STORES. Both LiL' Things and Baby Superstore carry name brand clothing at incredibly low prices. For example, we saw such famous labels as Baby Guess and Good Lad of Philadelphia—at prices well below regular department store prices. They also carry basic items from brands like Carter's, Baby Grow, and Little Me. The best part: you'll find a huge selection of brands and styles.

As for diapers, some mega-stores carry them and others don't. Baby Superstore, for example, had some of the best prices on disposables we've ever seen! On the other hand, LiL' Things has chosen not to carry diapers. Good news for cloth diaper users: both stores do stock a wide variety of diaper covers.

**4** WAREHOUSE CLUBS. Member-only warehouse clubs like Sam's and Price/Cosco sell diapers at rock-bottom prices. The selection is often hit-or-miss—sometimes you'll see brand names like Huggies and Pampers; other times it may be off-brands. While you won't find the range of sizes that you'd see in grocery stores, the prices will be hard to beat.

**5** MAIL-ORDER. There are a zillion catalogs that offer clothing for infants. The choices can be quite overwhelming, and the prices can range from reasonable to ridiculous. It's undeniably a great way to shop when you have a newborn and just don't want to drag your baby out to the mall. Cloth diapers and diaper covers are often available through mail order. Later in this chapter, we'll highlight some of the better catalogs offering these products.

**6** CONSIGNMENT OR THRIFT STORES. You might think of these stores as dingy shops with musty smells—purveyors of old, used clothes that aren't in great shape. Think again—many consignment stores today are bright and attractive, with name brand clothes at a fraction of the retail price. Yes, the clothes have been worn before, but most stores only stock high-quality brands that are in excellent condition. And stores that specialize in children's apparel are popping up everywhere, from Play it Again (718) 499-8589 in Brooklyn, New York, to Baby Bargains (602) 820-6406 in Phoenix, Arizona (no relation to this book, of course). Later in this chapter, we'll tell you how to find a consignment store near you.

## Baby Clothing

So you thought all the big-ticket items were taken care of when you bought the crib and other baby furniture? Ha! It's time to prepare for your baby's "layette," a French word that translated literally means "spending large sums of cash on baby clothes and other such items, as required by Federal Baby Law." But, of course, there are some creative (dare we say, sneaky?) ways of keeping your layette bills down.

At this point, you may be wondering just what does your baby need? Obviously it may be a few years before he or she wears your hand-me-downs. Sure you've seen those cute ruffly dresses and sailor suits in department stores—but what does your baby *really* wear everyday?

Meet the layette, a collection of clothes and accessories that your baby will use daily. While your baby's birthday suit was free, outfitting him in something more "traditional" will cost some bucks. In fact, a recent study estimated that parents spend $12,000 on clothes for a child by the time he or she hits 18 years old—and that sounds like a conservative estimate to us. That translates into a 20 *billion* (yes, that's billion with a B) dollar business for children's clothing retailers. Follow our tips, and we estimate that you'll save 20% or more on your baby's wardrobe. If you believe that $12,000 figure above, that translates into a savings of $2400!

## What Are You Buying?

 Once you've taken care of the furniture and bedding for your baby's new room, it's time to take care of the baby—and figuring out what your baby should wear is hardly intuitive to first-time parents. We had no earthly idea what type of (and how many) clothes a newborn needs, so we did what we normally do—we went to the bookstore to do research. We found three dozen books on "childcare and parenting"—with three dozen different lists of items that you must have for your baby and without which you're a very bad parent. Speaking of guilt, we also heard from relatives, who had their own opinions as to what was best for baby.

All of this begs the question: what do you really need? And how much? We learned that the answer to that last, age-old question was the age-old answer, "It depends." That's right, nobody really knows. In fact, we surveyed several department stores, interviewed dozens of parents, and consulted several "experts," only to find no consensus whatsoever. In order to better serve humanity, we have developed THE OFFICIAL FIELDS' LIST OF EVERY ITEM YOU NEED FOR YOUR BABY IF YOU LIVE ON PLANET EARTH. We hope this stems the confusion.

Feel free to now ignore those lists of "suggested layette items" provided by retail stores. Many of the "suggestions" are self-serving, to say the least.

Of course, even when you decide what and how much to buy for your baby, you still need to know what *sizes* to buy. Fortunately, we have this covered, too. First, recognize that most baby clothes come in a range of sizes rather than one specific size (newborn to 3 months or 3-6 months). We recommend you buy three to six-month sizes so your child won't grow out of his clothes too quickly. Stay away from newborn to three-month sizes. If you have a premature baby or an infant that is on the small side, we have identified a couple catalogs in Chapter 11 that specialize in preemie wear. And, if on the other hand, you deliver a 10-pounder, make sure you keep all receipts and packaging so you can exchange the clothes for larger sizes—you may find you're into six-month sizes by the time your baby hits one month old!

Remember, you can always buy more later if you need them. In fact, this is a good way to make use of those close friends and relatives who stop by and offer to "help" right after you've suffered through 36 hours of labor—send them to the store!

So, now, join with us as we travel on the Baby Clothes Super-Highway.

♣ *T-Shirts.* Oh sure, a t-shirt is a t-shirt, right? Not when it comes to baby t-shirts. These t-shirts could have side snaps, side ties, go on over the head (sometimes called "Jiffons"), or snaps at the crotch (also known as onesies or creepers). If you have a child who is allergic to metal snaps (they leave a red ring on their skin), you might want to consider over-the-head or side tie t-shirts.

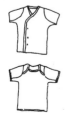

HOW MANY? T-shirts usually come in packs of three. Our recommendation is to buy two packages of three (or a total of six shirts) of the over-the-head variety. We also suggest buying one pack of side-snap shirts and one of side-tie shirts. This way, if your baby does have an allergy to the snaps, you have a backup.

♣ *Drawstring Gowns.* These are one-piece gowns with a drawstring or elastic at the bottom. They are used as sleeping garments in most cases, although we met one mom who used them when her baby had colic—the baby seemed to feel better when she had room to kick her feet. Most drawstring gowns are flame retardant, so you can use them as sleepwear. The drawstrings can be a serious choking hazard so either remove them by the time your baby is 10 weeks old or buy gowns that have an elastic insert instead of string or ribbon.

HOW MANY? In our opinion, drawstring gowns are unnecessary. We never used them, and neither did many of the parents we interviewed. Therefore, we recommend buying none of these. However, if you want to give them a try, buy just one or two to see what your baby thinks.

♣ *Sleepers.* This is the real workhorse of your infant's wardrobe, since babies usually sleep most of the day in the first months. Also known as stretchies, sleepers are most commonly used as pajamas for infants. They have feet, are often made of flame-retardant terry cloth and snap up the front.

HOW MANY? Because of their heavy use, we recommend parents buy at least four to six sleepers.

♣ *Blanket Sleepers.* These are heavy weight, footed one-piece garments. Used often in cool climates or when a baby is "cold natured," blanket sleepers usually have a convenient zipper down the front. The fabric should be treated for flame retardancy.

HOW MANY? If you live in a cold climate or your baby is born in the winter, you may want to purchase one or two of these items. As an alternative to buying blanket sleepers, you could put a t-shirt on underneath her sleeper or stretchie for extra warmth.

♣ *Coveralls.* One-piece play outfits, coveralls (also known as rompers) are usually cotton or cotton/poly blends that are not flame retardant and not intended for sleepwear. Small sizes (under 6 months) may have feet, while larger sizes don't.

HOW MANY? Since these are really playclothes and small infants don't do a lot of playing, we recommend you only buy two to four coveralls for babies under four months of age. However, if your child will be going into daycare at an early age, you may need to buy four to six outfits.

♣ *Booties/socks.* These are necessary for outfits that don't have feet (like drawstring gowns and coveralls). As your child gets older (at about six months), look for the kind of socks that have rubber skids on the bottom (they keep the baby from slipping).

HOW MANY? Three to four pairs are all you'll need at first, since your baby will probably be dressed in footed sleepers most of the time.

♣ *Sweaters.* What you think they are.

HOW MANY? Most people will find one sweater is plenty (they're nice for holiday picture sessions). Avoid all-white sweaters, since they show the dirt much faster.

♣ *Hats.* Believe it or not, you'll still want a light cap for your baby in the early months of life, even if you live in a hot climate. Babies lose a large amount of heat from their heads, so protecting them with a cap or bonnet is a good idea. And don't expect to go out for a walk in the park without the baby's sun hat either.

HOW MANY? A couple of hats would be a good idea—sun hats in summer, warmer caps for winter. We like the safari-style hats best (they have flaps to protect the ears and neck).

♣ Snowsuit/bunting. Similar to the type of fabric used for blanket sleepers, buntings also have hoods and covers for the hands. Most buntings are like a sack and don't have leg openings. On the other hand, snowsuits usually aren't sacks but rather have two legs. Snowsuits are easier to use in a car seat when you have to put the center buckle of your car seat between your baby's legs. Both versions usually have zippered fronts.

HOW MANY? Only buy one of these if you live in a climate where you need it. Even with the Colorado winter, we got away with layering clothes on our baby, then wrapping him in a blanket for the walk out to the warmed-up car.

♣ *Kimonos.* Just like the adult version. Some are zippered sacks with a hood and terry-cloth lining. You use them after a bath.

HOW MANY? Are you kidding? What a joke! These items are one of our "wastes of money." We recommend you pass on the kimonos and instead invest in good quality towels.

♣ *Saque Sets.* Two-piece outfits with a shirt and diaper cover.

HOW MANY? Forget buying these as well. The shirt tends to ride up on your baby anyway.

♣ *Bibs.* These come in two versions, believe it or not. The little, tiny bibs are for the baby that drools the volume of Lake Michigan. The larger versions are used when you begin feeding her solid foods (about six months). Don't expect to be able to use the drool bibs later for feedings, unless you plan to change her carrot-stained outfit frequently.

HOW MANY? Drool bibs are rather useless—skip them. When you get into feeding solids, however, you'll need at least three or four *large* bibs. Consider buying plastic bibs for feeding so you can just sponge them off after a meal.

 ♣ *Washcloths and hooded towels.* OK, so these aren't actually clothes, but baby washcloths and hooded towels are a necessity. Why? Because they are small and easier to use, plus they're softer than adult towels and washcloths.

HOW MANY? At first, you'll probably need only three sets of towels and washcloths (you get one of each per set). But as baby gets older and dirtier, invest in a few more washcloths to spot clean during the day.

♣ *Receiving Blankets.* You'll need these small, cotton blankets for all kinds of uses: to swaddle the baby, as a play quilt, or even for an extra layer of warmth on a cold day.

HOW MANY? We believe you can never have too many of these blankets, but since you'll probably get a few as gifts, you'll only need to buy three or four yourself. A total of seven to eight is probably optimal.

What about the future? While our layette list only addresses clothes to buy for a newborn, you will want to plan for your child's future wardrobe as well. For the modern baby, it seems clothes come in two categories: playclothes (to be used in daycare situations) and dress-up clothes. Later in this chapter, we'll discuss more money-saving tips and review several brands of play and dress-up clothes.

## Smart Shopper Tips
TIPS AND TRICKS TO GET THE BEST QUALITY

*"I've received several outfits from friends for my daughter, but I'm not sure she'll like all the scratchy lace and the poly/cotton blends. What should she wear, and what can I buy that will last through dozens of washings?"*

Generally, we recommend dressing your child for comfor̸. At the same time, you need clothes that can withstan̸ quent washings. With this in mind, here are our suggestions for finding the best clothing for babies.

**1** SEE WHAT YOUR BABY LIKES BEFORE INVESTING IN MANY GARMENTS. Don't invest $90 in eight layette gowns, only to find the baby hates them.

**2** WE GENERALLY RECOMMEND 100% COTTON CLOTHING. The exception: sleepwear should be made of flame-resistant fabrics like polyester.

**3** TEST POLY/COTTON BLENDS ON YOUR CHILD SPARINGLY WHEN SHE GETS OLDER (STARTING AT 3-6 MONTHS) to see if she finds them uncomfortable.

**4** IF YOU DISCOVER YOUR CHILD HAS AN ALLERGY TO METAL SNAPS (YOU'LL SEE RED RINGS ON HIS SKIN), CONSIDER ALTERNATIVES SUCH AS SHIRTS THAT HAVE TIES INSTEAD OF SNAPS. Another option is a t-shirt that pulls on over the head. Unfortunately, many babies don't like having anything pulled over their heads. Another alternative for allergic babies: clothes with plastic snaps or zippers.

**5** IN GENERAL, BETTER-MADE CLOTHES WILL HAVE THEIR SNAPS ON A REINFORCED FABRIC BAND. Snaps attached directly to the body of the fabric may tear the garment or rip off when changing.

**6** IF YOU'RE BUYING 100% COTTON CLOTHING, MAKE SURE ITS PRE-SHRUNK. Some stores, like Gymboree (see review later in this chapter), guarantee that their clothes won't shrink. In other shops, you're on your own. Our advice: read the label. If it says "wash in cold water," assume the garment will shrink. Care instructions that advise washing in warm water indicate the garment may already be preshrunk.

**7** BUY EXTRA WASHCLOTHS—you'll go through quite a few for diaper changes, etc. Another good tip: you can't get enough receiving blankets. We put a couple in the car and one in diaper bag for emergencies.

**8** GO FOR OUTFITS WITH SNAPS AND ZIPPERS ON BOTH LEGS, NOT JUST ONE. Dual-leg snaps or zippers make it much easier to change a diaper. Always check a garment for diaper accessibility—some brands actually have no snaps or zippers, meaning you would have to completely undress your baby for a diaper change!

**9** BE AWARE THAT EACH COMPANY HAS ITS OWN WARPED IDEA ABOUT HOW TO SIZE BABY CLOTHES. We found a "six month" size with one brand is more like a "12 month size" in another. Our advice: open packages to check the sizing, quiz friends for their experiences, ask salespeople for advice, and note whether items are pre-shrunk (if not allow for shrinkage). Beware of "one size fits all" clothes; they are often much bigger than you think. The best brands and mail-order catalogs have detailed sizing charts with height and weight information.

**10** IF YOU HAVE A LARGE CHILD, YOU MAY FIND YOURSELF OUTGROWING DIAPER-FRIENDLY CLOTHES. Most baby clothes include room for a diaper, but as they get larger (sometimes as as early as 3T sizes), the manufacturer assumes your child is already potty trained. We have a friend with this problem—her son was 23 pounds at just six months of age and was already wearing 18 to 24-month clothes! The solution may be buying ultra-thin disposable diapers or looking for larger, baggy pants.

**11** BEWARE OF APPLIQUES. Some applique work can be quite scratchy on the inside of the outfit (it rubs against baby's skin). Also, poor quality applique may unravel or fray after a couple washings.

## The Name Game: Reviews of Selected Manufacturers

 After each brand, we list the address and phone number of their corporate headquarters so you can contact them to find a dealer near you. In most cases, these companies do not sell direct to consumers—you must go through their retail dealers. The exception, of course, are manufacturers' outlets. We list the brands that have outlets later in this chapter, including the outlet's address and phone number.

There are over 700 stores that specialize in selling children's apparel—and that doesn't even count the department stores and discounters who also have baby clothing departments. As you visit these stores, here are some of the brands you'll encounter.

## The Ratings

★★★★ EXCELLENT—*our top pick!*
★★★ GOOD—*above average quality, prices, and creativity.*
★★ FAIR—*could stand some improvement.*
★ POOR—*yuck! could stand some major improve*

*Alexis* ..................................................★★★★
*Manufactured by Warren Featherbone Co., PO Box 383, Gainesville, GA 30503. (404) 535-3000.* This is one of those amazing brands that lasts through several children. In fact, we bought a "previously worn" Alexis outfit from our local consignment shop, and it looked just like new. As for brand-new clothes, we saw an Alexis safari outfit, complete with khaki shorts with suspenders, animal-print shirt, and straw hat for just $25—not bad considering you get that cute hat. The quality is impeccable and worth the price, even at full retail.

*Baby Dior* ..................................................★★
*1590 Adamson Pkwy., Morrow, GA. (404) 961-8722.* Manufactured by Carter's, Baby Dior is one of those upper-end lines that elicits many "oohs" and "aahs." We have mixed feelings about Baby Dior. On one hand, we like the quality of their towels and blankets ($21), but their clothes aren't necessarily any better than more affordable brands. For example, we purchased a Baby Dior terry sleeper ($18 to $21) that snagged badly in the wash and pilled up just as much as the less expensive Carter's sleepers. If you plan to buy any Baby Dior designs, try to catch them on sale or at the many Carter's outlet stores across the U.S. (later in this chapter, we'll review the Carter's outlets). In addition, be careful to check for crotch snaps—some Baby Dior designs lack diaper accessibility.

*Baby Gap* ..................................................★★¹/₂
*(415)952-4400.* An off-shoot of the Gap label, Baby Gap clothes are available at regular Gap stores and at the smaller Gap Kids shops. The Baby Gap label encompasses everything from coveralls to leggings to socks—and even sunglasses, hats, and shoes. On a recent visit to a Gap Kids, we noticed a cute shorts coverall outfit for $15—not bad. The coverall had a red checkered background (like a picnic tablecloth), covered with various condiments like catsup bottles, watermelon slices, and hot dogs. Plain purple leggings were $12.50, and a beautiful cardigan sweatshirt with an appliqued yellow pear was $18. While Baby Gap stores are all over the U.S., they are more numerous in the eastern states. Prices are moderate, and everything is 100% cotton.

*Brown* ..................................................★ ¹/₂
*....e., Chattanooga, TN 37406. (615) 629-*
*..1 is yet another brand we see just about*
*..cunately, they offer an over abundance of*
*blends, rather than all-cotton designs.*
*ir Snoopy-printed designs are cute; one cov-*

erall had Snoopy dressed in soccer garb. The $18 price tag, however, reminded us that we could find comparably priced all-cotton designs that would be more comfortable for our baby.

**Carter's** .................................................................. ★★★
*1509 Adamson Pkwy., Morrow, GA 30260. (404) 961-8722.*
We often hear from moms that Carter's is "a good brand for baby to spit up on"—and that's a compliment. Their affordable, all purpose playclothes are especially nice as "daycare wear" and for other uses when an expensive outfit would be overkill. We've seen Carter's just about everywhere, from department stores to baby specialty shops, outlets to discounters. Prices are always affordable, even when you don't find Carter's on sale. For example, we saw Carter's sleepers regularly priced at $20 on sale for $15.99. If you like Carter's, you'll also find *Baby Gro* (made by Kleinert's, Inc., 112 W. 34th St., Suite 1714, New York, NY 10120; 212-736-7030) interesting, another all-purpose brand name similar in quality and price. We saw one of their sleepers (in a simple design) for $17.

**Flapdoodles** ...............................................................★★ ¹/₂
*Delaware Industrial Park, Neward, DE 19713. (302) 731-9793.* Flapdoodles specializes in 100% cotton, pre-shrunk playclothes. We liked the reinforced crotches and the easy-to-use large buttons. We do have one bone to pick with this designer, however: we bought a Flapdoodles shorts outfit ($25) that was designed in such a way that it made diaper changes an Olympic sport. Why? While the outfit had snaps, you couldn't entirely unsnap it because of fabric bands around each leg. The upshot: diaper changes were hell. On the bright side, Flapdoodles has two outlets (see the "Outlets" section of this chapter for more details).

**Gerber** ...........................................................................★
*531 S. Main St., Greenville, SC 29601. (803) 240-2840.* We just don't get it. Why take a well-respected (or at least well-known) name like Gerber and slap it on a cheap line of baby clothing? We just didn't like their clothing, which tends toward synthetic fabrics (or blends) with styling that's just plain boring. They should stick to food.

**Good Lad of Philadelphia** .........................................★★★ ¹/₂
*431 E. Tioga St. Philadelphia,, PA 19134. (215) 739-0200.* If you're seeking outfits for dressier occasions (or even for an outing of miniature golf), you won't find a better designer than Good Lad of Philadelphia. We were impressed with their

high quality and (relatively) affordable dress outfits, which often include accessories like hats and suspenders. For example, one outfit that caught our attention was a girl's sailor dress with a navy blue and white sailboat print for $28—and that included a cute hat. Another big plus: their tags offer some of the most detailed sizing information we've seen. Good Lad designs are also available through several catalogs, including Olsen's Mill Direct (800-537-4979).

*Gymboree* ............................................................... ★★★
*700 Airport Blvd., Suite 200, Burlingame, CA 94010. (415) 579-0600.* Wow! What a great line of baby clothes! An offshoot of the famous play classes that go by the same name, Gymboree stores market their own brand of high-quality baby and children's clothes. We visited a local store (located in an up-scale mall) and found a wide selection of coordinating clothes for both boys and girls. The sizes are color coded (with age, height, and weight) and the fabrics are 100% cotton. Instead of dividing the clothes into boys and girls sections, Gymboree separates the primary color patterns from the pastel designs. For babies, we saw onesies for $14 and thick receiving blankets for $25. For girls, leggings are most popular ($16). A coordinating dress with a sailor collar runs $28. We liked their overall outfits ($22 for the overalls, $16 for the shirt), and they even have coordinating socks, hats, shoes, sunglasses, and purses. The designs are a refreshing change from the standard fare.

   If there isn't a Gymboree near you now, there probably will be one soon. The chain currently has about 200 stores and is opening 50 to 75 more each year. While you might expect this chain to have outlets in such populous states as Texas and California, they also have stores in states like Delaware, New Mexico, and Alabama (call the above number of the nearest location). Another interesting fact: Gymboree guarantees that their clothing will not shrink or fade—so even though it isn't cheap, you know it will last.

*Health-Tex by Triboro* .......................................... ★★
*172 S. Broadway, White Plains, NY 10605. (914) 428-7551.* Health-Tex is a "bread and butter brand" of kids clothing—basic playclothes that are priced affordably and that you won't mind your child destroying at daycare. A big plus is Health-Tex's excellent sizing information, clearly displayed on each tag. The only downside: many of the designs are poly/cotton blends, so if you prefer 100% cotton, check the label. A girl's bubble decorated with cartoon cows (in a poly-cotton blend) was $16.

**Le Top** ...................................................................★★ $^1/_2$

*Made by CK Enterprises. 2975 Technology Ct., Richmond, CA 94806. (800) 333-2257 or (510) 222-0477.* Widely available in department stores nationwide, Le Top specializes in 100% cotton designs that feature bright and colorful whimsical prints and large button detailing. We bought several Le Top outfits and really like them—our baby is very comfortable, and the prices didn't dent our wallet. For example, a shorts jumper and shirt outfit runs $25—and about 30% off on a holiday sale we attended. While we liked Le Top, another mom we interviewed didn't totally share our enthusiasm. She complained that Le Top's clothes aren't pre-shrunk. Her advice: be careful to buy a big enough size. She made the mistake of buying her daughter's usual size in a Le Top outfit—only then to have the outfit shrink so much that it became unwearable.

**Little Me** .................................................................★★★★

*Made by the Schwab Company, Upper Potomac Industrial Park, Cumberland, MD, (301)729-4488.* Little Me is wonderful brand of playclothes that feature great appliques, all-cotton and poly-cotton blends, and great prices. How great? All cotton onesies run about $10—that's about 40% less than Gymboree. Sizing is clear—each outfit comes with an easy-to-read tag that helps you select the right size. Best of all, Little Me is widely available in just about every size, including preemies. We've bought several Little Me outfits, including an adorable pale yellow creeper with matching booties and embroidered ducks for $25. Sleepers were priced at $22. We can't say enough nice things about Little Me—they wash well and are a very good value.

**OshKosh/Baby B'Gosh** .................................................★★★★

*112-T Otter Ave., PO Box 300, Oshkosh, WI 54901. (414) 231-8800.* Who hasn't seen a baby in those adorable denim overalls and thought, "Isn't that cute?" Okay, so we broke down and bought our son an Oshkosh overall outfit that makes him look like a little Iowa farmer—perfect for those grandparent photo-ops. OshKosh makes more than those famous overalls. The designer's label also adorns sweatsuits, pants, t-shirts, socks, shoes, coats, and hats—all with that too-cute OshKosh B'Gosh name. The overalls are all cotton in most cases, but, unfortunately, the shirts that coordinate are poly-cotton blends. We simply buy the overalls without coordinating tops. Cost: An overall set with poly/cotton t-shirt was $37. Just buying a pair of overalls was $18. Cotton onesie t-shirts were $8. By the way, we should mention that OshKosh also has a layette line for infants, called Baby B'Gosh. They offer sleepwear, socks, and onesies. OshKosh is available through several mail-order catalogs like Olsen's Mill Direct (800-537-4979), plus they have quite a large number of outlet stores (see the section on outlets later in this chapter for more details).

*Patsy Aiken Designs* .................................................★★★★
*4812 Hargrove Rd., Raleigh, NC 27604. (800) 828-2351 or (919) 872-8789.* This designer is one of our favorites for dressy kids clothes. Patsy Aiken makes the most beautiful, appliqued, 100% cotton designs on the market. They also wash well and may even last through several children. Although they can be very expensive (a shorts outfit can cost $40), Patsy Aiken's clothes are worth the money. They also make a great gift item (hint, hint, Grandma).

## Safe & Sound

 The number-one important safety issue regarding children's clothing has to be the flame retardancy of sleepwear. But what does "flame retardant" mean? Before we undertook the research for this book, we thought that it meant the fabric would not burn. We also heard rumors that the flame retardancy would wash out of the fabric, rendering it useless after several washings. Finally, we thought that cotton clothing was a better option for sleepwear because it wouldn't melt like polyester and burns more slowly.

Wrong on all three counts.

After researching this issue, we discovered "flame retardant" fabric does not mean it will not burn. In fact, the Consumer Product Safety Commission (CPSC) states that fabric labeled as flame retardant will only burn under a direct flame—but, most importantly, it will put itself out once the flame is removed. So it isn't a Superman-style second skin for your child.

The false assumption that the flame retardancy of children's sleepwear would wash out in the laundry stems from the belief that all flame retardant fabric is chemically treated. Actually, many of the fabrics used in children's sleepwear today are inherently flame retardant. The fabrics to look for are modacrylic, matrix, nylon, and polyester. Hence, we discovered the "wash out" rumor was just a myth.

What about the statement that cotton is a better sleep option because it doesn't melt like polyester or nylon and burns more slowly? We actually performed an informal burn test on a couple of our baby's outfits: one was a flame retardant sleeper that had been washed over 20 times and the other was a 100% cotton play outfit. The cotton fabric continued to burn even after we removed the match; the flame retardant polyester stopped burning immediately. And the cotton outfit did not seem to be burning any more slowly than the synthetic fabric. Yes, the polyester did melt somewhat, but we felt the advantages of flame retardancy outweighed this negative.

If you do choose to buy flame-retardant clothing, be sure to avoid washing such clothing in soap flakes. Soap flakes actually add a flammable chemical residue to the clothes. Instead, we recommend you use regular detergents. In fact, unless your child has severe reactions to detergent, you can usually wash all his clothes in a detergent that is free of colorings or perfumes, such as Tide Free. You can even use a dryer sheet like Bounce Free as well.

What about other safety hazards with children's clothing? Here are a few more to consider:

♣ *Check for loose strings.* These could become a choking hazard, or the strings could be wrapped around fingers or toes, cutting off circulation. Be careful about appliques as well. "Heat-welded" plastic appliques on clothes can come off and cause choking. Poorly sewn appliques can also be a hazard.

♣ *Avoid outfits with easy-to-detach, decorative buttons or bows*—these may also be a choking hazard. If you have any doubts, cut the decorations off.

♣ *With drawstring gowns, remove the strings or buy gowns with elastic on the bottom instead.*

## Money Saving Secrets

1 WAIT UNTIL AFTER SHOWERS AND PARTIES TO PURCHASE CLOTHES. Clothing is a popular gift item, and you may not need to buy much yourself.

2 STICK WITH BASICS—T-SHIRTS, SLEEPERS, CAPS, SOCKS AND BLANKETS. For the first month or more, that's all you need since you won't be taking Junior to the opera.

3 BE PRACTICAL. Make sure your baby is comfortable. 100% cotton clothes are your best bet. Yes, they cost more, but you won't waste money buying cheaper polyester clothes, only to discover you need to buy more comfortable cotton clothes later. Fancy lace bloomers that itch and bow ties are not needed.

> "*FLAME RETARDANT* FABRIC DOES NOT MEAN IT WILL NOT BURN."

4 TAKE ADVANTAGE OF BABY REGISTRIES. Many baby stores offer this service, which helps avoid duplicate shower gifts or too many of one item. This saves you time (and money) in exchanging gifts.

5 GO FOR THE SALES. The baby department in most department stores is definitely SALE LAND. At one chain we researched, the baby section has at least some items that are on sale every week! Big baby sales occur throughout the year, but especially in January. You can often snag bargains at up to 50% off the retail price. Another tip: consider buying for the future during end-of-season sales. If you're pregnant during the fall, for example, shop the end-of-summer sales for next summer's baby clothes.

6 CHOOSE QUALITY OVER LOW PRICE FOR PLAYCLOTHES AND BASICS. Sure that 100% polyester outfit is 20% cheaper than the cotton alternative. HOWEVER, beware of the revenge of the washing machine! You don't realize how many times you'll be doing laundry—that play outfit may get washed every couple of days. Cheap 100% polyester clothes pill or fuzz up and look like crap after just a few washings—making you more likely to chuck them. Quality clothes have longer lives, making them less expensive over time. The key to quality is thicker or more heavyweight 100% cotton fabric, well-sewn seams and appliques, and snaps on a reinforced fabric band.

7 ON THE OTHER HAND, WE RECOMMEND YOU GO FOR LESS-EXPENSIVE ITEMS WHEN IT COMES TO SLEEPERS. Let's get real here: babies pee and poop in their sleepers, plus the flame-resistant fabrics (which are synthetics like polyester) tend to pill and fuzz, no matter how expensive the brand. If you don't like the fuzzing or pilling, go for velour sleepers (they're better in cold climates anyway). A friend of ours who lives in Texas uses all-cotton onesies as sleepwear in the hot summer months. However, remember cotton is *not* flame resistant. Carter's is one brand that makes good quality and relatively affordable sleepwear (see a review earlier in this chapter).

8 RETURN USELESS SHOWER GIFTS AND EXCHANGE THEM FOR THE STUFF YOU NEED. Did you get three lace dresses? Return the impractical for the useful.

9 CAN'T RETURN IT? Consign it at a local thrift store. We took a basketful of clothes that we couldn't use or didn't like and placed them on consignment. We made $40 in store credit or cash to buy what we really needed.

**10** SPEAKING OF CONSIGNMENT STORES, HERE IS A WONDERFUL WAY TO SAVE MONEY: buy barely used, consigned clothing for your baby. We found outfits ranging from $5 to $7 from high quality designers like Alexis. In fact, when we planned to visit a warmer climate in the winter, we found several shorts outfits for our son at a consignment store. The cost was half off department store prices, and we couldn't have found shorts outfits in the baby stores at that time anyway, so it was twice as convenient. How can you find a consignment or thrift shop in your area specializing in high-quality children's clothes? Besides looking in the phone book, you could write to the National Association of Resale & Thrift Shops, 157 Halstead, Chicago Heights, IL, 60411, Attention: Children's Resources. Send a self-addressed, self-stamped envelope, and they'll mail you back a list!

**11** SHOP AT MARSHALLS (to find a store near you, call 1-800-MARSHALLS). We stopped at a Marshalls store in our town and found that they carry clothes by OshKosh, Carter's, Bugle Boy, Weebok, and Little Me. One Carter's sleeper we saw was only $6, regularly $11. An Oshkosh overall shorts set was $17, regularly $30. We also saw shoes from manufacturers like Buster Brown, Stride Rite, Converse, and Reebok. A leather tennis shoe design by British Knight was only $17.99, regularly $25. Of course, selection varies widely from store to store, but if you live near a Marshalls, it may be worth it to visit regularly.

**12** CHECK OUT KIDS R US STORES (call 201-262-7800 to find a store near you.) The clothing division of Toys R Us, Kids R Us has their own, free-standing stores that are packed with clothes from infants on up. They carry the usual brands like Carter's and OshKosh, as well as more premium names like Izod, Kids Jordach, and Health-Tex. One Izod sleeper with a sleeping bear applique was only $14, regularly $19. Basics like 100% cotton t-shirts and shorts were available at great prices as well (two t-shirts or shorts for $8). This is a store to shop for great daycare playclothes that don't cost an arm and a leg.

## Outlets

There's been a huge explosion in the number of outlet stores over the last few years—and children's clothing stores haven't been left out of the boom. Indeed, as we were doing research for this section, we heard from many manufacture that they had even more outlets on the drawing b Therefore, if you don't see your town listed belo numbers provided to see if they've opened any new outlets. Also, outlet locations open and close frequently—always call before you go.

There are two publications that list nearly every outlet store in the U.S. The first is *Outlet Bound* magazine, which is published by Outlet Marketing Group ($6.95, 800-336-8853). The magazine contains detailed maps for all areas of the U.S. and Canada, as well as store listings for each outlet center. We liked the index that lists all the manufacturers, and they even have a few coupons in the back.

A second good resource is *Joy of Outlet Shopping*, another magazine that chronicles the fast-growing outlet business. Center locations are clearly marked on maps, and the index even cross-references brands with their outlet stores. Best of all, the store listings include information on the discounts available. If that weren't enough, the magazine boasts 15 pages of coupons in the back, including a 20% discount coupon for OshKosh. You can order the Joy of Outlet Shopping ($5.95, published by Value Retail News) by calling (800) 344-6397 or (813) 536-4047.

## Sir Alec

*Location:* 428 Spring Valley, Dallas, TX 75244. (214) 458-8028.

Sir Alec makes beautiful, handmade dress clothes for babies and children. If you walked into one of the exclusive boutiques that sell this brand, you'd pay $55 to $100 for the fancy 100% cotton outfits. However, we found a Sir Alec outlet where you can get the same adorable clothes for just $16 to $70—a 20% to 70% savings. Tucked in an obscure office park in Dallas, the Sir Alec outlet takes great care of its clothes—all outfits are hung in plastic bags to keep them looking brand-new. Most of the designs are one piece jumpers and bubbles.

On a recent visit, we bought an outfit with butter-yellow corduroy short pants that buttoned to a cotton-pique white shirt (complete with Peter Pan collar and blue piping accents). Originally, this was $62. We paid $16. No kidding. If you're in the neighborhood, we definitely recommend Sir Alec.

## Carter's

*Locations:* Over 90 outlets.
C    1-8722 for the location nearest you.

ou how wild the outlet craze is when you realize
the famous brand that also makes Baby Dior)
tlets in the U.S. That's, right, 90. If you don't

have one near you, you probably live in Bolivia.

We visited a Carter's outlet and found a huge selection of infant clothes, bedding, and accessories. Terry-cloth sleepers, originally $20, were available for only $15.99. Baby Dior clothes were also available, although they are about 10% more than comparable Carter's designs. One Dior outfit that caught our eye was a footed design with embroidered bunnies on the yoke and a knit, spread collar. Cost: $17.99, regularly $26.

Be sure to look for Dior receiving blankets and towels while you're there as well. The Carter's outlets don't always have these in stock, but on one visit we found a few for 25% off the retail price. The extra thick receiving blankets are especially good buys.

As for baby bedding, we noted sets with quilt, bumpers, and pillow for only $70, while bumpers sold separately for $20 and comforters for $30 to $35. Fitted bassinet sheets were only $2.99 (regularly $5.50), Carter's brand receiving blankets were $6.99 (regularly $9.50), and towels were a mere $4.50 (regularly $7.50).

If you think those prices are great, check out the outlet's yearly clearance sale in January when they knock an additional 25% to 30% off their already discounted prices. A store manager at the Carter's outlet we visited said that they also have various items on sale every month. Regardless of what they have on sale, the Carter's outlets sell only first quality goods—no seconds or rejects. Run, do not walk, to the Carter's outlet near you for the best baby bargains.

## OshKosh

*Locations:* Call (414) 231-8800 for the location nearest you.

OshKosh, the maker of all those cute little overalls worn by just about every kid, sells their clothes direct at over 40 outlet stores. With prices that are 30% to 40% off retail, buying these playclothes staples is even easier on the pocketbook.

We visited our local OshKosh store and found outfits from infant sizes up to children's size 7. They split the store up by gender, as well as by size. Infant and toddler clothes are usually in the back of the store.

So, how are the prices? The famous denim overalls (regularly $18.50) were marked down to $14.80. A girl's skirted overall was a mere $13.35. Coordinating shirts were $8, and sweats were $8.75 for pants and $9.75 for shirts.

The outlet also carries OshKosh shoes, socks, hats, and even stuffed bears dressed in overalls and engineer hats. Seasonable ensembles are available, including shorts outfits in the summer and a snowsuit ($42) in the winter. Some clothes are irregulars, so inspect the garments carefully before you buy.

## Ava Kids

*Location:* 550 W. South Boulder Rd., Lafayette, CO 80026, (303) 673-9300; 17 Old Town Square #133, Ft. Collins, CO 80524, (303) 493-1900.

Ava Kids is the Colorado-based manufacturer of high-quality baby and toddler clothes usually sold at fancy retailers like Nordstroms, Neiman Marcus, and specialty boutiques. But why pay full price when you can save up to 66% by visiting the Ava Kids outlet, located in the town of Lafayette, Colorado (about 20 miles northwest of Denver).

When we visited the Lafayette outlet we saw woven and knit cotton designs in bright plaids, stripes, and florals. A blue flowered bubble with ruffled collar was only $14, while a purple and green plaid coverall with contrasting hood was a mere $8. Matching baseball caps were $5.62, and a neat fishing vest was only $16. While most of their clothes look a little dressy for daycare, they do also sell basics like t-shirts and bike shorts ($5) or leggings ($7).

The store itself looks more like a boutique than a warehouse outlet, complete with attractive displays of the clothing. Ava Kids even has a play area with toys and a changing table with wipes and diapers in the restroom.

Sizes range from newborn to 6X, with some youth sizes 7 to 14. The majority of baby clothes seem to start in the 12 month size range. The outlet does have periodic, 25%-off sales on end-of-season merchandise, plus two big warehouse sales each year.

If you come to Colorado on a vacation, we strongly suggest a detour to one of the Ava Kids outlet.

## Baby Guess

*Locations:* Eight outlets, under the names Baby Guess/Guess Kids. Gilroy, CA; Los Angeles, CA; Hilton Head, SC; Sunrise, FL; Orlando, FL; Philadelphia, PA; Jeffersonville, OH; Price William, VA.

To find the location near you, call (800) 228-4644 or (213) 892-1289.Baby Guess is famous for their funky/casual look, with acid-washed overalls and other playclothes for babies and children. Their eight outlets feature savings of 50% to 60%. While some of the garments have flaws, most are first quality. Sizing runs from six months up to youth sizes. A salesperson at one of the stores told us they tend to get their stock about a month or so after it hits the retail stores. We should note that Baby Guess asked us not to write about their outlet stores since "that's not something we want to promote." So just pretend that you didn't get this information from our book. Or better yet, tell them you did.

## Eagle's Eye Kids

*Locations*: Pigeon Forge, TN (615) 429-1605; Stafford, PA (215) 989-0440; Foley, AL (205) 943-3709; Silverthorne, CO (303) 262-2119; Destin, FL (904) 837-8989; Burlington, NC (910) 226-4847; Santa Fe, NM (505) 474-0488; Castle Rock, CO (303) 660-9810; Waipahu, HI (808) 671-6934; Dallas, TX (214) 692-6773; Loveland, CO (303) 593-0351.

Bright, upbeat fashions seem to be the hallmark of Eagle's Eye clothes, including the designs found in their kids outlets. The all-cotton, high-quality outfits are sold at the outlets at a 40% discount. By the way, the kids clothes are sometimes included in the adult Eagle's Eye stores. Unfortunately, they don't carry infant sizes.

## Esprit

*Locations:* Eight locations, with more to come. Dallas, TX; San Marcos, TX; San Francisco, CA (415) 957-2540; Colorado; Maine; Michigan; New York; Vermont. Call (800) 777-8765 or (415) 648-6900 for the location nearest you.

Not all of the Esprit outlets carry children's clothing, but those that do have sizes from 12 months through youth sizes. The designs include dresses, pant suits, and shorts. The prices are 30% to 70% off, and they sell only first quality overruns—no seconds. Call the outlet nearest you to see if it carries Esprit's children's line.

## Flapdoodles

*Locations:* Martinsburg, WV, (304) 263-6737 and the Lancaster/York, PA (717) 390-7073. New stores scheduled for Florida, Colorado, and Missouri. Call their corporate headquarters at (302) 731-9793 for the locations.

The 100%-cotton designs from Flapdoodles are a great value even at retail, but you can actually find the clothes at 20% to 40% off retail in their outlet stores. With first quality merchandise and sizes from six months up to youth size 14, Flapdoodles outlets are worth a peek for long-lasting, high-quality playclothes.

## Hartstrings

*Locations:* Strafford, PA (215) 971-9400 and Redding, PA (610) 376-8808.

Hartstrings' outlet stores specialize in first-quality apparel for infants, boys, and girls and even have some mother/child outfits. Infant sizes start at three months and go up to 24 months. The savings range from 30% to 50%.

## Health-Tex

*Locations:* 45 outlets. Call (800) 772-8336 or (610) 378-0408 for the location near you.

Health-Tex children's clothing is owned by Vanity Fair Corporation, which also produces such famous brands as Lee jeans, Wrangler, and Jansen. The company operates nearly four dozen outlets under the names VF Factory Outlet or Outlet Marketplace. They sell first-quality merchandise; most are discontinued items. VF Outlets discounts 50% everyday, while Outlet Marketplace sells at 30% to 70% off retail. Both outlet chains sell the Health-Tex brand.

## Storybook Heirlooms

*Locations:* Gilroy, CA (408) 842-3880 and Las Vegas, NV (702) 896-4663.

If you've ever received Storybook Heirlooms' catalog, you probably know that they have very fancy and very expensive children's clothing. Thankfully, they also have two factory outlets in California and Nevada to help you save a little money. The outlets sell most items shown in their catalog, including last season's merchandise, left-overs in sizes, and even current merchandise. They offer a 25% discount off their catalog prices, plus clearance sales with discounts as low as 70% off retail. Sizes start at 12 months and range up to youth size 14.

## Florence Eiseman

*Locations:* Michigan City, IN (219) 879-1767 and Lancaster/York, PA (717) 295-9809.

Florence Eiseman's children's clothing designs are carried at Neiman Marcus, Saks, and Nordstroms, just to name a few places . . . so you can imagine they aren't exactly cheap. That's why a visit to one of their two outlets may be worth the effort.

The outlet store carries infant through youth sizes, with some layette designs as small as newborn. Florence Eiseman specializes in party dresses and swimwear, but this designer also carries casual outfits as well. The savings at the outlet stores is an impressive 30% to 40% off retail—all of it first-quality merchandise.

## Kid's Zone

*Locations:* 22 outlets. Call (918) 599-9553 to find the location nearest you.

Owned by the Children's Source, the Kid's Zone outlets sell brand name clothing at 30% to 40% discounts off the retail price. They have layette (and even preemie sizes) in sleepers and dresses, plus a wide assortment of other clothing. Brands include Bryan, Beginnings, Children's Hour, and Ruth Scharf. All items are first-quality merchandise, and Kid's Zone has end-of-season clearances and manager's specials from time to time. Most of the outlets are in the South, West and Midwest, although there is one in New York. Some of the outlet stores go under the name "Today's Child."

## Nathan J.

*Locations:* City of Commerce, CA (213) 725-1781; Lake Elsinore, CA (909) 245-5533; and Huntington Beach, CA (714) 895-6266.

You might see Nathan J.'s 100% cotton baby clothing in such toney department stores as Bloomingdales, Neiman Marcus, and Nordstroms. But if you want it at 30% to 60% off, you'll have to go to one of their three outlets in California. Nathan J. sells layette items, dresses, rompers, underwear, booties, hats, receiving blankets, sacque sets, and more. A "frequent buyer" discount is available. Look for their ad in *Parenting Magazine* for a 10%-off coupon.

## Pattycakes

*Locations:* 2669 Santa Rosa Ave., Santa Rosa, CA 95407. (707) 575-5020.

Pattycakes' outlet store offers their creative children's apparel at 50% to 80% off the retail price. Sold in high-end department stores and boutiques, Pattycakes concentrates on casual playwear in bright prints and pastels. Sizes start at three months and go up to size 10. Although generally first-quality, current merchandise, the outlet does have one rack of seconds in the store. Another plus: they take additional markdowns from time to time, so the savings you find may be even better.

## *Pixie Playmates*

*Locations:* 2300 S. Belcher, Largo, FL. (813) 531-1411. The store is connected to the manufacturing facility and is only open Tuesday through Friday, 10:00 am-5:00 pm .

Although Pixie Playmates' clothes are normally sold through K-mart and Wal-Mart stores at already decent prices, they offer an amazing 50% savings at their outlet store in Largo, Florida. The clothes are a mix of 50/50 blends and all-cotton designs in sizes 12 months through toddlers. Pixie Playmates specializes in basics like t-shirts and sportswear in bright prints and solid colors. They also sell fabric by the yard.

## *Polly Flinders*

*Locations:* They have 48 outlets. For a location near you, call (800) 543-0373 or (513) 721-7024.

Looking for beautiful hand-smocked dresses at a discount? Polly Flinders sells these and more at their outlets for 40% to 70% off retail prices. For example, one dress we priced was only $24.99 (others range from $10 to $37). Sizes start at three months and go up to youth sizes. Although dresses are their specialty, they also carry sportswear, nightwear, and some boys outfits. Polly Flinders' outlets also have occasional sales, offering even bigger discounts.

## *Schwab Factory Outlet (Little Me clothing)*

*Locations:* Upper Potomac Industrial Park, Cumberland, MD. (301) 729-0602.

While we like the Little Me brand, we have to give thumbs down to the obnoxious service at their outlet store, the Schwab Factory Outlet (which is Little Me's parent company). The "helpful" salesperson who answered the phone couldn't tell us their address, didn't know what highway they are located on, and generally had the IQ of a house plant. Combine this with the fact that the discounts are a meager 10% to 20% off retail, and you may want to only visit this outlet if you happen to be in the neighborhood.

Did you discover an outlet that you'd like to share with our readers? Call us at 303-442-8792!

## *Waste of Money #1*

**❗** CLOTHING THAT LEADS TO DIAPER CHANGING
GYMNASTICS

*"My aunt sent me an adorable outfit for my little
girl. The only problem: it snaps up the back making diaper
changes a real pain. In fact, I don't dress her in it often
because it's so inconvenient. Shouldn't clothing like this be
outlawed?"*

It's pretty obvious that some designers of baby clothing have
never had children of their own. What else could explain outfits that snap up the back, have super tiny head, leg and arm
openings, and snaps in inconvenient places (or worse, no
snaps at all)? One mother we spoke with was furious about
outfits that have snaps only down one leg, requiring her baby
to be a contortionist to get into and out of the outfit.

Most babies are already unhappy when you put them on
the changing table. But add in an outfit that requires you to
turn the baby over to unsnap it or one that you need a crow-
bar to get the shirt over his head, and you've got a "negative
parenting experience." You may feel like "au naturale" is
your best bet here.

Our advice: stay away from outfits that don't have easy
access to the diaper. Look instead for snaps or zippers down
the front of the outfit or on the crotch. If your baby doesn't
like having things pulled over his head, look for shirts with
wide, stretchie necklines instead.

## *Waste of Money #2*

THE FUZZ FACTOR

*"My friend's daughter has several outfits that aren't very old
but are already pilling and fuzzing. They look awful and my
friend is thinking of throwing them out. What causes this?"*

Your friend has managed to have a close encounter with
that miracle fabric known as polyester. Synthetics such as
polyester will often pill or fuzz, making your baby look a little
rag-tag. Of course, this is less of a concern with sleepwear—
the flame retardancy of the fabric outweighs the garment's
appearance. Besides, your baby won't be wearing sleepwear
over to grandma's house anyway.

However, when you're talking about a play outfit, we recommend sticking to all-cotton clothes. They wash better, usually last longer, and generally look nicer—not to mention that
they feel better to your baby. Cotton allergies are rare, unlike

> "STAY AWAY FROM OUTFITS THAT DON'T HAVE EASY
> ACCESS TO THE DIAPER."

sensitivities to the chemicals used to make synthetic fabrics. You will pay more for all-cotton clothing, but in this case, the extra expense is worth it. Remember, just because you find the cheapest price on a polyester outfit doesn't mean you're getting a bargain. The best deal is not wasting money on outfits that you have to throw away after two washings.

## *Waste of Money #3*
DO I REALLY NEED THESE?

*"My mother bought me a zillion drawstring gowns before my baby was born, and I haven't used a single one. What the heck are they for?"*

*"The list of layette items recommended by my local department store includes an item called a saque set. I've never seen one, and no one seems to know what they're for. Do I really need one?"*

*"A kimono with matching towel and washcloth seems like a neat baby gift for my pregnant friend. But another friend told me it probably wouldn't get used. What do you think?"*

All of these items come under the heading "Do I Really Need These?" Heck, we didn't even know what some of these were when we were shopping for our baby's layette. For example, what in the world is a saque set? Well, it turns out it's just a two-piece outfit with a shirt and diaper cover. Although they sound rather benign, saque sets are a waste of money. Whenever you pick up a baby under the arms, it's a sure bet her clothes will ride up. In order to avoid having to constantly pull down the baby's shirt, most parents find they use one-piece garments much more often than two-piece ones.

As for drawstring gowns, the jury is still out on whether these items are useful. These seem kind of silly, but a parent we interviewed did mention that she used the gowns when her baby had colic. She believed that the extra room in the gown made her baby more comfortable. The choice is up to you; however, we definitely recommend buying only a few to start with so you don't sink too much money into such a questionable purchase.

There is no question in our minds about the usefulness of a kimonos, however. Don't buy them. For a baby who will only wear it for a few minutes after a bath, it seems like the quintessential waste of your money. Instead, invest in some good quality towels and washcloths and forget those cute (but useless) kimonos.

## Waste of Money #4
### COVERING UP THOSE LITTLE PIGGIES

*"I was looking at shoes for my baby the other day, and I saw a $35 pair of Nikes at the store! This must be highway robbery! I can't believe babies' shoes are so expensive. Are they worth it?"*

Developmentally, babies don't need shoes until after they become quite proficient at walking. In fact, it's better for their muscle development to go barefoot or wear socks. While those expensive Baby Nikes might look cute, they're really a waste of time and money.

One mother we interviewed insisted her daughter wear shoes whenever they went out. If you, too, feel uncomfortable if your child goes shoe-less, at least look for shoes that have the most flexible soles. You'll also want fabrics that breathe and stretch, like canvas and leather—stay away from vinyl shoes. The best brands we found: "Cutiecakes" soft-sided shoes (available from the One Step Ahead catalog, (800-274-8440) run $7.95 and have non-skid soles. Another good brand: Storkenworks (available from the Natural Baby Catalog, 609-771-9233) cost $17.95 and are soft shoes made of natural leather. Booties and moccasins are available from many catalogs and retail stores. The best moccasins we found are from Herb Farm Moccasins (PO Box 28, Parlin, CO 81239). Prices range from $21 for infants to $29 for one year olds if you order directly from the company.

## Waste of Money #5
### TO DROOL OR NOT TO DROOL

*"I received a few bibs from my mother-in-law as gifts. I know my baby won't need them until she's at least four months old when I start feeding her solids. Besides, they seem so small!"*

What you actually got as a gift from your mother-in-law was a supply of drool bibs. Drool bibs are tiny, little bibs intended for small infants who start teething and hence drool all over everything. Our opinion: they're pretty useless, even if you use them for their intended purpose. When we decided we needed a few bibs for drooling, we got larger, more absorbent versions that we could reuse later when we started feeding solids to our baby.

When you do buy bibs, stay away from the ones that tie. Bibs that snap or have velcro are much easier to get on and off. Also, stay away from the super-size vinyl bibs that cover your baby's arms. We've been told that babies can get too hot in them. However, we do recommend you buy a few regular-style vinyl bibs for traveling. You can wash them off much more easily than the standard terry-cloth bibs.

We did come across one great resource for large, terry-cloth bibs: Sunshine Bibs (800-221-8799, 714-692-8696) offers large, 100% cotton bibs with bright designs—tigers, pandas, dinosaurs, college logos, etc. We have a couple of these bibs and have been very impressed with their great quality. They are super-absorbent (they're made by a towel company), wash well, don't fade, and have adjustable snaps. The cost is about $6 each.

Another interesting option: the Kangeroo Bibs from the Perfectly Safe Catalog (800-837-5437). These plastic bibs have "specially shaped pockets" to catch spills and cost about $6 each.

> "DROOL BIBS ARE PRETTY USELESS. GET LARGER, MORE ABSORBENT VERSIONS YOU CAN REUSE LATER WHEN SOLIDS ARE INTRODUCED INTO YOUR BABY'S DIET."

## Do it by Mail

### After the Stork.

*To Order Call:* (800) 333-5437 or (505) 243-9100;
Fax (505) 243-6935.
*Shopping Hours:* 24 hours a day, seven days a week.
*Or write to:* After the Stork, 1501 12 St. NW, PO Box 26200, Albuquerque, NM 87125.
*Credit Cards Accepted:* MC, VISA, AMEX, Discover.

 After the Stork is one catalog that actually offers great prices on kids' cotton clothing. While they may not be fancy, the clothes in here are good, well-made basics, like the $18.50 henley coverall we saw (sizes 6 months up to 4T). In three solid colors and one bright peach pattern, this is a perfect staple for your kid's closet.

After the Stork offers a small discount when you purchase two or more of an item. For example, a basic cotton tank top is $5.95, or just $4.95 if your buy two or more. Other clothes are discounted off department store prices. A sleeveless, empire-waist, floral dress in sizes 2T to 6X was priced at only $12.50 (compared to $22 in stores).

## Biobottoms.

*To Order Call:* (800) 766-1254 or fax (707) 778-0619.
*Shopping Hours:* Monday-Friday 5:00 am-9:00 pm; Saturday 6:00 am-6:00 pm; Sunday 8:00 am-4:00 pm Pacific Time.
*Or write to:* Biobottoms, PO Box 6009, Petaluma, CA 94953.
*Credit Cards Accepted:* MC, VISA, AMEX, Discover.

This California-based catalog started out selling "lamb-soft wool" diaper covers called Biobottoms for babies in cloth diapers. Along the way, they branched out into colorful, 100% cotton clothing in bold patterns and bright colors.

The bulk of the Biobottoms catalog showcases their cheerful, fun clothing. Check out the Cloud Coverall ($29) with matching socks ($5.50), or the sunbonnet ($13) in pink or blue. Other whimsical designs include farm animal t-shirts ($15.50), gingham-checked high-top tennies ($18), and plaid seersucker rompers ($26).

We purchased clothes for our baby from Biobottoms and found them to be well made and long lasting. The clothes didn't shrink or fade after many washings, and our son found them very comfortable. The prices aren't a bargain, but the fun designs and high quality make them worth the purchase price.

## Hanna Anderson.

*To Order Call:* (800) 222-0544; Fax (503) 222-0544.
*Shopping Hours:* 5:00 am to 7:00 pm Pacific Time, seven days a week.
*Or write to:* Hanna Anderson, 1010 NW Flanders, Portland, OR, 97209.
*Credit Cards Accepted:* MC, VISA, AMEX, Discover.

Hanna Anderson offers some of the highest quality children's clothing on the market today. The catalog features beautiful, all-cotton layette clothing basics like side-tie t-shirts ($15). Hanna Anderson also offers bright colored playclothes like plaid coveralls ($38), sweaters ($39), and even basic sweatpants ($19).

These are clothes you can dress your child in for daycare or for a more formal outing. The basics like sweats and bib overalls aren't cheap, but they will last much longer than those cheaper, "disposable" brands we reviewed earlier in the chapter. This is what makes Hanna Anderson one of the most popular kids clothing catalogs around—and we couldn't agree more.

## Olsen's Mill Direct.

*To Order Call:* (800) 537-4979, (800) 452-3699 or
Fax (414) 426-6369
*Shopping Hours:* 7:00 am to 11:00 pm Central Time, seven days a week.
*Or write to:* Olsen's Mill Direct, 1641 S. Main St,
Oshkosh, WI 54901.
*Credit Cards Accepted:* MC, VISA, Discover.

One of the best organized catalogs we've seen, Olsen's Mill Direct offers an attractive selection of such famous brands as Good Lad of Philadelphia, Hartstrings, Monster Wear, Sara's Prints, OshKosh, and more.

Another plus: the catalog has large photos of the clothes, so you can see what you're getting. For example, a beautiful, bold-patterned set of outfits by Good Lad included a girl's sailor dress and hat ($28-30), boy's suspendered sailor shorts ($30-32), and coordinating baby bubbles for boys and girls with cute hats ($26-30).

## Playclothes.

*To Order Call:* (800) 362-7529; (800) 222-7725; Fax (913) 752-1095.
*Shopping Hours:* 24 hours a day, seven days a week.
*Or write to:* Playclothes, PO Box 29137, Overland Park, KS 66201.
*Credit Cards Accepted:* MC, VISA, AMEX, Discover.

As the name implies, Playclothes focuses on affordable, attractive, and comfortable clothing in bright, bold patterns. For example, we saw an outrageously colorful coverall covered with jungle animals that cost only $18. This 100% cotton outfit also had a matching baseball cap for $6.

Sizes start at 12 months and go up to girl's size 14 and boy's size 16. Infant clothes were scattered throughout the catalog rather than grouped into one section. Playclothes carries name brands including Good Lad of Philadelphia.

Glancing through a recent catalog, we especially liked the bright animal prints and cheerful florals (giant strawberries and sunflowers were standouts). The catalog even showcased licensed sports apparel, like a Florida Marlins romper with matching hat for $25. Other teams include Colorado Rockies, New York Yankees, and Atlanta Braves—what! No Mets? Despite this transgression, we give Playclothes two thumbs up.

*For more catalogs featuring baby clothing, check out the catalog reviews in Chapter 11.*

## Diapers

The great diaper debate still rages on: should you use cloth or disposable? On one side is the environmental argument that landfills are clogged, and disposables are at least partially to blame. On the other hand, it's hard to beat the convenience of disposables. After all, you don't have to keep hauling around those wet disposables after changing your baby the way you do with cloth diapers.

Perhaps the biggest problem with cloth diapers is leaks. Super-absorbant disposable diapers just don't leak as much, meaning less laundry and headaches. One mother we interviewed who abandoned cloth diapers after three weeks complained that the laundry was overwhelming. You can count on going through a diaper cover with every poopy diaper, she said. With her baby, that meant washing three to five diaper covers each day.

But what about all those environmental concerns? Yes, disposables do take up space in our landfills, but if it makes you feel any better, they only constitute about 2% of the trash according to a recent University of Arizona study.

And just how environmentally friendly are cloth diapers? Consider all the water and energy used to wash and dry diapers, not to mention the gasoline used by diaper services to deliver them. All those frequent washings and truck trips can't be good for the planet. Moreover, the chlorine bleach used to sanitize diapers may be released into our environment through water treatment systems.

The bottom line: it's a wash. Your decision may depend on where you live. We live in the arid West, where water is scare and landfill space is abundant. Hence, disposables might make more environmental sense than cloth—folks out here would rather keep precious clean water in their favorite trout stream than divert it for use cleaning diapers. However, in the East, the situation may be the opposite; there's lots of water but not as much landfill space. The conclusion if you live there: cloth diapers may make more environmental sense.

## The Name Game: Reviews of Selected Manufacturers

 We have to admit that our nonscientific diaper test was probably biased since we have a boy. Our son had an uncanny way of leaking from some of the best diapers in this world. We did learn eventually that if you fold down the front of the diaper to form a little pocket, you'll have fewer leaks. Luckily, girls don't tend to "shoot off" upwards and therefore have few leaks from the top of the diaper. One mother did mention that her daughter had a tendency to "blow out" the back of her diapers during bowel movements. (And you thought being a parent was just deciding what lace dress your girl should wear).

Overall, we really liked the new "ultra thin" styles of diapers. These use new technology that avoids all the bulkiness of past disposables. Your baby can now look slim and trim, instead of bottom heavy.

All disposables, even generic store brands, now come in male and female designs and a variety of sizes to correspond with your baby's growth. Even though they claim to be super absorbent, you should still change your baby's diaper frequently to help avoid diaper rash. One way to determine if the diaper is wet without taking it off is to pinch it. If it springs back, it's not wet; otherwise, it's time for a change.

Here are our reviews of the best known names in the diaper business. We'd love to hear your comments on diapers as well. Call us at (303) 442-8792. Or write to us at 1223 Peakview Circle, Boulder, CO, 80302. We value your feedback and will include any comments in future editions of this book.

### Huggies .................................................................★★★★
Of all the brands we sampled, we liked Huggies the best. Their diapers have leak protection on the sides of the diapers (special edging that holds in the liquid). Our only complaint: the leak protection in the back was somewhat lacking, allowing poop "blow outs" from time to time.

New to the Huggies line are the "Huggies Supreme" brand diapers. These claim to have an outer covering that looks more like fabric. Now you can walk the mall and have your baby at least look politically correct.

The Huggies Supremes also have velcro fasteners rather than the standard tapes. They suggest that this way you can check and recheck your baby's diaper and still be able to re-close it time after time. This seems like a first-time parent gimmick to us—after changing a thousand diapers, you'll know when your baby needs a change.

### Pampers.................................................................★★ $1/2$
We used Pampers for boys and found that the extra fabric in front made it difficult to fold down. Hence, leaks actually occurred with more frequency than with the Huggies. Pampers diapers also have leak pockets on the sides and in the front and back. This should have helped, but we found the pockets to be pitifully shallow. As a result, the diapers just don't stop leaks that well.

The bright-colored pictures on the front of the diaper feature a bevy of cute, multi-cultural babies (how P.C.).

Unfortunately, under lightweight clothes, the designs were more visible than I would have liked. All in all, we give Pampers a mixed review. If you have a girl, the leaking problems might not be as pronounced. Yet, we were somewhat disappointed in our test.

Another negative for Pampers: we found their sizing to be somewhat off—one mother we interviewed said Pampers "newborn"-size diapers didn't fit her eight-pound newborn infant.

*Luvs* ....................................................................................★★
Luvs offered decent absorbancy and protection against leaks in our field test. Like Pampers, the extra fabric up front for boys was more of an annoyance than a help. However, our biggest beef with Luvs is the little sailboat pattern splashed over the entire diaper. Unlike Pampers and Huggies (which limit their designs to the front waistband), Luvs has apparently decided that plain white diapers are passe. Our complaint: those sailboats are too visible and ruin the "cute look" of outfits we paid a fortune for. Call us vain, but we won't buy Luvs for that reason.

*Cloth Diapers* ....................................................................★★
Are cloth diapers cheaper than disposables? Surprisingly, the answer is no. Diaper services charge about 9¢ to 19¢ per diaper. That includes delivery, diapers, a hamper and liners, deodorizer, and pickup. In our area, the going rate is 16¢ per diaper.

Yet we found disposables as low as 15¢ per diaper at some of the discount outlets we list below. Sure, grocery stores sell disposable diapers for high prices that work out 20¢ to 25¢ per diaper, but you can find cheaper sources.

*Tushies* ..............................................................................★★
*To find a dealer near you, call (203) 454-8831 or write to PO Box 5200, Westport, CT 06881.* What if you want the convenience of disposables but the political correctness of cloth? You may want to check out Tushies, a disposable diaper that is made of natural ingredients (no chemicals). The filling is 30% cotton and 70% wood pulp. We found Tushies at a specialty baby store, and they were definitely not cheap. A box of 48 diapers runs $15 (or 31¢ per diaper). Perhaps you can buy a box to impress your friends (and then refill it with cheaper disposable diapers).

## Money Saving Secrets

1 BUY IN BULK. Don't buy those little packs of 20 diapers—look for the 80 or 100 count packs instead. You'll find the price per diaper goes down when you buy larger packs.

**2** Go for warehouse clubs. Both Sam's and Price/Cosco wholesale clubs sell diapers at incredibly low prices. At Sam's, we found a 160-count package of Pampers Phase 1 for $27.99. Their own "store brand" was just $5.89 for 50 diapers (that's just 11¢ per diaper). And Price/Cosco sells a 100-count package of Huggies Step 1 for just $15. We also found great deals on wipes at the wholesale clubs. Sam's had a package of 336-count Baby Fresh Wipes for $7.83. A store brand with 462 wipes was just $6.97.

**3** Consider Toys R Us. Sure, you may not have a wholesale club nearby, but you're bound to be close to a Toys R Us. And we found them to be a great source for affordable name-brand diapers. Both Pampers and Huggies were $7.67 for a 50-count package. The Toys R Us store brand was even cheaper, at $6.99 for 54 diapers. If you like Luvs, you'll love the price: $6.77 for 54-count package.

**4** When your baby is nearing a transition point, don't stock up. Quick growing babies may move into another size faster than you think, leaving you with an excess supply of too-small diapers.

**5** Don't buy diapers in grocery stores. We compared prices at grocery stores and found them to be sky-high. Most were selling diapers in packages that worked out to 20¢ to 25¢ per diaper.

**6** Use coupons. You'll be amazed at how many coupons you receive in the mail, usually for 75 cents off diapers and 50 cents off wipes. One tip: to keep those "introductory" packages of coupons coming, continue signing up to be on the mailing lists of the maternity chain stores (apparently, these chains sell your name to diaper manufacturers, formula companies, etc.). One mother we know did this, and she swears it works.

---

Looking for Preemie Diapers?
The Preemiewear Catalog (208-733-0442 or
800-992-8469) suggests these sources:
Disposable diapers: Pampers (800) 543-4932
Cloth diapers: Diaperaps (800) 477-3424

---

## Do it By Mail

 Yes, there are several catalogs that sell cloth diapers and diaper covers by mail. Here are some of the best:

## Biobottoms.

*To Order Call:* (800) 766-1254 or fax (707)778-0619.
*Shopping Hours:* Monday-Friday 5:00 am-9:00 pm; Saturday 6:00 am-6:00 pm; Sunday 8:00 am-4:00 pm Pacific Time.
*Or write to:* Biobottoms, PO Box 6009, Petaluma, CA 94953.
*Credit Cards Accepted:* MC, VISA, AMEX, Discover.

Biobottoms got their start as purveyors of cloth diapers and diaper covers. They make their own brands of diaper covers called "Classic Biobottoms," and "Cotton Bottoms." Classic Biobottoms are made of "lamb-soft wool developed especially for babies." The price is $18 each, and they have three versions: plain, rainbow-colored trim, and rainbow trim on a bikini-style cover.

The Cotton Bottoms diaper covers are made of 100% cotton, with an inner lining of polyester. The catalog claims these covers are "so durable you can practically cook them in the dryer." Cost: $14.50 to $15 depending on size.

And what about the cloth diapers you're supposed to put inside those diaper covers? Well, Biobottoms offers their own "double duty" diapers that have 4 to 5 layers of absorbancy and come prefolded. Infant diapers are $18 for 12 and toddler sizes are $25 for 12. For extra absorbancy, Biobottoms sells "soak-it-up" liners that "put absorbancy where it's needed without double-diaper bulk." A big plus: the catalog's sizing chart is easy to follow and understand.

## Bosom Buddies.

*To Order Call:* (914) 338-2038
*Or write to:* Bosom Buddies, PO Box 6138, Kingston, NY 12401.
*Credit Cards Accepted:* MC, VISA.

Bosom Buddies offers one brand of diaper cover called Snibbs. Imported from Sweden, these covers are made of PVC film that is tied on. The catalog claims the covers have a special texture which "allows air to come through to prevent sticking." Snibbs cost $5.25 each and are recyclable.

## Motherwear.

*To Order:* (800) 633-0303, (413) 586-3488; Fax (413) 586-2712
*Shopping Hours:* Monday-Thursday 9:00 am-8:00 pm; Friday and Saturday 9:00 am-5:00 pm.
*Or write to:* Motherwear, Order Department, PO Box 114, Northampton, MA 01061.
*Credit Cards Accepted:* MC, VISA, Discover.

Motherwear offers hourglass-type cloth diapers for $32 per dozen—by far the most expensive brand we've found. Thankfully, they offer a little discount ($3 off per dozen) if you buy three or more dozen. Prefolded flannel diapers are also pricey at $29 per dozen.

Nikky diaper covers are available for $17.25 for wool and $15 for cotton. Nylon covers are $5. Bumkins, an all-in-one washable diaper and diaper cover, is $10 for one or $59 for six. The prices in the Motherwear catalog are steep, so you better be committed to cloth diapers before you sink this much money into these supplies.

## I Dream of the Diaper Genie

Excuse us for a moment while we wax rhapsodic about the Diaper Genie, the neatest invention for parents since the baby-sitter. This sleek white plastic can has done what years of diaper pails have failed to do: take the stink out of stinky diapers.

Here's how it works: you pop in a disposable diaper and give the lid a twist. That's it! No brain damage! The Diaper Genie seals the diaper in air-tight, deodorized plastic and stores it in the container base. There are no batteries or motorized parts to worry about: just hit a lever on the base and a chain of sealed diapers emerges for easy disposal (the container holds up to 20 diapers). Best of all, there's no smell and no deodorant cartridges to replace.

The Diaper Genie retails for $40, but we've seen it as low as $19.95 in the Baby Superstore (for a store near you, call 803-675-0299), $24.95 in LiL' Things (817-649-6100), and about $30 in Toys R Us. And then you've got to buy the refill cannisters that hold the plastic wrap—these retail for $7, but you can find them for $5 at Toys R Us and just $3.97 from the Baby Catalog of America (800-752-9736).

Now, one of those refill cannisters wraps 150 to 180 diapers—or about 10 days to two weeks worth of diapers. So, if you use the Diaper Genie for a year, your total cost would be about $150 (including the cost of the Genie itself). That isn't cheap and probably explains the resistance of some parents to the Diaper Genie, who don't want to part with that much cash to keep their nursery odor-free.

However, we've used the contraption for a while now and think it is worth the money. It's relatively easy to use, although it does take a little getting used to. The process of emptying the diapers out of the canister is relatively straightforward (you twist a cutter on top and the chain of diapers plops out the end), but the switching of cannisters is a little more complicated. It takes a few times before you'll get the hang of it, but since you'll be changing as many as 100 diapers a week in the beginning, you'll adjust pretty fast.

Even if you don't buy a Diaper Genie, you'll need some type of diaper pail (which run $10 to $25). And, in the fancy models, every three months you still have to replace those charcoal filters that keep the odors down (at a cost of $4 to $5 each).

So, we give the Diaper Genie a big "thumbs up." It's not cheap, but the convenience factor is hard to beat. (The Diaper Genie is made by Mondial Industries, 8765 Freeway Dr., Macedonia, OH 44056. For a dealer near you, call 216-467-4443.)

### Natural Baby: Alternative Products for Children and Their Parents.

*To Order Call:* (609) 771-9233 or Fax (609) 771-9342
*Shopping Hours:* Monday-Friday 9:00 am-8:00 pm; Saturday 10:00 am-4:00 pm Eastern Time.
*Or write to:* The Natural Baby Co. Inc., 816 Silvia St. 800 B-S, Trenton, NJ 08628.
*Credit Cards Accepted:* MC, VISA, Discover.

The diapers available through Natural Baby Co. are not the usual square cloth diapers you see in stores. No, they have a unique hourglass shape that doesn't require any fancy folding. All this doesn't come cheap. The prices range from $15.50 to $28.95 per dozen.

The Natural Baby Co. sells Nikky diaper covers, in either cotton or wool. Cotton runs $14.95, while wool is $19.45. A third style of Nikky diaper cover (with 80% cotton and 20% polyester) costs $9.95 each. The catalog also offers its own brand of diaper cover for only $3.95 each.

## THE BOTTOM LINE:
### A Wrap-Up of Our Best Buy Picks

 In summary, we recommend you buy the following layette items for your baby:

| Quantity | Item | What it Will Cost You (Prices at discount) |
|---|---|---|
| 6 | T-shirts/onesies (over the head) | $22 |
| 2 | T-shirts (side snap or side tie) | $25 |
| 4-6 | Sleepers | $64-$96 |
| 1 | Blanket Sleeper* | $10 |
| 2-4 | Coveralls | $40-$80 |
| 3-4 | Booties/socks | $12-$16 |
| 1 | Sweater | $16 |
| 2 | Hats (safari and caps) | $30 |
| 1 | Snowsuit/bunting* | $20 |
| 4 | Large bibs (for feeding) | $24 |
| 3 sets | Wash clothes and towels | $30 |
| 7-8 | Receiving blankets | $42-$48 |

**TOTAL**          **$340 to $422**

* *If you live in a cold climate.*

These prices are from discounters, outlet stores, or sale prices at department stores. What would all these clothes cost at full retail? $450 to $550, at least. The bottom line: follow our tips and you'll save $100 to $200 on your baby's layette alone. (Of course, you may receive some of these items as gifts, so your actual outlay may be less.)

Which brands are best? We recommend Carter's for sleepers and Little Me for onesies. As for casual playwear, the top names we like are Gymboree, Le Top, and the products available in the catalogs Biobottoms and Hanna Anderson. Going out on the town? Look to Good Lad of Philadelphia for boys and Patsy Aiken for girls.

In general, we found that 100% cotton clothes are best (except for sleepwear). Yes, you'll pay a little more for cotton, but it lasts longer and looks better than clothes made of polyester blends. Other wastes of money for infants include drawstring gowns, kimonos, saque sets, and shoes.

What about disposable diapers? Huggies is our favorite brand, although Pampers are acceptable and Luvs a good buy. The best way to save money on diapers is to buy in bulk (100-diaper packages) from a warehouse club or Toys R Us. Believe it or not, you could easily go through 10 to 12 diapers a day, or a total of 1800 to 2200 by the end of six months. Buy those at discount (from our sources), and you'll spend $270 to $330. Pop into a grocery store, and you'll have to shell out $450 to $550. Hence, you'll save a total of $200 or more on disposable diapers alone—and that's just for the first six months!

 Questions or comments? Did you discover a layette bargain you'd like to share with our readers? **Call the authors at (303) 442-8792!**

# Chapter 5

## Maternity/Nursing Clothes & Breastfeeding

L ove 'em or hate 'em, every mother-to-be needs maternity wear at some point in her pregnancy. Still, you don't have to break the bank to get comfortable, and, yes, fashionable maternity clothes. In this chapter, we tell you which sources sell all-cotton, casual clothes at unbelievably low prices. Then, we'll review the top maternity chains and reveal our list of top wastes of money. You'll learn which outlet stores offer tremendous savings on career wear. Finally, learn all about breastfeeding, including five sources for help, and the low-down on which breast pumps work best.

## Maternity & Nursing Clothes

### Getting Started:

It may seem obvious that you'll need to buy maternity clothes when you get pregnant, but the irony is you don't actually need all of them immediately. The first thing you'll notice is the need for a new bra. At least, that was my first clue that my body was changing. Breast changes occur as early as the first month, and you may find yourself going through several different sizes along the way.

Next, your belly will begin to "swell." Yes, the baby is making its presence known by making you feel a bit bigger around the middle. Not only may you find that you need to buy larger panties, but you may also find that skirts and pants feel tight as early as your second or third month. Maternity clothes at this point may seem like overkill, but some women do begin to "show" enough that they find it necessary to head out to the maternity shop.

If you have decided to breastfeed (more on this later in this chapter), you'll need to consider what type of nursing bras you'll want. Buy two or three in your eighth month so you'll be prepared. You may find it necessary to buy more nursing bras after the baby is born, but this will get you started. As for other nursing clothes, you may or may not find these worth the money. Don't go out and buy a whole new wardrobe right off the bat. Instead, get a couple of nursing shirts before you deliver and try them out once the baby has arrived. You can always pick up more later.

## Sources:

1 MATERNITY WEAR CHAINS. Not surprisingly, there are quite a few nationwide maternity clothing chains. Visit any mall and you'll likely see the names Pea in the Pod, MothersWork, Pageboy, Mimi Maternity, and Motherhood, to mention a few.

We visited several of the stores and will review them later in this chapter.

2 MOM AND POP MATERNITY SHOPS. These small, independent chains sell a wide variety of maternity clothes, from affordable weekend wear to high-priced career wear. Some baby specialty stores carry maternity wear as well. The chief advantage to the smaller stores is the personalized service— we often found salespeople who were knowledgeable about the different brands. In addition, these stores often offer other services; for example, some rent formal wear for special occasions, saving you big bucks. Of course, you will pay for the extra service with higher prices. Whether you want all that service is a personal decision.

3 CONSIGNMENT STORES. Many consignment or thrift stores that specialize in children's clothing may also have a rack of maternity clothes. In visits to several such stores, we found some incredible bargains (at least 50% off retail) on maternity clothes that were in good to excellent condition. Of course, the selection varies widely, but we strongly advise you check out any stores in your area.

4 DISCOUNTERS. When we talk about discounters, we're referring to chains like Target and K-Mart. Now, let's be honest here. When we think of good places to buy clothes, those chains may not come to mind first. Yet, you'll be surprised about their maternity clothes, especially the casual wear. Later, we'll tell you about the incredible prices on these all-cotton clothes.

5 DEPARTMENT STORES. Most folks think of their local department store first when looking for maternity clothes. And many department stores do carry maternity clothes. The big disadvantage: the selection is usually rather small. This means you'll often find unattractive jumpers in abundance and very little in the way of fashionable clothing. Even worse, maternity clothes almost never go on sale.

6 MAIL ORDER. Even if you don't have any big-time maternity chains nearby, you can still buy the clothes they sell. Many chains offer a mail-order service (later in this chapter, we'll give you more details). We also found several mail-order catalogs that specialize in maternity clothes. In the "Do It By Mail" section of this chapter, we'll give you the run-down on these options.

7 NON-MATERNITY STORES. Here's a great way to save money: buy large clothes from non-maternity stores. Chains that specialize in over-sized shirts and the like often have prices that are way below the maternity shops. Sales are more numerous here, too.

## *What Are You Buying?*

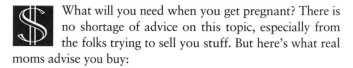 What will you need when you get pregnant? There is no shortage of advice on this topic, especially from the folks trying to sell you stuff. But here's what real moms advise you buy:

♣ *Maternity Bras.* Maternity bras are available from specialty maternity shops and department stores. We aren't sure what makes them "special," but one style I bought promised to adjust as you change. Problem is, they aren't cheap (about $25 to $30 each). You may prefer to buy regular bras throughout your pregnancy.

HOW MANY? Two in each size as your bustline expands. I found that I went through three different sizes during my pregnancy, and buying two in each size allowed me to wear one while the other was washed.

♣ *Sleep Bras.* What do you need a bra to sleep in for, you ask? Well, some women find it more comfortable to have a little support at night as their breasts change. Toward the end of pregnancy, some women also start to leak breast milk (to be technical, this is actually colostrum). And once the baby arrives, a sleeping bra (cost, about $10) will keep those breast pads in place at night (to keep you from leaking when you inadvertently roll onto your stomach—yes, there will come a day when you can do that again). Don't buy anything bulky here; just stick with light support that closes in front (this provides easy nursing access later on).

HOW MANY? Two sleep bras are enough—one to wear, one to wash.

♣ *Underpants.* In the movie "She's Having a Baby," Kevin Bacon laments the fact that his pregnant wife (Elizabeth McGovern) stops wearing her sexy, skimpy bikini underwear and instead dons humongous "granny" briefs. Well, sorry to say, those bigger undies are more comfortable. For as long as I could, I rolled my regular underpants down under my expanding tummy, but, by the sixth month, I broke down and bought some plain cotton maternity underpants. While not glamorous, they were more comfortable and accommodated my tummy better. The good news: the styles have become slightly more attractive, although the prices are rather expensive (at some shops, $4 to $5 a pop). See "Money-Saving Secrets" for tips on how to pay less for maternity underwear.

HOW MANY? I don't like to do lots of laundry, so I bought eight pairs. Remember, you may be wearing them even after your baby is born, so get some that will last.

♣ *Nursing Bras.* I doubt these contraptions were actually invented by women. Built like tanks, these bras have special flaps that unhook and fold down to expose you to the world. The result: you look like an extra from a Frederick's of Hollywood ad. Nevertheless, if you plan to nurse, you should probably buy at least two during your eighth month (they cost about $20 to $30 each). Why then? Theoretically, your breast size won't change much once your baby is born and your milk comes in. I'd suggest buying one with a little larger cup size (than your eighth month size) so you can compensate for the engorgement phase. You can always buy more later and, if your size changes once the baby is born, you won't have invested too much in the wrong size. If you want more advice on nursing bras, you can call Playtex (800-537-9955) for a free guide.

HOW MANY? Buy two to three bras in your eighth month. After the baby is born, you may want to buy a couple more. Another good tip: buy two to three pairs of breast pads (to prevent leaks) before the baby is born.

♣ *Career Clothing.* Our best advice about career clothing for the pregnant mom is to stick with basics. Buy yourself a coordinating outfit with a skirt, jacket, and pair of pants and then accessorize.

Now, we know what you're saying. You'd love to follow this advice, but you don't want to wear the same old thing several times a week—even if it is accessorized. I don't blame you. So, go for a couple dresses and sweaters too. The good news is you don't have to pay full price. We've got several money-saving tips and even an outlet or two coming up later in this chapter.

At some point, you'll notice that regular clothes just don't fit well, and the maternity buying will begin. When this occurs is different for every woman. Some moms-to-be begin to show as early as three months, while others can wait it out until as late as six months. But don't wait until you begin to look like a sausage to shop around. It's always best to scope out the bargains early, so you won't be tempted to buy outfits at the convenient (and high-priced) specialty store out of desperation.

♣ *Casual clothes.* Your best bet here is to stick with knit leggings or sweat pants and big tops. You don't necessarily have to buy these from maternity stores. In fact, later in this chapter, we'll talk about less-expensive alternatives. If you're pregnant in the summer, dresses can be a cooler alternatives to pants and shorts.

♣ *Dress or formal clothes.* Forget them unless you plan to have a full social calender or have many social engagements associated with your job. Usually, you can find a local store that rents formal wear for the one or two occasions when you might need it.

### Smart Shopper Tip
BATTLING YOUR WACKY THERMOSTAT

*"It's early in my pregnancy, and I'm finding that the polyester-blend blouses that I wear to work have become very uncomfortable. I'm starting to shop for maternity clothes—what should I look for that will be more comfortable?"*

You've discovered what we all tend to go through when we get pregnant. Your body's thermostat has gone berserk. All those lovely little pregnancy hormones cause your body temperature to increase. You may find you perspire more because of it. And those polyester-blend clothes may not be so comfortable anymore.

We recommend sticking with natural fabrics as much as possible, especially cotton. Unfortunately, a lot of lower-priced maternity clothing is made of polyester/cotton blend fabrics. Makes you kind of wonder who the designers are at these companies.

To make matters worse, you may also find that your feet swell and are uncomfortable as your pregnancy progresses. Stick with shoes that have low or no heels for maximum comfort.

# The Name Game: Reviews of Selected Maternity Stores

 Usually this section is intended to acquaint you with the clothing name brands you'll see in local stores. When it comes to maternity wear, however, the biggest players are actually the stores themselves. National chains like MothersWork and A Pea in the Pod have their own store brands. Here's a wrap-up of what's available. We've also included Japanese Weekend, which is a maternity wear manufacturer not associated with its own chain of shops.

## The Ratings

★★★★ EXCELLENT—*our top pick!*
★★★ GOOD—*above average quality, prices, and creativity.*
★★ FAIR—*could stand some improvement.*
★ POOR—*yuck! could stand some major improvement.*

---

***A Pea in the Pod*** ........................................................★★ ¹/₂
*1309 Noble St., Philadelphia, PA 19123. (215) 625-9259.*
With over 70 stores in 29 states, A Pea in the Pod offers a nice mix of casual and career wear, along with other items, such as underwear and bathing suits. Most of the clothes are made exclusively for the chain by such designers as Carol Little and Adrienne Vittadini. Prices are moderate to expensive; on a recent visit, we saw a floral denim overall shorts outfit for $68. A coordinating t-shirt seemed a bit pricey at $38, even though it was 100% cotton.

As far as career clothes go, a double-breasted, six-button rayon dress in periwinkle blue was $200 and a silk suit with skirt and jacket ran $284. While A Pea in the Pod's extensive career collection is a strength, it's also a weakness—with office fashion trending toward the casual (leggings, big blouses, boxy sweaters), you can often find the same looks for less at other "regular" clothing stores.

Despite the prices, we like Pea in the Pod. Their personal shopper service is certainly neat—if you don't live near a store or are just too busy, they send you a selection of clothes, you pick out what you like and then send back the ones you don't want. What a plus for busy moms-to-be (call the 800 number listed above to find a store near you that can give you all the details).

And how's the service at Pea in the Pod? We had mixed feelings after several visits. At times, the salespeople seemed too "in-your-face," so aggressive and overly attentive that I felt pressured. Like static cling, one saleswoman followed me around and asked one too many questions about my pregnancy. As soon as you walk in, it takes less than five seconds for someone to offer you spring water—a contrived, albeit nice, gesture. On the upside, the salespeople knew their merchandise, a refreshing change from other mall stores. All in all, the place is worth a visit. If you can get past the prices, the styling and fabrics are top-notch. And you can get all the spring water you can drink.

*Japanese Weekend.* ...................................................... ★★★★
*To find a store near you that carries this brand of clothing, call (800) 808-0555, (415) 621-0555, or write to 22 Isis St., San Francisco, CA 94103. You can also ask for a catalog.*

Japanese Weekend is a line of women's maternity clothing that emphasizes comfort. They are best known for their unusual "OK" belly-banded pants, which have a waistband that circles under your expanding tummy for support (rather than cutting across it).

In recent years, Japanese Weekend has expanded its line beyond pants to include jumpers, tops, catsuits, nightgowns, and skirts. We really like the simple, comfortable style of the clothes and highly recommend them. For once, a company has created all-cotton clothing for moms-to-be, avoiding the all too common polyester blends.

One nice plus: Japanese Weekend will send you a list of stores that carry their clothes (call the above number for more information). In addition, the designer has a company store in San Francisco (415-989-6667).

*Mimi Maternity* ...............................................................★★★
*1309 Noble St., Philadelphia, PA 19123. (215) 625-9259.*
Looking for high-fashion maternity clothes? That's the concept behind Mimi Maternity, a 35-store division of MothersWork. On a recent visit, we were impressed with the collection of career and casual wear—although the prices made us squirm.

We first noticed a nice selection of all-cotton knit items. For example, a $48 pair of leggings was paired with a Southwestern-style vest detailed with silver buttons for $78. The white cotton t-shirt that completed the outfit was $38. Next, we meandered over to the career wear section and found some sale items, like a Donna Ricco suit with spread collar jacket and slip skirt (in case you're wondering, this garment consists of a nylon tank top undergarment attached to a skirt). The outfit was on sale for $119, regularly priced at $198. In fact, an impressive rack of clothes was on sale the day we visited. The shop itself was well layed out and featured large dressing rooms.

The salesperson, who was friendly and helpful, explained that Mimi Maternity is the "fashion-forward" division of Motherswork. We suppose "fashion forward" explains why an all-cotton t-shirt is $40. I guess we prefer fashion backward prices.

*Mothercare* ................................................................★★★
*Over 120 stores. Call (312) 263-6700 for a store near you.*

Mothercare Maternity stores offer medium-priced maternity clothing with a wide selection of casual and work clothes. For example, we saw a blue and white check trapeze shirt for $42, paired with matching blue stirrup pants for $24. Considering that we've seen leggings and stirrups for as much as $50 in other maternity shops, Mothercare is a bit easier on the pocketbook.

Dresses and suits are also available. If you're looking for a high-style pant suit, we noticed a teal outfit with gold-button detailing for only $64. A rayon floral print dress was only $69. Undergarments and swim suits are also reasonably priced.

As an interesting side note, Mothercare is owned by the same parent company that operates the Dan Howard Maternity Factory Outlets (see review later in this chapter).

*Motherhood* ................................................................★★$^1$/2
*For a store near you call (800) 929-4428.*

Yet another national chain of maternity shops with a mix of weekend casual and workday suits. The standouts? A beautiful silk print blouse accented with pearl buttons ($62) and a coordinating slip skirt ($36). As for the casual look, the blue denim jumpsuit was cute with its rolled cuffs. The price was less cute: $62.

Once again, we were not impressed with the hefty price tags. At least the fabrics were mostly natural, and the designs put comfort first.

*MothersWork* ................................................................★★★$^1$/2
*1309 Noble St., Philadelphia, PA 19123. Call (215) 625-9259 for a store location or a catalog.*

MothersWork combines the best of all maternity worlds: superior styling, high quality, and decent service. Another major plus: even if you're not near one of their stores, MothersWork's catalog offers many of the same fashions through the mail.

Career wear is the specialty here; most of the shops have a large part of their selling space devoted to suits and dresses. We liked their coordinating outfits with matching jackets, skirts, and jumpers. As we suggested in the money-saving section of this chapter, coordinating pieces like these may be the way to go during your pregnancy. Instead of buying different outfits and having to accessorize them separately, a small number of coordinating pieces can be more versatile—and affordable.

For example, you can buy a navy jacket from MothersWork for $148, a pleated slip skirt ($68), or a straight slip skirt ($58). Other pieces include a coordinating floral dress ($138) or jumper ($114). Figure out what pieces you want, add a few blouses to the mix, and you've got a whole wardrobe. Although the prices aren't cheap, you'll be able to limit the clothes you buy to items that coordinate.

As for the rest of the selection at MothersWork, we saw beautiful evening dresses with empire waists or swing tops, knit leggings, vests, and t-shirts. My favorite: a pansy-covered sundress ($58) that my father-in-law graciously bought for me during my pregnancy. The 100% cotton dress was one of the most comfortable outfits (and certainly the most colorful) of all my summer maternity clothes. It washed well and is still in great shape.

*Some late-breaking changes:* As we went to press on the first edition of this book, there some "mergers and acquisitions" in the maternity wear world.

MothersWork acquired the Pea in the Pod chain. Now the same parent company (MothersWork) owns Mimi Maternity, Pea in the Pod, Maternite' by MothersWork and the Maternity Works stores. What's prompted all the consolidation? Many maternity stores were hit with declining sales in the '90's as women looked to less expensive outlets and catalogs to shop for maternity wear. Will all these mergers mean better-run shops and lower prices? We'll have to wait and see.

## Wastes of Money

### Waste of Money #1
MATERNITY BRA BLUES

"My old bras are getting very tight. I recently went to my local department store to check out larger sizes. The salesperson suggested I purchase a maternity bra because it would offer more comfort and support. Should I buy a regular bra in a larger size or plunk down the money for a maternity bra? When I saw the $28 price tag on the maternity bra, I wasn't sure it was worth it."

It may not be worth it. I wore both regular bras and "special" maternity bras. The biggest difference really seemed to be the price. In fact, we've become suspicious that a maternity bra is just a regular bra with a "maternity" tag slapped on it—as well as a higher price. I found perfectly comfortable all-cotton bras that were just as nice as the all-cotton maternity bras, at prices 20% to 30% less.

## *Waste of Money #2*
### ORANGE YOU GOING TO WEAR HOSE?

*"Have you seen the horrendous colors available in maternity hose? I can't wear those orange things to work!"*

Don't. You don't have to buy maternity hose—those thick, itchy horrors only sold in four shades of orange (ugly, sheer ugly, super-duper ugly, and son of ugly). Maternity hose must have been invented by a third world country looking for a new torture device; now, it takes its rightful place next to the bridesmaid's dress as one of the most dreaded apparel items for women.

Here's our advice: Be creative. With a few modifications, you may be able to wear regular hose during your pregnancy. Try rolling the waistband down under your tummy. It works, believe me. When I was six months pregnant and invited to a formal occasion, I wore regular hose in that manner and had no problem. Or you may find that cutting the waistband of your hose gives you some breathing room for a few months. If you wear only long skirts and dresses, knee-hi hose are an option; no one will know you're not wearing full hose. Some women swear by self-supporting stockings, the kind with rubberlike grippers around the bands. Women we spoke with found them uncomfortable, but ask around—you may find a brand you like.

Finally, if all else fails, there is one company that makes maternity hose in attractive colors: Hue, made by Leslie Fay Co. To find a store near you that carries this brand, call (212) 947-3666. Hue's maternity hose retail for $14 per pair.

## *Waste of Money #3*
### OVER THE SHOULDER TUMMY HOLDER

*"I keep seeing those 'belly bras' advertised as the best option for a pregnant mom. What are they for and are they worth buying?"*

Belly bras were invented to provide additional support for your back during your pregnancy. They envelop your whole torso and look like a tight-fitting tank top. No one can argue that, in many cases, the strain of carrying a baby and the additional weight that goes with it is tough even on women in great physical shape. So, if you find your back, hips, and/or legs are giving you trouble, consider buying a belly bra or support panty.

However, in our research, we noticed most moms don't seem to need or want a belly bra. The price for one of these puppies can range from $35 to an incredible $55. The bottom line: hold off buying a belly bra or support panty until you see how your body reacts to your pregnancy. Also, check with your doctor to see if she has any suggestions for back, hip, and leg problems.

## *Waste of Money #4*
### OVEREXPOSED NURSING GOWNS

*"I plan to nurse my baby and all my friends say I should buy nursing gowns for night feedings. Problem is, I've tried on a few and even though the slits are hidden, I still feel exposed. Not to mention they're the ugliest things I've ever seen. Can't I just wear a regular gown that buttons down the front?"*

Of course you can. And considering how expensive nursing gowns can be ($35 to $50 each), buying a regular button-up nightshirt or gown will certainly save you a few bucks. Every mother we interviewed about nursing gowns had the same complaint. There isn't a delicate way to put this: it's not easy to get a breast out of one of those teenie-weenie slits. Did the person who designed these ever breastfeed a baby? I always felt uncovered whenever I wore a nursing gown, like one gust of wind would have turned me into a poster child for a nudist magazine.

And can we talk about nursing shirts with those "convenient button flaps for discreet breastfeeding"? Convenient, my fanny. There's so much work involved in lifting the flap up, unbuttoning it, and getting your baby positioned that you might as well forget it. My advice: stick with shirts you can pull up or unbutton down the front. These are just as discreet, easier to work with, and (best of all) you don't have to add some expensive nursing shirts (at $30 to $50 each) to your wardrobe.

---

THE FOUR SHADES OF MATERNITY HOSE
"UGLY, SHEER UGLY, SUPER-DUPER UGLY AND SON OF UGLY—
OUTCLASSED ONLY BY BRIDESMAIDS DRESSES AS ONE OF THE
MOST DREADED APPAREL ITEMS FOR WOMEN."

## Money-Saving Secrets

**1** CONSIDER BUYING "PLUS" (LARGE LADIES) SIZES FROM A REGULAR STORE. Thankfully, fashion styles of late include leggings and oversized tops and sweaters. This makes pregnancy a lot easier since you can buy the same styles in larger ladies' sizes to cover your belly without compromising your fashion sense or investing in expensive and often shoddily made maternity clothes. We found the same fashions in large-ladies' stores for 20% to 35% less than maternity shops (and even more during sales).

One drawback to this strategy: by the end of your pregnancy, your hemlines may start to look a little "high-low" in front—your expanding belly will raise the hemline in front. This may be especially pronounced with skirts and dresses. Of course, that's the advantage of buying maternity clothes: the designers compensate with more fabric in front to balance the hemline. Nonetheless, we found that many moms we interviewed were able to get away with large-lady fashions for much (if not all) of their pregnancy. And how much money can you save? We priced a pair of cotton-blend leggings from Mimi Maternity at $44. Meanwhile, we found that Eddie Bauer carries cotton/spandex leggings for only $30—and we'd hardly call Eddie Bauer a cheap source for clothes. And the chain sells leggings through their catalog in petites, talls, extra large, and extra, extra large sizes.

Another tip: one pregnant mom we interviewed recommended wearing her husband's shirts. And they're free, so to speak.

**2** DON'T BUY EXPENSIVE BRAS WHEN YOU'RE PREGNANT. As your pregnancy progresses, your bra size is going to change at least a couple times. Running out to buy five new bras when you hit a new cup size is probably foolish—in another month, all those bras may not fit. The best advice: buy the bare minimum (two or three). And forget maternity bras—investing $20 to $30 each is ridiculous. As we mentioned above, we couldn't tell much, if any, difference between maternity bras and regular bras. So just buy what's comfortable and save your money. By the way, Victoria's Secret (call 800-888-8200 for a store near you) often has "buy two get the third free" sales on bras—a great way to save a few bucks.

**3** DON'T SHOP AT MATERNITY STORES FOR UNDERWEAR. Shop around for the best price. For example, when I was pregnant, both Motherhood and Target carried 100% cotton maternity panties. They appeared to be made by the same manufacturer, but labeled with different brand names. The only difference: Target's brand (LuvPats) was priced at about a dollar less per pair.

Another example of money-savings: a friend of ours told us she bought maternity panties from her local maternity shop and paid $4 each. Later, she noticed that her local J.C. Penney store carried a similar style for $3.25 each. She was infuriated that the maternity shop had marked their panties up 20%. As you can see, by buying a week's worth of panties at non-maternity stores, you'd save at least $5. And similar savings are available on nursing bras, slips, hose, and more.

**4** CONSIDER TARGET AND K-MART FOR CASUAL CLOTHES. Okay, I admit that I don't normally shop at K-Mart and Target for my wardrobe. But I was surprised to discover both chains carry casual maternity clothes in 100% cotton at very affordable prices. Let's repeat that—they have 100% cotton t-shirts, shorts, pants, and more at prices you won't believe. Most of these clothes are in basic solid colors—sorry, no fancy prints. At Target, for example, I found cotton chambray maternity shirts and shorts at just $10 each. At $20 per outfit, you can't beat it. We found 100% cotton maternity shirts in K-Mart for just $8.98. Hello? Try to find that price at a chain maternity store.

While Target and K-Mart don't carry any career wear (as you might expect), you'll save so much on casual/weekend clothes that you'll be ecstatic anyway. Witness this example. At A Pea in the Pod, we found a cotton knit tank top and shorts outfit in solid yellow. The price: a heart-stopping $82. A similar all-cotton tank top/shorts outfit from Target was $20. Whip out a calculator, and you'll note the savings is an amazing 75%. Need we say more?

**5** RENT EVENING WEAR—DON'T BUY. We found that many maternity stores rent evening wear. For example, a local shop we visited had an entire rack of formal wear for rent. An off-white lace dress (perfect for attending a wedding) rented for just $50. Compare that with the purchase price of $175 retail. Since you most likely would need the dress for a one-time wearing, the savings of renting versus buying would be $125.

**6** CHECK OUT CONSIGNMENT STORES. You can find "gently worn" career and casual maternity clothes for 40% to 70% off the original retail! Many consignment or second-hand stores carry only designer-label clothing in good to excellent condition. If you don't want to buy used garments, consider re-couping some of your investment in maternity clothes by consigning them after the baby is born. You can usually find listings for these stores in the phone book. (Don't forget to look under children's clothes as well. Some consignment stores that carry baby furniture and clothes also have a significant stock of maternity wear.)

7 FIND A DAN HOWARD MATERNITY OUTLET. One of the best places to find maternity clothes at significant savings is at the over 90 Dan Howard Maternity Factory Outlets. Call their main number (312) 263-6700 to find a store near you. To get a free catalog of their clothes, dial (800) 966-6847. Dan Howard and other maternity outlets are discussed in greater detail in the following section.

## Outlets

### Dan Howard Maternity Factory Outlet

*Locations:* Over 90 stores. Call (312) 263-6700 to find a store near you or call (800) 966-6847 for a catalog.

Dan Howard, manufacturer of a line of career, dress, and casual clothes, is the most visible of the maternity outlet stores, with over 90 locations in North America, including seven in Canada. Dan Howard advertises savings of up to 50% off comparable retail.

On a recent visit to a Dan Howard outlet, we noticed that their specialty seems to be career wear, with an emphasis on dresses. One example was a lavender rayon dress with empire waist and pearl button detailing for $59 (compare at $84). An attractive black and cream checked suit also caught our eye. The jacket, in an acetate and rayon blend, was $88 (regularly $126), and the matching skirt was $34 (compare at $49).

Dan Howard also carries casual clothing and even nursing shirts ($34). We noticed leggings, bike shorts, cotton knit designs, undergarments, and even bathing suits. If your career requires a hefty investment in maternity clothes, check out Dan Howard's frequent buyer club, which offers additional discounts.

We actually bought several outfits from the Dan Howard outlet and were pleased with the style and quality. If we had one bone to pick with Dan Howard, it would be their "suggested retail" prices, which seemed a bit high. Since most of the clothes they carry are their own private label, it's hard to confirm the exact savings. Nevertheless, considering the quality, the prices are somewhat lower than retail—just probably not the 50% claimed in Dan Howard's ads.

## MothersWork Outlets

*Locations:* Outlets in Massachusetts, Pennsylvania, Texas, Virginia, and Colorado. For exact addresses and new locations call (215) 625-9259.

The offspring of the catalog and retail stores of the same name (see our review in "Do It By Mail" later in the chapter), MothersWork outlets have started springing up in outlet malls across the country. On a recent visit, the outlet featured markdowns from 20% to 75% on the same top-quality designs you see in the catalog or the retail stores.

For example, we noticed a cotton knit jumper at MothersWork for $59 that was regularly priced at $98. Knit stirrup pants were on sale for $39, almost 20% off the regular price of $48. A suit jacket was priced at a mere $39 (regularly $158), and the matching skirt was only $29 (regularly $58). That's right, you could pick up this whole outfit for just $68, instead of the $226 retail price.

The outlet also carried a decent selection of party dresses, undergarments, and casual wear.

## Mothercare

*Location:* Secaucus, NJ (201) 392-1237.

Even though Mothercare is the retail division of Dan Howard Maternity, the chain has its own outlet store in Secaucus, New Jersey. In addition to carrying casual and career maternity clothes, Mothercare also sells children's clothing (from newborn to 24 months sizes). The discounts are rather slim, however, averaging about 20% off retail.

# Do it By Mail

## Garnet Hill.

*To Order Call:* (800) 622-6216; Fax (603) 823-9578.
*Shopping Hours:* Monday-Friday 7:00 am-11:00 pm; Saturday and Sunday 10:00 am-6:00 pm Eastern Time.
*Or write to:* Garnet Hill, 262 Main St., Franconia, NH 03580.
*Credit Cards Accepted:* MC, VISA, AMEX, Discover.

 Unfortunately, Garnet Hill is a good example of how expensive maternity clothes can get. Sample impressions from a recent catalog: a denim maternity shirt was a whopping $58. We also saw leggings for $52, a jumper for $66, and a knit dress for $72.

Well, at least the clothes are stylish. While we like Garnet Hill's contemporary and fresh designs (they sell only natural fabrics), their casual wear is overpriced. On the upside, they do occasionally offer a discount for new customers. And look for sale catalogs—those $52 leggings were last seen selling for $24.

## J.C. Penney.

*To Order Call:* (800) 222-6161. Ask for the following catalogs: Baby and You, For Baby, and Starting Small.
*Shopping Hours:* 24 hours a day, seven days a week.
*Credit Cards Accepted:* MC, VISA, JC Penney, AMEX, Discover.

J. C. Penney offers a free "mini-catalog" called "Baby and You." A recent edition featured 44-pages of maternity clothes, plus a small selection of cribs, linens, and furniture.

Perhaps the best aspect of Penney's offerings is their collection of career maternity wear at affordable prices. For example, a rayon and polyester-blend pantsuit with a cardigan jacket was just $82. Other "career essentials" included three-piece ensembles (jacket, pants, and skirt) for $69 to $72. As for more casual clothes, simple cotton/rayon chemise dresses in "spring prints" were just $39 to $42. A selection of nightgowns, swim suits, lingerie, and hose round out the offerings in this catalog.

## Mother's Place.

*To Order Call:* (800) 829-0080; (216) 826-1712.
*Shopping Hours:* Monday-Friday 8:00 am-10:00 pm;
Saturday 9:00 am-8:00 pm.
*Or write to:* Mother's Place,  6836 Engle Rd., PO Box 94512, Cleveland, OH 44101.
*Credit Cards Accepted:* MC, VISA, Discover.

Mother's Place maternity catalog claims to save mothers-to-be up to 50% off the cost of maternity clothes. With such hefty advertised discounts, we had to investigate.

At a slim 13 pages, the catalog is nevertheless crammed full of maternity outfits, most suited for career dressing. The cover featured a two-piece outfit in a poly/rayon blend with a white collar and white accent buttons. Priced at only $35.99 (regularly $49.99), the outfit seemed like a great deal.

Designs range from smock tops and leggings, to jackets and pleated skirts. The standard drop-waisted jumpers (like a striped chambray number for $24.99) are there, as is the occasional party dress (a burgundy two-piece dress with white lace collar was a standout for only $34.99).

It's obvious that these prices are fantastic. Our only complaint is the heavy use of synthetic and blended fabrics—it would have been nice to see more cotton offerings.

## MothersWork.

*To Order Call:* (800) 825-2286 or (215) 625-9259;
Fax (215) 440-9845.
*Shopping Hours:* 24 hours a day, seven days a week.
*Or write to:* MothersWork, 1309 Noble St., 6th Floor, Dept. PG,
Philadelphia, PA 19123.
*Credit Cards Accepted:* MC, VISA, AMEX.

You won't find any polyester pants in MothersWork, the catalog division that also operates retail locations and outlet stores. But if it's style you want for maternity clothes (and if price isn't much of an object), that's what you'll get.

For example, we found the perfect career option for pregnant moms in MothersWork's three-piece suit and companion pieces. The three pieces include a 100% wool crepe cardigan jacket ($148), long-sleeve white blouse ($54), and wool crepe "adjuster" skirt ($88). Companion pieces range from a pleated slip skirt ($74) to maternity pants ($78). The catalog claims that some of the pieces can even be worn after pregnancy. At these prices, it sure would be nice—but don't bet on it.

Besides career wear, MothersWork offers evening designs (such as a red crepe evening dress with a pearl-accented neckline) and casual clothes. We liked the black knit jumpsuit with stirrups ($88), as well as the black and white checked swing top with red trim ($74) seen in the latest catalog. These prices aren't a bargain, but if your career requires an investment in stylish maternity clothes and you don't have a decent maternity shop nearby, MothersWork might be the answer.

---

### Maternity Wear for the Real World

Tired of t-shirts emblazoned with the word "baby" and an arrow pointing down to your tummy? Seen one too many cute denim overall outfits? Then have we found the designer for you: Lauren Sara M.

You've probably seen designer Lauren Sara's clothes on such famous celebrity moms-to-be as Paula Zahn and Demi Moore. Lauren told us she was inspired to design the line after a wealthy New York socialite (who was five months pregnant) hired her to design an evening gown. The dress was a smashing success, and Lauren set out to design a line of maternity wear with style.

The collection includes career wear like suits (jackets run $320 to $385, and skirts and pants cost $150 to $225), daytime dresses ($250), and even a few evening gowns (about $500). Sure, the prices aren't cheap, but we challenge you to find a more fashionable alternative. Most of the specialty stores that carry the Lauren Sara M designs are on the East Coast; you can call (212) 730-0007 to find a dealer near you. A catalog is also available.

## *Breastfeeding*

Suppose we told you that you could take a miracle pill during pregnancy that would do amazing things for your baby.

What things? How about a higher IQ? Yes, this miracle drug would do that, as well as lessen your child's chance of respiratory and gastrointestinal infections. The same pill would mean fewer and less severe allergies, and your baby would have better jaw and teeth development. Speech problems and ear infections in childhood? This pill would help eliminate them, as well as provide protection from illnesses like rubella, chicken pox, bronchitis, and polio. If that weren't enough, taking this pill would even reduce the chance your child would be obese as an adult. Not only would this miracle pill do all that for your baby, but it would also lower the chance of breast cancer and heart disease in you, the mother.

Surprise! There is no pill that does all that! But there is something you can do for your baby that does everything described above and more: breastfeeding.

We used this analogy to make a point. What mother wouldn't want to give her baby the best chance to live a healthy and productive life? And if there were such a pill, you know there would be a line a mile long outside your nearest drug store.

Certainly, comparing breastfeeding to taking a pill during pregnancy isn't entirely fair. While breastfeeding may seem intuitive to some women, most have to work to get it right—and those first few days can seem like hell. So, it's important to know how to find help. This section will provide you with tips and tricks to successfully breastfeed, including a list of products and organizations that can make the process easier.

### *Breastfeed Your Baby and Save $500*

Since this is a book on a bargains, we'd be remiss in not mentioning the tremendous amount of money you can save if you breastfeed rather than use formula. Just think about it: no bottles, no expensive formula to prepare, no special insulated carriers to keep bottles warm, etc.

So, how much money would you save? Obviously, the biggest money-saver would be not having to buy formula. Even if you were to use the less expensive powder, you would still have to spend nearly $8 per 16-ounce can. (For reference, we used our local grocery store's price of $7.79 per can as a price point.) Since each can makes 116 ounces of formula when mixed with water, the cost per ounce of formula is about 7¢.

That doesn't sound too bad, does it? Unless you factor in that a baby will down 32 ounces of formula per day by 12 weeks of age. Your cost per day would be $2.15. Assuming you breastfeed for the first six months, you would save a grand total of $387. Not only is breastfeeding better for your baby's health, it is much kinder to your wallet.

To be fair, there are some optional expenses that might go along with breastfeeding. The biggest dollar item: you might decide to rent a piston electric breast pump if (or when) you return to work in order to express milk every day. The cost? About $50 per month. You can also buy a mini-electric breast pump for about the same money it takes to rent a larger pump for a month.

If $387 doesn't sound like a lot of money, consider the savings if you had to buy formula in the concentrated liquid form instead of the cheaper powder. A 13-ounce can of Similac liquid concentrate costs about $2.30 at a grocery store and makes just 26 ounces of formula. The bottom line: you could spend over $500 on formula for your baby in the first six months alone! Even if you ignore the fantastic health benefits from breastfeeding your baby, it's hard to argue against the money it saves.

## What's a Breastfeeding Mom's Biggest Misconception?
"I'M NOT MAKING ENOUGH MILK"

In some ways, a mom who feeds her baby formula has it easy. She measures out a certain amount of formula and can see her baby's progress as she empties the bottle. Breastfeeding, however, is based a little more on faith. You can't see how much milk you have, nor can you tell how much milk your baby has had. The truth is most women have breasts that make plenty of milk. The nagging fear that your baby isn't eating enough is often just that: a fear.

To be frank, however, we should note that in a small number of cases mothers may not have milk to breastfeed their babies. According to a report in the *Wall Street Journal*, "insufficient-milk syndrome may occur as much as 5% of the time, affecting about 200,000 mothers a year in the U.S. Some physicians say certain breasts are structurally incapable of producing enough milk; in addition, women who have had breast surgery are at risk. Some infants, meanwhile, are incapable of learning how to breast-feed."

The result: mothers with the best of intentions can actually starve their babies. Two infant deaths caused by insufficient-milk syndrome were reported in the first half of 1994. Since the signs of dehydration can be subtle, the best advice may to see your doctor immediately if your think your baby is not getting enough milk in the first few days. Of course, failing to breastfeed your baby does not mean that you're a failure as a mother.

Fortunately, this syndrome is quite rare. Most women have no problem producing enough milk for their baby. The biggest obstacle to breastfeeding may be mental. Many moms start out with the best of intentions, only to abandon breast-feeding because of lack of support or self-confidence. The next part of this chapter addresses this problem.

## *Sources: Where to Find Help*

 The basis of breastfeeding is attachment. Getting your new little one to latch onto your breast proper-ly is not a matter of instinct. Some babies have no trouble figuring it out, while many others need your help and guidance. In fact, problems with attachment can lead to sore nipples and painful engorgement. Of course, you should be able to turn to your pediatrician or the nurses at the hospital for breastfeeding advice. However, if you find that they do not offer you the support you need, consider the following sources for breastfeeding help:

1 LA LECHE LEAGUE (800-LA LECHE). Started over 35 years ago by a group of moms in Chicago, La Leche League has traditionally been the most vocal supporter of breastfeeding in this country. You've got to imagine the amount of chutzpah these women had to have had in order to promote breastfeeding at a time when it wasn't fashionable (to say the least).

In recent years, La Leche has established branches in many communities, providing support groups for new moms inter-ested in trying to nurse their children. They also offer a cata-log full of books and videotapes on nursing, as well as other child care topics. Their famous book *The Motherly Art of Breastfeeding* is the bible for huge numbers of breastfeeding advocates (we review the book in Chapter 10).

Although we admire the work La Leche League has done to help nursing mothers and to change society's attitudes toward them, we disagree with some of the group's tenets. For example, their approach toward parenting includes an unhealthy dose of negativism when it comes to working moms. Let's get real, folks. Most moms today have to work, at least part-time—to have such a prestigious organization as La Leche promoting a traditional stay-at-home role model is anachronistic. Another gripe: the group's books and materials rarely mention the father and any positive role he may play in raising an infant.

Of course, these are minor points of disagreement. All in all, La Leche provides an important service and, coupled with their support groups and catalog of publications, is a valuable resource for nursing mothers.

2 NURSING MOTHERS' COUNCIL (408-272-1448). Similar in mission to La Leche League, the Nursing Mothers' Council differs on one point: the group emphasizes working moms and their unique needs and problems.

3 LACTATION CONSULTANTS. Lactation consultants are usually nurses who specialize in breastfeeding education and problem solving. You can find them through your pediatrician, hospital, or the International Lactation Consultants Association (708-260-8874). At our local hospital, resident lactation consultants are available to answer questions by phone at no charge. If a problem persists, you can set up an in-person consultation for a minimal fee.

Unfortunately, the availability of lactation consultants seems to vary from region to region. Our research shows that, in general, hospitals in the western U.S. are more likely to offer support services, such as on-staff lactation consultants. Back east, however, the effort to support breastfeeding seems spotty. Our advice: call area hospitals before you give birth to determine the availability of breastfeeding support. If your local hospital has no such program, request it. Maternity wards are a profit center for most hospitals; many administrators have realized that the competitive advantage of on-staff breastfeeding support translates into bigger profits. Letting a hospital know you picked a competitor to deliver your baby because of this service sends a strong signal to the medical community.

4 HOSPITALS. Look for a hospital in your area that has breastfeeding-friendly policies. What are these? Hospitals that allow 24-hour rooming in (where your baby can stay with you instead of in a nursery) and breastfeeding on demand are best. Pro-nursing hospitals do not supplement babies with a bottle and don't push free formula samples. Their nurses will also respect your wishes concerning pacifier usage, which is important if you are concerned about nipple confusion.

Stay away from hospitals that insist on rigid feeding schedules for your baby, don't allow rooming in, and hand out formula samples right and left. As we mentioned earlier, hospitals on the East Coast are more likely to fall into the anti-breastfeeding camp than those in the West.

### Baby Formula Manufacturers:
### Modern Convenience or Sinister Conspiracy?

We got an interesting package in the mail the other day. It was from Enfamil, one of the country's largest formula makers. This wasn't any special treatment because we had authored this book. Nope, it appears to be standard practice. What was inside this special delivery? A case of six cans of formula and, get this, a pamphlet with tips on *breastfeeding*. We were appalled. It was sort of like Marlboro sending us a booklet on how to quit smoking—along with a case of cigarettes.

We've got nothing against formula, per se. Sure, we're firm believers in breastfeeding, but we're not foolish enough to think it's right for everyone. For example, one woman we interviewed had to return to work after six weeks of maternity leave. She wanted to continue breastfeeding her baby, but her employer didn't offer any day-care on site. And trying to pump at work each morning to leave her baby a supply of breast milk was too difficult.

Formula does have a useful purpose on planet Earth. It's the way that formula companies *market* their product that most irks us. If you knew what was going on behind the scenes in the formula war, it might make you sick. Among the more interesting activities we discovered: formula makers shower hospitals with all kinds of gifts and free samples—all in the hope that the nurses will pass the word to you and other new mothers. One company offers gift incentives to nurses who hand out the most formula packets to new moms. Another firm has even shamelessly produced a video on breastfeeding, with a plug for their formula tactfully inserted at the end. Hospitals get the video free of charge and send one home with each new mom.

You can always spot the new parents when they check out of a maternity ward—they're the ones weighed down with free diaper bags, rattles, and toys, all emblazoned with the fancy logos of the formula makers.

All this makes us think, what kind of message are they trying to send? Sure, you should breastfeed, but if you have any problems, we want to make sure a convenient can of formula is never that far away. One of our favorite examples of this duplicity was a rattle we received as a gift, once again at the hospital. Emblazoned with the name Enfamil, it featured a picture of a rabbit feeding its baby with a *bottle*! We don't know about you, but we haven't seen any rabbits in the Wild Kingdom who bottle-feed their young.

Consider a recent advertising campaign for Carnation's Good Start formula: a new mom looks into the camera and says something like "Remember, breast milk is best, but Carnation's Good Start is made to be gentle for your baby." Sort of like a beer company saying "Don't drink and drive, BUT if you're going to get sloshed, make it a Coors."

Frankly, we think the baby formula companies are taking advantage of new mothers, plying us poor souls (who are already short of sleep) with slick pitches for "convenient" solutions to our babies' feeding problems. In our opinion, there's no difference between them and companies that market sugar-packed wine like Mad Dog 20-20 to the down and out.

What's our solution to this marketing muddle? Require a doctor's prescription to get baby formula. No free samples, no fancy marketing campaigns. Companies like Gerber and Carnation would be banned from marketing directly to consumers. Surprisingly, many other western countries already require this, and the result is breastfeeding gets a better shake. Would that hurt the formula companies, causing job losses among formula farmers? Who cares? A couple of major formula makers (namely, Mead/Johnson and Ross) already restrict their marketing to the medical community, and they don't seem the worse for it.

Formula companies aren't run by dummies. They realize that when a breastfeeding mother switches to formula within her baby's first year, odds are she will have to continue formula feeding for the rest of that first year. Contrast that with the fact that moms who never breastfeed often switch to whole cow's milk after just six months. Hence, it's more lucrative for these companies to target breastfeeding moms, since getting them to switch racks up bigger profits in the long run.

Considering the overwhelming evidence that breastfeeding is infinitely better for babies, it is time this country took a hard look at regulating the out-of-control marketing of baby formula.

5 BOOKS. Here's a list of books recommended by our local lactation specialist. Although they aren't a substitute for support from your doctor, hospital, and family, these books will provide plenty of information and encouragement.

♣ *Politics of Breastfeeding* by Gabriel Palmer
♣ *Breastfeeding Your Baby* by Sheila Kitzinger
♣ *Nursing Mother's Companion* by Kathleen Huggins
♣ *Breast Feeding: Getting It Right For You* by Mary Renfrew, Chloe Fisher & Suzanne Arms
♣ RECOMMENDED VIDEO: *Breastfeeding: A Special Relationship*

These titles are available through the La Leche League catalog (708-519-7730) or check your local bookstore.

## Smart Shopper Tips

### Smart Shopper Tip #1
PUMPED UP

*"My husband and I would really like to go out to dinner sometime before our daughter is 15 years old. I've been looking at different breastpumps—which really works best?"*

Expressing milk is a science in itself. You'll notice a wide variety of pumps, from manual pumps that cost a few dollars to huge, piston electric pumps that run into the hundreds of dollars (most women rent rather than buy these). Here's a run-down of the four options:

♣ *Manual Expression:* There are several good breastfeeding books that describe how to express milk manually (see Chapter 10 for more information). Most women find that the amount of milk expressed, compared to the time and trouble involved, hardly makes it worth using this method. A few women (we think they are modern miracle workers) can manage to express enough for an occasional bottle; for the majority of women, however, using a breastpump is a more practical alternative.

♣ *Manual Pumps:* Non-electric, hand-held pumps create suction by squeezing on a handle. While they're cheap, manual pumps are also the least efficient—you simply can't duplicate your baby's sucking action by hand. Though if you're a professional tennis player or in training to be one, a manual pump is probably good exercise. Target sells an Evenflo manual pump for $16, while Toys R Us sells the same model for $20.

*Recommendation:* Egnell's Mother's Touch One-Handed Breast Pump ($27.95). It's easier to use and is available through La Leche League's catalog (708-519-7730), or call the company at (800) 323-8750 or (708) 639-2900 for a store that carries the pump. Another brand to look for at your local baby store is the Medela Manualectric Breast Pump/Feeding System ($24.95, call 800-435-8316 or 815-363-1246 for a dealer near you).

♣ *Mini-Electrics:* I bought one of these, and it was probably a waste of money. I thought these battery-operated breast-pumps would be good for expressing an occasional bottle. Unfortunately, the sucking action is so weak that I quickly discovered it took twenty minutes *per side* to express a signifi-cant amount of milk. And doing so was not very comfortable, to say the least. Why is it so slow? Most models only cycle nine to fifteen times per minute—compare that to a baby who sucks the equivalent of 50 cycles per minute! Some of the most inefficient mini-electric breastpumps just so happen to be manufactured by formula makers (like Gerber). Coincidence? We wonder.

*Recommendation:* The Medela Mini Electric (about $70 to $80 retail) is one of the few battery operated breastpumps that actually operates at 50 cycles per minute. Call Medela at (800) 435-8316 for the store nearest you. Sure, you can find other mini-electrics for $30 to $50 at discount and drug stores, but be sure to check the cycles per minute before you buy.

♣ *Piston Electric Pumps*: The Mercedes Benz of breast-pumps—and you may have to hock the Mercedes if you want to buy one. Fortunately, you don't have to shell out the $1200 or so that piston electric pumps cost. . . most commu-nities have a source where you can rent one on a daily, week-ly, or monthly basis.

We can't sing the praises of the piston electric pumps enough. In just 10 minutes, you can pump *both* breasts. And they are much more comfortable than mini-electrics. In fact, at first I didn't think the piston electric pump I rented was working well because it was *so* comfortable. The bottom line: there is no bet-ter option for a working woman who wants to provide her baby with breast milk.

A wide variety of sources rent piston electric breastpumps. We called a lactation consultant at a local hospital who gave us a list that included maternity stores, small private companies, and home-care outfits. Another possibility is to call the La Leche League (see number earlier in this chapter) or other lactation support groups for a referral to a company that rents piston electric pumps.

What does it cost? One company we surveyed rented pumps for $60 for one month or $45 per month if you rent for two or more months. In general, we found rental charges ranged from $1 to $2.50 per day, with the lower rates for longer rentals. You'll also have to buy a kit of the collection bottles, shields, and tubes (this runs about $30 to $35).

We rented the Medela Classic, which weighs 22 pounds. The Medela Lactina is more portable at five pounds, but our lactation consultant didn't recommend this model since its suction may not be strong enough (depending on the way a mother sets up the machine). Both models pump at 50 cycles per minute.

### *Smart Shopper Tip #2*
NIPPLE CONFUSION?

*"When I check the catalogs and look in baby stores, I see bottles with all different shaped nipples. Which one is best for my baby? How do I avoid nipple confusion?"*

Nipple confusion occurs when a baby learns to suck one way at the breast and another way from a bottle. This happens because the "human breast milk delivery system" (i.e., the breast and nipple) forces babies to keep their sucking action forward in their mouth. The result: they have to work harder to get milk from a breast than from a conventional baby bottle.

So, what bottle and nipple do the experts recommend? Playtex Nursers. That's right, Playtex offers a nipple that helps keep your baby's sucking in the natural position. Longer bottle nipples push the sucking action farther back into the baby's mouth, so when you switch baby back to the breast, she might get confused and frustrated. The medical specialists we interviewed also prefer Playtex Nursers because they encourage better oral motor skills.

What about pacifiers? Ironically, the pacifiers labeled "orthodontic" are the worst, according to the experts we interviewed. These pacifiers have a short, flat nipple that supposedly helps oral development—it would be nice if it were true. The lactation consultants, nurses, and pediatricians whom we consulted would like to get these pacifiers banned. A better bet: pacifiers that have "normal," round nipples (brands like Playtex and Mini-Mams are examples).

## ! *Waste of Money*

Even Cows Opt for the Electric Kind

*"I'll be going back to work a couple of months after my baby is born. My co-worker who breastfeeds her baby thinks manual breastpumps are a total waste of money. What do you think?"*

While they may be useful to relieve engorgement, manual pumps aren't very practical for long-term pumping when you're at work. They are very slow, which makes it hard to get much milk. Mini-electric breastpumps are better (and more expensive) but are really best only for occasional use. They do extract more milk but may be painful and still too slow.

Your best bet if you plan to do some serious pumping is to rent a piston electric pump. These monsters maintain a high rate of extraction with amazing comfort. A breastfeeding consultant we interviewed said piston electric pumps can empty both breasts in about 10 to 15 minutes—contrast that with 20 to 30 minutes for mini-electrics and 45 minutes to an hour for manual pumps. We'll discuss them at greater length later in this chapter in our section on breastfeeding.

## *FACTOID*

Introduce the Bottle Early

If you plan to introduce a bottle to your baby so you can go out on the town or back to work, do it between the third and sixth week of age. Most parenting books tell you about this, but they don't stress how important it is to keep giving a bottle regularly—perhaps two or three feedings per week. In our case, we didn't give a bottle consistently, and by the time our son was about four months old, he absolutely refused to take a bottle at all. Oops! That made going out to dinner and a movie alone a lot tougher. A word to the wise: keep up the occasional bottle.

## *Breastfeeding in Public: Exposing Yourself for Onlookers' Fun and Your Baby's Health*

Here's a controversial topic to discuss around the office water cooler: breast-feeding in public. Since our society tends to see a woman's breasts as sexual objects rather than as utilitarian milk delivery systems, we often run into disapproval of breastfeeding, especially in public. Ironically, this is one of the chief advantages of breastfeeding—it's very portable. No hauling and cleaning bottles, mixing and warming formula, and your child gets nourishment exactly when he wants it.

Amazingly, some parts of this country still manage to equate breastfeeding in public with indecent exposure. Florida just recently repealed a law forbidding public breastfeeding after several woman were cited by the "breast" police for whipping it out at a local mall. It's hard to believe that until just recently laws in this country branded one of life's most basic needs—eating—as illegal. You can call your local La Leche League or other breastfeeding sources to find out if your city or state still has laws like these. If they do, consider getting involved in trying to get them repealed. For example, Austin, Texas, managed to pass an ordinance allowing breastfeeding in public after moms let their feelings be known.

The irony is that breastfeeding in public involves very little flashing of flesh. As an admitted public breastfeeder, I can attest to the fact that it can be done discreetly. Here are some suggestions:

1   IF THE THOUGHT OF BREASTFEEDING IN PUB-LIC IS NOT YOUR CUP OF TEA, CONSIDER BRINGING A BOTTLE OF EXPRESSED MILK WITH YOU. We know one couple who did this and never seemed to have a problem.

2 USE THE SHAWL METHOD. Many women breastfeed in public with a shawl or blanket covering the baby and breasts. While this works well, you must start practicing this early and often with your baby. Otherwise, you'll find that as she gets more alert and interested in her surroundings, she won't stay under the shawl.

3 FIND ALL THE CONVENIENT REST ROOM LOUNGES IN YOUR TOWN. Whenever we visit the local mall, I nurse in one of the big department store's lounge areas. This is a great way to meet other breastfeeding moms as well. Of course, not every public rest room features a lounge with couches or comfy chairs, but it's worth seeking out the ones that do.

Another creative alternative: stores will usually let you use a dressing room to breastfeed. Of course, some stores are not as "breastfeeding friendly" as others. New York City, for example, has 10 million people and about seven public rest rooms. In such places, I've even breastfed in a chair strategically placed facing a wall or corner in the back of a store. Not the best view, but it gets the job done.

4 YOUR CAR. My son knows the back of both of our cars extremely well now. I found it easier and more comfortable to feed him there, especially when he started to become distracted in restaurants and stores. The car holds no fascination for him, so he tends to concentrate on eating instead of checking out the scenery. I suggest you keep some magazines in the car since you may get bored.

## *FACTOID*
### CLUSTER FEEDING

Did you know that babies often want to nurse more frequently at night than during the day? This is called "cluster feeding," and it may be because breast milk is not as rich at night as it is in the morning (after it's "recharged"). I had no idea about this cluster feeding phenomenon and kept trying to stretch my son out during the evening to conform with a three or four-hour feeding interval. When I realized feeding more often at night was normal, I relaxed, fed the baby when he wanted it, and everyone was happy. Another helpful tip: if your baby seems hungry but when put to the breast won't nurse, try nursing while you stand or walk around.

## *THE BOTTOM LINE:*
### *A Wrap-Up of Our Best Buy Picks*

For career clothes, we thought the best deals were at the Dan Howard Maternity Outlets. With dresses for $60 or less and suits (jacket and skirt) in the $100 to $150 range, the prices can't be beat. Shop at a retail maternity chain, and you'd shell out $200 to $300 for the same items.

If your place of work allows more casual dress, check out the prices at large ladies stores. A simple pair of leggings that could cost $45 to $50 at a maternity shop are only $30 or less at "regular" stores.

For the weekend, we couldn't find a better deal than the 100% cotton shirts and shorts at discounters like Target and K-Mart. Prices are as little as $8.98 per shirt—compare that to the $40 price tag at maternity chain stores for a simple cotton shirt.

Invited to a wedding? Rent that dress from a maternity store and save $100 or more. In fact, if you follow all our tips on maternity wear, bras, and underwear, you'll save $200 to $300. Here's the breakdown:

**1. Career Wear        $450**
Includes three dresses ($60 each), one suit ($125), and three blouses ($45 each), plus various accessories. Prices are from the Dan Howard Maternity Outlet.

**2. Casual Clothes      $100**
Five outfits of 100% cotton t-shirts and shorts/pants. Prices from Target.

### 3. Underwear                    $225

Eight pairs of maternity underwear, plus ten bras, including regular, sleep and nursing bras. Prices from J.C. Penney.

**Total damage: $775.** If you think that's too much money for clothes you'll only wear for a few months, consider the cost if you outfit yourself at full-retail maternity shops. The same selection of outfits would run $1200 to $1400.

If you plan to breastfeed, we strongly recommend renting a piston electric pump (about $45 per month). The other pumps (manual and mini-electrics) are inefficient and a waste of money. And don't forget all the money-savings from breastfeeding itself. You'll spare yourself from spending at least $500 on formula in the first six months alone.

Questions or comments? Did you discover a maternity or nursing bargain you'd like to share with our readers? **Call the authors at (303) 442-8792!**

# Chapter 6

## Around the House: Monitors, Toys, Bath, Food, High Chairs, & Swings

What's a "Flatobearius"? Which baby monitor looks like a space ship? Why do baby foods look like a sinister science experiment gone wrong? In this chapter, we explore everything for baby that's around the house. From a basic list of toys to which baby monitors are best, we'll give you tricks and tips to saving money. You'll learn seven safety tips for toys and which new brand of baby food is sweeping the country. Finally, we've got reviews of the best high chairs, a new swing that's pretty cool, and even tips for making sure pet and baby get along.

### Getting Started: When Do You Need This Stuff?

 The good news is you don't need all this stuff right away. While you'll probably purchase a monitor before the baby is born, other items like high chairs, activity seats, and even bathtime products aren't necessary immediately (you'll give the baby sponge baths for the first few weeks, until the belly button area heals).While you may not need some items immediately, it still may be more convenient to shop for home and bath items before the baby is born. In each section of this chapter, we'll be more specific about when you need certain items.

### What Are You Buying?

 Here is a selection of items that you can use when your baby is three to six months of age. We've divided them into three categories: toys, bathtime, and the baby's room.

### Toys

1 BASIC SET OF STACKING CUPS. Once your baby starts to reach for objects, a nice set of stacking cups can supply endless hours of fun—although we had second thoughts

about whether we'd later regret teaching our son to knock over objects. Sage insight or the ramblings of a first-time parent? Anyway, the Hand in Hand Professional Catalog (800-872-3841) has a set of colorful stacking cups designed "in consultation with Dr. T. Berry Brazelton to be developmentally stimulating and fun." Price: $9.95.

Also, Toys R Us sells sets of stacking cups for about $5.

2 MOBILE FOR CRIB. Sure, a mobile sounds like the perfect accessory for any crib, but how do you choose one? Here's our best advice: look at it from underneath. It's surprising to see the number of flat two-dimensional mobiles out there—get underneath them and look from the baby's perspective and what do you see? Nothing—the objects seem to disappear! The best mobiles are more three-dimensional. Our favorite brand: Dakin, 1649 Adrian Rd., Burlingame, CA 94010, (800) 227-6598 or (415) 692-1555. Their colorful and fun mobiles retail for $50 to $60 and are widely available. We liked the Panda Bear/Stars mobile the best. Another, less expensive brand of mobile we liked was made by Dolly (320 N. Fourth St., Tipp City, OH 45371, or call 800-758-7520). At only $20, the three-dimensional design was a great buy. For more money-saving ideas on mobiles, see our money-saving tips section later in the chapter.

3 FISHER PRICE ACTIVITY CENTER. Ah, the old stand-by. This venerable toy ($14.99 at Toys R Us) features various spinning balls, bells, phone dialer, squeakers, etc.—all attached to molded plastic. This toy has been around since 1973. While the current version features bright, primary colors, we've seen older ones in consignment stores dating back to the '70s—in such baby-friendly colors as avocado green and harvest gold. We wonder if playing with toys in such colors contributed the warped sensibilities of Generation X. Just a thought.

On a more practical note, the Fisher Price activity center (like other toys) has a strap that enables you to attach it to the crib. We found two problems with this: first, it's hard to do, since the crib's bumper pads are in the way. Also, such crib toys make it difficult to put the baby down to sleep—any time you touch the crib, the toy makes a sound, and the baby might wake up. Our advice: plan on using "noisy" toys outside the crib. We put a couple of small stuffed animals (babyproofed, of course, with no ribbons, choking hazards, etc.) in the crib for the baby to play with.

4 GYMFINITY BY TODAY'S KIDS. What most impressed us about the Gymfinity is its versatility. First, it's an infant

toy bar, which dangles high-contrast (read: black and white) toys for the baby to play with from underneath. Then, it converts to a toddler play table, with puzzle pieces, interlocking gears, and other fun activities for kids through age three. The only drawback to the Gymfinity: its hefty retail price ($45.95) is somewhat hard to swallow. The best price we saw: $37.99 from the Baby Catalog of America (1-800-PLAY-PEN). Even when you factor in the shipping and handling at $6.95, you still come out somewhat ahead. We should also note we've seen the Gymfinity on special at local stores from time to time ($29.99 at Toys R Us).

**5** ACTIVITY SEAT WITH TOY BAR. An activity seat provides a comfy place for baby while you eat dinner, and the toy bar adds some mild amusement. The Playtime Bouncer Seat with Toy Bar by Summer runs about $50 retail. Optional accessories include matching canopies (about $15) and head rests ($12). Once again, the Baby Catalog of America (1-800-PLAY-PEN) has the Playtime Bouncer for only $29.98 (seat only). Here's another money-saving tip: turn your infant carrier into an activity center with an attachable toy bar. The One Step Ahead catalog (1-800-274-8440) sells a toy bar with rattles and spinning toys for just $12.95 (order #4104). Two elastic straps attach to any brand infant carrier. Another plus: your baby is safer in an infant car seat carrier than in other activity seats, thanks to that industrial-strength harness safety system.

**6** TAPE PLAYER. Gotta have something to play those Barney tapes on. Actually, there is quite a selection of musical tapes for babies that won't irritate you like some purple dinosaurs might. (Check out the Music for Little People catalog, 800-727-2233, reviewed in Chapter 10). The Right Start catalog (800-548-8531) sells a "Cow-sette Player" for $19.95 that features a (you guessed it) plastic cow on the front.

**7** SELECTION OF BOOKS. As book authors, we'd be remiss if we didn't recommend that you buy lots of books for your baby. Visit your local bookstore, and you'll find stiff board books (easier for young hands to turn or, at least, not destroy) as well as squishy cloth books. There are even books made of vinyl to make bathtime more fun. Although you can find such books at general bookstores, many towns have bookstores that specialize in children's books; look under "bookstores" in the phone book to find one near you.

**8** FLATOBEARIUS. Our hip California cousins Ken and Elizabeth Troy turned us on to this adorable line of small stuffed animal rattles. "Flatobearius" is a flat, squishy bear rattle, part of the "Flato" series from North American Bear Co. (to find a dealer near you, call 800-682-3427 or 312-329-0020). Once you get hooked, you'll have to acquire the entire collection of animals/rattles—flatopup, flatjack (a rabbit), and squishy fish. The small flato rattles are about $9 to $12 (not cheap, but worth it), and they even have a couple of larger versions that cost $25 to $55.

## *Bath*

**1** Toys/Books. What fun is it taking a bath without toys? The Sesame Street Tub Puzzle from Hand in Hand Professional (800-872-3841) features five soft squeezable figures of Bert & Ernie, Cookie Monster, Big Bird, and more. Cost: $12.95. Some of those vinyl bath books are entertaining, too, although soaking your bath rug by kicking large volumes of water out of the tub may seem like more fun.

**2** Toiletries. Basic baby shampoo like the famous brand made by Johnson & Johnson works just fine, and you'll probably need some lotion as well. The best tip: first try lotion that is unscented in case your baby has any allergies. Also, never use talcum powder on your baby—it's a health hazard.

What about those natural baby products that are all the rage, like the Mama Toto line from the Body Shop? We got a gift basket for our baby of the Body Shop's expensive potions, and—sorry, all you granola heads out there—we didn't like them. The shampoo dried out our baby's hair so much he had scratching fits. Another negative: they don't have a no-more tears formula, which is no fun whatsoever. We suppose the biggest advantage of these products is that they don't contain mineral oil and petroleum by-products. Also, most don't have perfumes, but then, many regular products now come in unscented versions. The bottom line: it's your comfort level. If you want to spend the money, give the natural products a shot. However, we think they're a waste of money.

**3** The Medicine Cabinet. In Chapter 8, we go into more detail about what you need in your baby's medicine cabinet.

## *Baby's room*

**1** A diaper pail. As you know, we're big fans of the Diaper Genie. Yet, if you feel traditional, even regular diaper pails today come equipped with charcoal filters that not only eliminate diaper odors, but even fry up a decent burger (just kidding). The Odor Free Diaper Pail by Gerry ($24.99, available at most baby stores) has not one but two charcoal filters that last about three months (refills run $5).

**2** MONITOR. Later in this chapter, we have a special section devoted to monitors, including some creative money-saving tips.

**3** THE CHANGING TABLE. The well-stocked changing table features much more than just diapers. Nope, you need wipes and lots of them. Our favorite brand is Baby Fresh (about $4 for a 126-count box at Toys R Us). Store brands of wipes are cheaper, but are of inferior quality—they're thinner, less absorbent, etc. Other mothers we've interviewed like Huggies Wipes ($3.69 for a 120-count box at Toys R Us). We stocked up with 10 boxes of wipes before the baby was born and soon found ourselves at the store to buy more. Why? You can go through four to eight wipes per diaper change. Most brands come in scented and unscented versions and some have aloe or lotion. None we've researched have alcohol.

Now that you've got the poop on wipes (sorry), here's the next item you'll want: a diaper-wipe warmer. Ever change a baby's diaper with a cold wipe at three am? If so, you'd fork over the $25 for one of these devices, which wrap around the wipe box and warm it to a toasty 99 degrees. The Comfy Wipe Warmer features a machine-washable, quilted cover that attaches to wipe boxes with Velcro. Retail is $24.99, but we found it for $19.50 from the Baby Catalog of America (800-752-9736). The same catalog sells a portable wipe warmer (Wipes R' Warm) for the same price that also keeps bottles and baby food warm.

Other products to consider for the diaper changing station include diaper covers (if you're using cloth), diaper rash ointment (A & D, Desitin, etc.), lotion or cream (we like Lubriderm unscented lotion and Eucerin cream for our baby's eczema), cotton swabs, and rubbing alcohol to care for the belly button area.

## *Money-Saving Secrets*

**1** CHILDREN'S BOOK CLUBS OFFER BIG SAVINGS. For example, we joined the Dr. Seuss book club and received eight hardcover books for $1.99. You agree to buy eight more at $4.99 per book—a 28% savings off the retail price. The bottom line: you get 16 books for about $3.50 per book (including shipping); they even throw in a free stand. And we're talking all the classics, like "Green

Eggs and Ham." Write to Dr. Seuss and His Friends, the Beginning Readers' Program, Grolier Books, PO Box 1774, Danbury, CT 06816-1772, for more information.

2 BUY AN INTERCOM INSTEAD OF A BABY MONITOR. Since both cost about $40, you could save $40 by just buying an intercom. That way you could monitor the baby's room and have two-way conversations with the base station. The only disadvantage: the units aren't portable, so you can't wander into the garden and listen to the baby like you could with a battery-operated monitor. Another negative: most intercoms do not have light displays, which provide a visual display of your baby's crying (helpful when you're in a noisy room).

3 SHOP AT BABY MEGA-STORES. For the best prices on monitors, toys, high chairs, and just about everything else you need around the house, check out the prices of those baby mega-stores like LiL' Things (for the store nearest you, call (817) 649-6100 and Baby Superstore (803) 675-0299. We found their prices to be 20% to 30% less than specialty shops—and even less than traditional discounters like Wal-Mart and K-Mart. Best of all, they have the best name brands, which you can't find at the discount stores.

4 CHECK OUT TOYS R US. They don't always have the lowest price, but we like Toys R Us for their selection. Sure, you'd expect lots of toys, but we were surprised by the wide assortment of items like baby monitors and swings. Best of all, they tend to keep everything in stock, so you can get it and go. Unfortunately, the service (or lack thereof) means you're pretty much on your own. Nonetheless, if you know what you're looking for, it's hard to beat Toys R Us.

5 DON'T FORGET CONSIGNMENT STORES. A great item to find at second-hand stores specializing in children's clothing and products: mobiles. Most aren't handled by babies so they're in excellent condition—at prices that are typically 50% or more off retail. We found quite a few in our local baby consignment store for $10 to $20; compare that to the $50 retail price these fetch at specialty stores. Since you tend to use a mobile for such a short period of time (at most, five months because after that time they become a strangulation hazard), you can then re-consign it at the shop and get some money back! Of course, these stores sell much more than mobiles—you can pick up toys, high chairs, and, of course, clothes at tremendous savings. Check your phone book under "Consignment" or "Thrift Stores"; many also list under "Clothes & Accessories—Infant & Child—Retail."

6 GO FOR REFILLABLE PACKAGES. Take diaper wipes, for example. You can often buy refillable packages of wipes to fit into those plastic boxes. The savings: about 20% off the cost of buying a new box. And you save another plastic box from the landfill.

7 GET A PRICE QUOTE FROM THE BABY CATALOG OF AMERICA. The catalog (which can be ordered by calling 800-752-9736) has fantastic prices on high chairs, toys, swings, and even baby monitors. They also carry items that aren't in the catalog; call to see if they carry the brand you're looking for.

8 CHECK OUT SUAVE BABY CARE PRODUCTS. In 1994, Helen Curtis introduced an entire line of baby care products under their Suave brand name—and the prices are amazing. In Celina, Ohio, a Wal-Mart store sells Suave baby wipes for just $1.87 (80-count box). Compare that to Baby Fresh at $2.37 for the same quantity—a 20% savings! You can also find great deals on Suave baby lotion, shampoos, and powders. Suave's baby care slogan: "Gentle care for your baby doesn't have to cost a fortune." And we have to agree.

## Wastes of Money

1 FANCY TOYS. We interviewed one couple who bought a fancy set of expensive toys for their infant daughter, only to be dismayed that she didn't want to play with them. What did baby really like to play with? Their keys. The lesson: sometimes it's the simple, inexpensive things in life that are the most fun.

2 FANCY BOOKS. Walk through any children's section in your local bookstore and you'll see a zillion children's books, all lavishly illustrated and beautifully packaged. And do you know what most babies want to do with books? Eat them. We liked the suggestion that one mom discovered when it came to books: shop at used bookstores to save money. Also, many popular hardcover children's books come in soft-cover or paperback versions, at substantially lower prices. That way if Junior decides his favorite book looks like lunch one day, you're not out as much money. Board books (and even cloth books) are good to chew on too.

3 FANCY BURP PADS. Do you really need to spend $5 on a burp pad—a scientifically designed piece of cloth for you to put on your shoulder to keep spit-up off your clothes when Junior burps? No, just put a cloth diaper on your shoulder (average price 50¢ or less each) and save the money.

4 BLACK AND WHITE MOBILES. Yes, they are all the rage today. True, your baby is attracted to high-contrast black and white images in the first four months, and such mobiles may be quite fascinating. But $20-$40 seems like a lot of money to be spent on an item that's used for just four months. We liked the money-saving suggestion from one dad we interviewed: he drew patterns with a black pen on white index cards and then attached the cards to a regular color mobile. The baby liked the improved version just fine, and the parents saved $20 to $40. (One safety tip: make sure the cards are attached firmly to the mobile. And, as always, remove all mobiles from the crib after five months when you're baby can reach for them). Another solution: buy a mobile with black pandas holding bright colored stars. That way they get both the black and white and color stimulation in one package.

5 BABY BATH TUB. Save the $15 to $25 that these tubs cost and just give your baby a bath in the kitchen sink. Or bring the baby into the bathtub with you. While we think baby bath tubs are a waste of money, "bath rings" (which are sort of like a seat that is affixed to the bottom of the tub with suction cups) are more useful—you can start to use them when your baby can sit up. We got the Fisher Price "Stay n' Play Bath Ring" for about $20 and found it relatively easy to use. The only disadvantages: it isn't easy to put together at first, and it's bulky to store. Perhaps a better option: the Splash Seat ($14.95) from the Hand in Hand Professional catalog (800-872-3841) has a front that opens for easy access; the seat also folds up for quick storage.

## *Monitors*

For her first nine months, your baby is tethered to you via the umbilical cord. After that, it's the baby monitor that becomes your surrogate umbilical cord—enabling you to work in the garden, wander about the house, and do many things that other, childless human beings do, while still keeping tabs on a sleeping baby. Hence, this is a pretty important piece of equipment you'll use every day—a good one will make your life easier and a bad one will be a never-ending source of irritation.

> "A GOOD ONE WILL MAKE YOUR LIFE EASIER
> A BAD ONE WILL BE A NEVER-ENDING SOURCE OF
> IRRITATION."

## *Smart Shopper Tips for Monitors*

### Smart Shopper Tip #1
BUGGING YOUR HOUSE

*"My neighbor and I both have babies and baby monitors. No matter what we do, I can still pick up my neighbor's monitor on my receiver. Can they hear our conversations too?"*

You better bet. Let's consider what a baby monitor really is: a radio transmitter. The base unit is the transmitter and the receiver is, well, a receiver. So anyone with another baby monitor can pick up your monitor—not just the sound of your baby crying, but also any conversations you have with your mate about diaper changing technique.

You'll notice that many monitors have two channels "to reduce interference," and some even have high and low range settings—do they help reduce interference eavesdropping? No, not in our opinion. In densely populated areas, you can still have problems.

We should note that you can also pick up baby monitors on many cordless phones—even police scanners can pick up signals as far as one or two miles away. The best advice: remember that your house (at least, your baby's room) is bugged. If you want to protect your privacy, don't have any sensitive conversations within earshot of the baby monitor. You never know who might be listening,

### Smart Shopper Tip #2
BATTERY WOES

*"Boy, we should have bought stock in Duracell when our baby was born! We go through dozens of batteries each month to feed our very hungry baby monitor."*

Most baby monitors have the option of running on batteries or on regular current (by plugging it into a wall outlet). Our advice: use the wall outlet as often as possible. Batteries don't last long (maybe a day or two with constant use) in baby monitors. What about those rechargeable batteries? They're more hassle than they're worth—you have to change (and recharge) them so often, it's not worth the savings. We haven't experimented yet with the new alkaline rechargeable batteries, but we still think using the wall outlet as much as possible is prudent advice.

## Smart Shopper Tip #3
CORDLESS COMPATIBILITY

*"We have a cordless phone and a baby monitor. Boy, it took us two weeks to figure out how to use both without having a nervous breakdown."*

If we could take a rocket launcher and zap one person in this world, it would have to be the idiot who decided that baby monitors and cordless phones should share the same radio frequency. What were they thinking? Gee, let's take two people who are already dangerously short of sleep and make them real frustrated!

After hours of experimentation, we have several tips. First, make sure your cordless phone has the ability to switch among 10 channels to find the clearest reception. If you don't have this feature, you may find your phone and monitor are always in conflict, no matter how times you flip that "Channel A or B" switch on the baby monitor.

Another tip: consider buying one of those new cordless phones that work on the 900 Mhz frequency—then you'll be assured there won't be any interference since they won't share the same frequency. (For techno-heads out there, most cordless phones and all baby monitors work on the 46 to 49 Mhz radio frequency). The only disadvantage to this tip is that the new 900 Mhz cordless phones are somewhat difficult to find and can be as much as twice the cost of regular cordless phones.

Always keep the receipt for any baby monitor you buy— you may have to take it back and exchange it for another brand if you find the interference is too much for you. It sure would be nice if manufacturers of cordless phones and baby monitors would label their products with the radio frequency they use, so you could spot conflicts before they happen.

## Smart Shopper Tip #4
THE ONE-WAY DILEMMA

*"Our baby monitor is nice, but it would be great to be able to buzz my husband so he could bring me something to drink when I'm feeding the baby. Are there any monitors out there that let you communicate two ways?"*

Nope, not that we found in our research. To get two-way communication, you need to buy an intercom. We decided it was worth the investment after we got tired of shouting back and forth between the baby's room and our living room.

Radio Shack sells a basic intercom for about $40—you can

"call" the other unit and have two-way conversations. Most also have a "lock" feature that you can leave on to listen to the baby when he's sleeping. Of course, the only disadvantage to intercoms is that they aren't portable; most must be plugged into a wall outlet. (Baby monitors, on the other hand, can run off of batteries and most even have a belt clip to make transport easier). Since we work out of our home office, we found an intercom to be a major convenience; we use our baby monitor to listen in on the baby at night.

## *The Name Game: Reviews of Selected Manufacturers*

 If you've ever looked at monitors, you might ask what's the difference? Most models have all the neat features that you want—belt clips, flexible antennas, two switchable channels. But, there are some differences. Not all monitors have a light display that shows you the intensity of your baby's cry—especially helpful if you're in a noisy environment and can't hear the monitor. Some models have rounded antennas on the parent's unit, making them more portable.

By the way, most of these monitors are available at Toys R Us, where we found the best selection and lowest prices. We should also note that the phone numbers listed below are so you can find the dealer nearest to you (most manufacturers don't sell directly to the public).

## *The Ratings*

★★★★  EXCELLENT— our top pick!
★★★  GOOD—above average quality, prices, and creativity.
★★  FAIR—could stand some improvement.
★  POOR—yuck! could stand some major improvement.

*Fisher Price* ............................................................★★★★
*(800) 828-4000 or (716) 687-3000.* The "Sound 'N Lights" monitor is our favorite—it's got everything you want at a decent price (about $40). The variable light display is great. We've used the monitor for several months and are quite pleased. The unit also features "high/low range selector for added privacy," a belt clip, and more. Our only complaint: when you adjust the volume on the parent's unit, it makes a loud, squawking sound—not a pleasant experience at 3:00 am. To get around this, we tend to set the unit at a decent volume before we go to bed.

*Sony* .................................................................... ★★1/2
*Like most gadgets that Sony sells, their "Baby Call" monitor is an attractive unit but grossly overpriced.* We liked the rounded antenna (on both the transmitter and receiver), but it's missing a sound-activated light display. And the price (about $45 to $50) is too much for us to handle. We should note, however, that we did find it at the Baby Superstore for $39. To find a store near you, call (803) 675-0299.

*Safety 1st* .................................................................... ★
*(800) 962-7233 or (617) 964-7744.* We got a Safety 1st monitor as a gift and used it for about a week before we couldn't resist the urge to smash it into electronic pulp. Why? The monitor didn't have a continuous transmission system; when the baby would cry, it would trip the monitor, which would turn on with a loud BRAAPPP! It sounded like a CB radio from hell, but much more obnoxious. We could only take so much torture before we permanently unplugged it. To be nice, we should note that Safety 1st came out with a new model (the Sight N' Sound Nursery Monitor, $30) that fixes this problem and now has "continuous transmission." But our experience with Safety 1st has left such a bitter aftertaste that we just can't recommend their baby monitors.

*Gerry* .................................................................... ★★1/2
*(800) 525-2472 or (303) 457-0926.* If you're looking for a low-cost monitor, the Gerry "Premier" monitor might fit the bill. It's just $26 (at Toys R Us). Unfortunately, you don't get much for that price; no light display or high/low range setting. It does come with a round antenna on the parent's unit, though. If you don't need all the bells and whistles, this monitor is a pretty good buy. We should also note that Gerry sells a "Look 'N Listen" monitor with a light display and a range indicator that lights up when the parent's unit is out of range (which is pretty cool). Retail for this fancier unit is a whopping $60, but we saw it for $43.23 in the Baby Catalog of America (800-752-9736).

*Century* .................................................................... ★★
*(216) 468-2000.* Century's claim to fame is that their monitor also features a night light. Its space saucer-looking base unit certainly is unique. Yet, we found the price (about $40) a little steep, considering it doesn't have a sound-activated light display. At least the night light has an on/off timer.

## Do It by Mail

Several of the catalogs that we mention in Chapter 11 sell monitors. Here's a wrap-up of some of the more unusual offerings:

1 IF YOU'RE LOOKING FOR A DELUXE INTERCOM, CHECK OUT THE NOVI COMMAND WIRELESS INTERCOM FROM SAFETY ZONE (800-999-3030). It isn't cheap (about $80), but you do get all kinds of fancy features, including the ability to select among three different channels (cheaper intercoms just use one).

2 THE BIGGEST PROBLEM WITH BABY MONITORS: IT ALWAYS SEEMS YOU'RE IN A ROOM WHERE THE RECEIVER ISN'T. Well, the Perfectly Safe catalog (800-837-5437 or fax orders to 216-494-0265) has a solution—The Eavesdropper additional listening station. Just $12.95, this gadget is compatible with all best-selling monitors. Its "Accutuner" dial can be adjusted precisely to eliminate static and interference. Perfectly Safe also has its own brand of nursery monitor—the "Pansy Ellen" for $49.95. In their tests, the catalog claims it was the only monitor that did not pick up interference in highly populated areas.

3 If you're really paranoid about what your baby is doing at night, you can get the "Baby Watch" system, also from the Perfectly Safe catalog. Now you can see your baby cry, instead of just hear it. This "personal video observation system" includes a low-light camera with microphone and a black and white five-inch screen. Cost: $300.

## Toys

Walk through any toy store and the sheer variety will boggle your mind. Buying toys for a newborn infant requires more careful planning than for older children. Here are seven tips to keep your baby safe and sound:

## Safe and Sound

1 Make sure stuffed animals have sewn eyes. A popular gift from friends and relatives, stuffed animals can be a hazard if you don't take a few precautions. Buttons or other materials for eyes that could be removed by the baby present a choking hazard—make sure you give the stuffed animal the once over before putting it in the crib.

2 BEWARE OF RIBBONS. Another common decoration on stuffed animals, make sure you remove any ribbons before giving the toy to your baby.

3 MAKE SURE TOYS HAVE NO STRINGS LONGER THAN 12 INCHES—another easily avoided strangulation hazard.

4 WOODEN TOYS SHOULD HAVE NONTOXIC FINISHES. If in doubt, don't give such toys to your baby. The toy's packaging should specify the type of finish.

5 BATTERY COMPARTMENTS SHOULD HAVE A SCREW CLOSURE. Tape players (and other battery-operated toys) should not give your baby easy access to batteries—a compartment that requires a screw driver to open is a wise precaution.

6 BE CAREFUL OF CRIB TOYS. Some of these toys are designed to attach to the top or sides of the cribs. The best advice: remove them after the baby is finished playing with them. Don't leave the baby to play with crib toys unsupervised, especially once she begins to stand on her own. Toys can then be used a step to help her climb out of the crib. We keep a couple stuffed animals (that have been baby proofed, of course) in our baby's crib.

7 DO NOT USE WALKERS. And if you get one as a gift, take it back to the store and exchange it for something that isn't a death trap. Exactly what are these invitations to disaster? A walker suspends your baby above the floor, enabling him or her to "walk" by rolling around. The only problem: babies tend to "walk" right into walls, down staircases, and into other brain damage-causing obstacles. It's a scandal that walkers haven't been banned by the Consumer Products Safety Commission. How many injuries are caused by these things? Are you sitting down? 20,000 a year! Why juvenile products manufacturers continue churning out these death traps is beyond us.

What are the alternatives to walkers? Several companies are marketing "stationary activity centers" that provide all the fun with none of the injury. One of the best is the Exersaucer by Evenflo—babies can bounce, rock, stand, sit, and play, thanks to a rotating seat that has three height adjustments. The only disadvantages: it's bulky (you need a pretty big area to set it up), and it's expensive—$70 retail. Yet we've seen it for $55 in Toys R Us and just $49.20 in the Baby Catalog of America (800-752-9736). Our baby gave it a test drive at a LiL' Things (their price was also $49.99; to find the store nearest you call 817-649-6100), and he seemed quite amused. We give the Exersaucer a big thumps up.

# Solid Foods

At the tender age of four to six months, you and your baby depart on a magical journey to a new place filled with exciting adventures and never-before-seen wonders. Yes, you've entered the SOLID FOOD ZONE.

Fasten your seat belts and get ready for a fun ride. As your tour guide, we would like to give a few pointers to make your stay a bit more enjoyable. Let's take stock:

## Smart Shopper Tips on Mealtime Accessories

### Smart Shopper Tip #1
TRACKING DOWN UFFOS (UNIDENTIFIABLE FLYING FOOD OBJECTS)

*"We fed our baby rice cereal for the first time. It was really cute, except for the part when the baby picked up the bowl and flung it across the kitchen! Should we have bought some special stuff for this occasion?"*

Well, unless you want your kitchen to be redecorated in Early Baby Food, we do have a few suggestions. First, a bowl with a bottom that suctions to the table is a great way to avoid flying saucers. Plastic spoons that have a round handle are nice, especially since baby can't stick the spoon handle in her eye (yes, that does happen). Spoons with rubber coatings are also nice; they don't transfer the heat or cold of the food to the baby's mouth and are easier on his gums.

### Smart Shopper Tip #2
AVOIDING MEALTIME BATHS

*"Our baby loves to drink from a cup, except for one small problem. Most of the liquid ends up on her, instead of in her. Any tips?"*

Tommie Tippie cups (about $5) have been around for years and are helpful for young infants to get the hang of this drinking thing. The cups have a weighted bottom to prevent spills and a sipping spout to provide an interim learning step for baby. After your baby gets more used to a cup, we've found that ones that are made from clear plastic are a good idea. Why? Your baby can see out the bottom and not feel like someone has turned out the lights.

> "FASTEN YOUR SEAT BELTS—YOU'VE ENTERED THE SOLID FOOD ZONE."

## The Name Game: Reviews of Selected Manufacturers

 Here's a round-up of some of the best known names in baby food. We should note that while we actually tried out each of the foods on our baby, you may reach different conclusions than we did. Unlike our brand name ratings for clothing or other baby products, food is a much trickier rating proposition. We rated the following brand names based on how healthy they are and how much they approximate real food (aroma, look, and, yes, taste). Our subjective opinions reflect our experience—always consult with your pediatrician or family doctor if you have any questions about feeding your baby. (Special thanks to our baby for his help in researching this topic.)

## The Ratings

★★★★  EXCELLENT—*our top pick!*
  ★★★  GOOD—*above average quality, prices, and creativity.*
   ★★  FAIR—*could stand some improvement.*
    ★  POOR—*yuck! could stand some major improvement.*

*Gerber*............................................................................★
Dominating the baby food business with a whopping 75% market share (that's right, three out of four baby food jars sold sport that familiar label), Gerber sure has come a long way from its humble beginnings. Back in 1907, Joseph Gerber (whose trade was canning) mashed up peas for his daughter, following the suggestion of a family doctor. We imagine those peas looked quite different from Gerber's peas today. Now, thanks to scientific progress, Gerber's peas are put through such a rigorous canning process that they don't even look like peas, but more like green slime. And it's not just the look, have you actually smelled or tasted any of Gerber's offerings? Yuck. Sure it's cheap (about 30¢ for a 2 1/2 ounce jar of Gerber 1st Foods), but we just can't feed our baby this stuff with a clear conscience.

*Earth's Best* .............................................................★★★*1*/2
*PO Box 887, Middlebury, VT 05753. (800) 442-4221.* If you're looking for jarred baby food but don't like brands that add sugar, salt, and other additives, then you've got to try Earth's Best. Based in Vermont, this company has a complete line of "natural" baby foods—all vegetables and grains are certified to be organically grown, and meats are raised without antibiotics or steroids. Earth's Best foods have no added

sugars, salt, or modified food starches. Unfortunately, it isn't cheap—about twice as much as Gerber charges for a four-ounce jar (59¢ in one store we priced). We tried out Earth's Best and were generally pleased. Our only complaint: they tend to do a lot of "combo" foods, like the Vegetable Turkey Dinner with carrots, apples, turkey, and barley flour. The problem is you are supposed to introduce new foods to baby one food at a time. If the baby had an allergic reaction, was it the carrots or the turkey? Also, some of the dinners have corn, a highly allergenic food that is not supposed to be introduced until your baby is 12 months old. Despite this problem and the lack of single food options, we really like Earth's Best—a much-needed natural alternative to the standard fare that babies have been fed for far too many years.

*Growing Healthy*...........................................................★★★★
*2905 Northwest Blvd. #250, Plymouth, MN 55441. (800) 755-4999 or (612) 557-6088.* Hands down, our pick for the best baby food is Growing Healthy, a fantastic line of frozen, all-natural baby food. Yes, you read right—it's frozen. Each package contains two individual trays that can be popped into the microwave to thaw. Best of all, it looks and tastes like real food . . . the carrots have a real orange color, the applesauce tastes like, well, applesauce. How do they do it? Well, they start with all-natural ingredients, don't add empty fillers and then "gently simmer and freeze" to retain "more of the nutrients and a delicious taste." Our baby just loves this stuff. We do wish there were more varieties, though. Growing Healthy divides its foods into three categories (strained fruits and cereals, strained vegetables, and dinners) and has just 21 varieties total. As you might expect, it costs more than the jarred stuff, but we think it's worth it. The fruits run 79¢ for two, two-ounce servings, the veggies cost 91¢, and the dinners cost $1.30. To ease the pain, the company offers coupons (call the number listed above for more information).

Perhaps the worst thing we can say about Growing Healthy is that it just isn't available in many places yet. Besides their home base of Minneapolis/St. Paul, the food is available in some stores in Illinois, Indiana, Texas, California, Arizona, and Colorado. That's it. They're planning to add some more East Coast cities as we go to press, but that still leaves too much of country uncovered. Our advice: ask your grocer to get it in and make sure to check the freezer section—Growing Healthy is often separated from the rest of the other jarred baby foods since it is frozen. If you're turned off by jarred baby food and are looking for a more healthy option, we can't recommend Growing Healthy highly enough.

### *Other Brands We Discovered:*

Like the book of the same name (see a review in Chapter 10), Mommy Made and Daddy Too is a line of all-natural baby foods available primarily on the East Coast. Check with your local supermarket or grocery store to see if they stock it.

In some parts of the country, you can also get jarred baby food made by Beech-Nut—a brand that is very similar to Gerber. We will never buy any baby food from Beech-Nut, thanks to the company's decision to market sugar water as "100 percent pure apple juice" in the early 1980s. Two executives from the company were indicted in 1986, and Beech-Nut pled guilty on 215 felony counts of fraud. The company paid over $2 million in fines and pledged not to sell fake juice, but we won't ever give them our money.

Another big brand of commercially prepared baby food is Heinz, which is more popular in Europe than it is here in the U.S. In their book on baby products, *Consumer Reports* notes that Heinz is about 25% cheaper than Gerber, but also contains additives like modified starches and sugar.

Have you found a brand of baby food that you (and your baby) just love? Since many brands are produced by small, regional manufacturers, we found tracking them down to be difficult. As a result, we'd love to hear from you if you've discovered a great brand. Call us at (303) 442-8792 to spread the word.

What about formula? According to the research we've seen, most of the brands are quite similar . . . the same ingredients, just different colored labels. You can buy formula both in powder and liquid concentrate forms. One tip: don't start with the liquid concentrate and try to switch to the power form. Babies can get hooked on a particular form of formula and find it hard to switch later.

## Safe & Sound

1 FEED FROM A BOWL, NOT FROM THE JAR. Why? If you feed from a jar, bacteria from the baby's mouth can find their way back to the jar, spoiling the food much more quickly. Also, saliva enzymes begin to break down the food's nutrients. The best strategy: pour the amount of baby food you need into a bowl and feed from there (unless it's the last serving from the jar).

2 DON'T STORE FOOD IN PLASTIC BAGS. If you leave it on the baby's high chair, they can be a suffocation hazard. A better solution: store left-over food in a small, plastic containers.

3 Do a taste test. Make sure it isn't too hot, too cold, or spoiled. If you've actually seen most of the baby food that comes in jars, you may find this a somewhat difficult suggestion to swallow (so to speak). Yet, as you read above, we've found a couple great-tasting alternatives to traditional baby food.

4 For formula, once you mix a bottle, you must use it within 48 hours. Also check freshness dates on the bottom of each can. The best safety motto: if in doubt, throw it out. Also, never let a baby fall asleep with a bottle—your baby could get "bottle mouth," which contributes to tooth decay.

## Money-Saving Tips

 ♣ *Believe it or not, Toys R Us sells baby food.* If you think your grocery store is gouging you on the price of baby food, you might want to check out the prices at Toys R Us. We found Gerber 1st Foods in a four-pack of 2.5 ounce jars for $1.13—that works out to about 28¢ per jar or about 5% to 10% less than grocery store prices. Toys R Us also sells four-packs of assorted dinners from Gerber's 2nd and 3rd Food collections. If that weren't enough, you can also buy a case of Gerber formula (a dozen 13-ounce cans of concentrated liquid) for just $23.88—that's only $1.99 per can!

♣ *Coupons! Coupons! Coupons!* Yes, we've seen quite a few cents-off and buy-one-get-one-free coupons on baby food and formula—not just in the Sunday paper but also through the mail. One of the best deals: Growing Healthy mails out coupons to get five free packages of their frozen food (call the 800 number above for more information). Our advice: don't toss that junk mail until you've made sure you're not trashing valuable baby food coupons. Another coupon trick: look for "bounce-back" coupons. Those are the coupons put in the packages of baby food to encourage you to bounce back to the store and buy more.

♣ *Formula freebies.* Did you know that most pediatricians are besieged with free cases of formula to give out to their patients? One mom we interviewed in Arizona received several cases of the stuff free from her doctor, who simply kept requesting more samples from the formula companies. We say take advantage of their generosity and ask your doctor if she has any spare cases she could part with.

# *High Chairs*

As soon as Junior starts to eat solid food, you'll need this symbolic piece of baby furniture—the high chair. Surprisingly, this seemingly innocuous product generates nearly 9000 injuries each year. Hence, in this section, we'll look at how to buy a safe high chair and provide tips for proper use. And, as always, we'll give you some money-saving tips and a review of some of the most popular brands out there today.

## *Smart Shopper Tips for High Chairs*

### *Smart Shopper Tip #1*
HIGH CHAIR BASICS 101

*"My mother insists I buy a high chair that looks like Captain Kirk's chair from Star Trek. I prefer something simpler, but every chair I see in the stores has to have some high-tech gimmick, converting into a toaster and so on. What's really important?"*

Basically, the most important thing to look for in a high chair is one that doesn't tip over—the cause of many high chair injuries. The best chairs have a wide base. Another important item to check in the store is the tray release. Many brands advertise "one hand release," but the ease with which the tray really releases varies from maker to maker. Another wise tip: make sure the tray mechanism can't pinch your baby's fingers. Take it from a parent who has pinched his son's fingers once on a hook-on high chair, it's not a fun experience.

Beyond the basics, the hot trend in high chairs is convertibility—models that transform into hook-on seats, youth chairs, and even a table and chair set (sorry, no toasters, yet). The big decision you'll have to make: do you want a high chair that is height-adjustable? Without this feature, you'll spend $50 to $60. Chairs that adjust run $65 to $120. Is it worth it? We think so—you can adjust it to different table heights, using it in the standard position when the baby is young and then lowering it to table height as a youth chair when she gets older. If this feature is important to you, go for a chair that is fully height adjustable (not just a couple of pre-set positions).

What about colors? As you're about to learn, white is the hot color for high chairs. But how practical is this? We have a white high chair, and it's great at showing dirt. On the other hand, it goes with everything and doesn't stick out like a sore thumb in our kitchen. So the question may be, what is more important—can you live with the fact that it's always going to look filthy, or is it more important to match your home's decor? One possible compromise: high chairs now come in subtle patterns (white with sea shells, for example) that might hide the grunge better.

### Smart Shopper Tip #2
TRAY CHIC AND OTHER RESTAURANT TIPS

*"We have a great high chair at home, but we're always appalled at the lack of safe high chairs at restaurants. Our favorite cafe has a high chair that must date back to 1952— no straps, a metal tray with sharp edges, and a hard seat with no cushion. Are these people nuts or what?"*

We think so. Restaurateurs must search obscure third world countries to find the world's most hazardous high chairs. The biggest problem? No straps, enabling babies to slide out of the chair, submarine-style. The solution? The Right Start (800-548-8531) sells a Seat Supporter ($9.95) that braces the baby. Also, the same catalog sells Sit'n Secure, which secures a baby to a chair with Velcro straps. Cost: $11.95.

## *The Name Game: Reviews of Selected Manufacturers*

What's hot with high chairs? White, it appears. In order to match today's neutral kitchens, high chairs in white are flying out of the stores. An alternative: some couples go with patterns that match their baby's bedding.

Beyond color (or the lack of it), many high-tech high chairs feature height adjustments and extra-large feeding trays. While most are made of plastic and metal, there are still fans out there who like traditional wood chairs. In the southern U.S., wood chairs by Simmons and Child Craft (yes, they're the same names you saw in Chapter 2 in the crib reviews) still sell well, despite their lack of fancy features (you can't adjust the height, it doesn't fold up, etc.). Contrast that with fancy baby stores in East Coast cities where they can't keep foreign-made, fancy brands like Peg Perego in stock. In order to make everyone happy, here's a round-up of the different brands you'll encounter on your high-chair shopping excursion:

---

### HIGH CHAIRS
LOOK FOR ONE THAT DOESN'T TIP OVER AND HAS A DECENT TRAY RELEASE THAT WON'T PINCH FINGERS

## *The Ratings*

★★★★  EXCELLENT—*our top pick!*
★★★  GOOD—*above average quality, prices, and creativity.*
★★  FAIR—*could stand some improvement.*
★  POOR—*yuck! could stand some major improvement.*

---

*Baby Trend*................................................................. ★★★★
*1928 W. Holt Ave., Pomona, CA 91768. (800) 328-7363 or (909) 469-1188.* Our pick as one of the best high chairs available today is the Home and Roam (model 8213) by Baby Trend. We like the thickly padded seat, the extra-wide tray, and six-position height adjustment. But what's really cool is it detaches from its base to become a hook-on chair for the table top. While we don't drag it to restaurants (it's too bulky for that), we do take it to Grandma's house. Styling is good; the chair comes in white or a jungle print (which was a little too loud for us). The one-handed tray release works OK (it could be a little easier to release). The price is $109, not cheap but less than those fancy foreign imports. We've seen it discounted about 10% to 15% at baby mega-stores like the Baby Superstore (see Chapter 2 for a review). We've also seen Baby Trend in catalogs like the Right Start (800-548-8531) or One Step Ahead (800-274-8440).

*Cosco* ................................................................................★★
*2525 State St., Columbus, IN 47201. (812) 372-0141.* They're not fancy, but Cosco's high chairs feature large trays and an easy-to-fold frame. The Superflair by Cosco has a decent amount of padding, although we didn't like the design, which featured amoeba-like creatures on a white background. At least the cost is reasonable at $50 to $60.

*Evenflo* ........................................................................★★ *1/2*
*1801 Commerce Dr., Piqua, OH 45356. (800) 837-9201 or (513) 773-3971.* This well-known brand offers four high chair styles. The "Right Height" (about $70) high chair features a one-hand height adjustment system. We weren't wild about the tray with its high sides to prevent splashing (forget it; if Junior wants to throw his food, a little two-inch high tray ain't going to stop him). The padding also looked a little skimpy, and the chair's base doesn't roll. The Celebrity (about $100) fixes the latter problem with rolling casters and even has a few extra features. Both chairs offer one-hand tray releases. Evenflo also makes a couple of cheaper models without height adjustment or chair padding (the Happy Days and

Sidewinder models, $29.99 to $49.99). Overall, we just weren't impressed with Evenflo's high chairs; the styling is alright, but the choice of fabrics (including some truly hideous patterns) leaves much to be desired.

*Gerry*...............................................................................★★★
*12520 Grant Dr., Denver, CO 80241. (800) 525-2472 or (303) 457-0926.* One of the hotter names in high chairs is Gerry, the Colorado-based maker of various juvenile products. Perhaps their hottest model is the Adjust-A-Height Chair, which has five height levels. We saw this chair at Toys R Us for $65—not bad considering the features (it folds for easy storage). The only negatives: the padding looked a little skimpy, and the purple pastel styling didn't do much for us. While we liked the Adjust-A-Height, we were less impressed with the Two-in-One High Chair ($99 retail, $75 at Toys R Us). This chair, which has a somewhat narrow wooden base, converts to a table and chair set.

*Graco* ................................................................................★★
*Rt. 23, Main St., Elverson, PA 19520. (215) 286-5951.* Graco seems to have taken this black and white trend to excess lately. Their Puppy Paws High Chair features a cute spotted dog with a red bandana (it matches the Puppy Paws bedding, stroller, swing, toys, and diaper bags, of course). As the owner of a Dalmation, we have an affinity for things with black and white spots, but this might be overkill. The high chair does have six positions (even the footrest has three levels), but the trays (like all Graco high chairs) didn't seem very deep. If you don't want to see spots, Graco also offers several other fabric choices in muted pastels. Prices range from $50 to $60 (available at Toys R Us).

*Peanut Butter & Jelly* ................................................★★★ *1/2*
*4900 Main, 11th Floor, Kansas City, MO 64111. (816) 561-6328.* Looking for something different? Tired of boring white high chairs? Well, we have the company for you: Peanut Butter & Jelly Furniture. Their art-deco, all-wood high chairs are something to see. With cute names like the "Mak-N-Toshy" and the "Hi-Q," owners Chad and Tray Humphrey sure have crafted some funky high chairs. Of course, you might ask, how practical are they? Well, the seats do have a cushion, but the backs are not padded. And, like all wooden high chairs, you'd better like the height because you can't change it. Chad pointed out to us that they designed the chair to be the height of a formal dining room table—so you can take off the tray when the baby gets older and have him join you there. (We should note that the company plans a full line

of funky kid's furniture, with tables and chairs, rockers, and changing tables. So, are the high chairs worth it, at prices ranging from $159 to $199? For people who don't like to run with the pack, there probably isn't a better option.

*Peg Perego*................................................................ ★★★★
*3625 Independence Dr., Ft. Wayne, IN 46808. (219) 482-8191.* Parents we interviewed raved about Peg Perego's high chairs, lauding their high quality and super-thick padding. The Deluxe model is similar to Baby Trend's Home and Roam; both have six different height positions, a deep tray, and a wide base on rollers. Unfortunately, at about $140 retail, it's about 20% more expensive than the Baby Trend (although we saw it for $121.19 in the Baby Catalog of America, 800-752-9736).

*Playschool* .........................................................................★
*108 Fairway Ct., North Vale, NJ 07647. (800) 777-0371 or (201) 767-0900.* It's an infant recliner. And it's a high chair. And a toddler chair. Playschool's 1-2-3 High Chair combines all these into their fast-selling high chair, which retails for $100 but is discounted to about $75 at most stores, including Toys R Us. But do you really need an infant recliner, which is supposed to make bottle feeding easier? I don't know about you, but I thought that holding your baby while feeding is one of those parental bonding experiences that you're not supposed to miss. Also, we've read that babies aren't supposed to be in a reclining position while feeding because of the choking hazard. Nevertheless, as a high chair, the 1-2-3 does have a six-position height adjustment and even a storage compartment. However, considering how expensive it is, we thought the padding is a little skimpy and the tray a trifle small.

### Other Brands We Encountered:

If you're looking for a high chair that needs to fit into a small space, Chicco's modular metal high chairs might do the trick. (Chicco is sold at some Bellini stores; see Chapter 2). Another hot import brand is Italian-made Brevi (marketed in the U.S. by C&T International, 201-461-9444). The Brevi Maxi is similar to the Peg Perego, but has even more features, such as extra large trays and super-thick padding.

## Safe and Sound

Considering the number of injuries caused by high chairs, it's important to understand the safety basics when it comes to these products. Here's the scoop:

♣ *Most injuries occur when babies are not strapped into their chair.* Sadly, four to five deaths occur each year when babies "submarine" under the tray. Other babies are injured when they tip over the chair by pushing against the wall. Make sure your high chair is not placed near a wall or object that the baby might be able to push off on.

♣ *The safety standards for high chairs are voluntary.* In a recent report, Consumer Reports claimed that not all high chairs meet these voluntary standards. Perhaps the safest bet: look for JPMA-certified high chairs. JPMA requires a battery of safety tests, including checks for stability, a locking device to prevent folding, a secure restraining system, no sharp edges, and so on.

♣ *Inspect the seat—is it well upholstered?* Make sure it won't tear or puncture.

♣ *Look for stability.* It's basic physics: the wider the base, the more stable the chair is.

♣ *Carefully inspect the restraining system.* Belts should hold the baby so she can't stand or slide out under the tray. Straps around the hips and between the legs do the trick.

♣ *The truth about trays.* Besides checking the release (How easy does it release in the real world?), consider the fact that trays with wide rims are better at containing spills.

♣ *Some high chairs offer different height positions,* including a reclining position that supposedly makes it easier to feed a young infant. The problem? Feeding a baby solid foods in a reclining position is a choking hazard.

---

### *Living the High Life*

Hook-on chairs and booster seats are close relatives to the familiar high chair. Depending on your needs, each can serve a purpose. Hook-on chairs do exactly what they say—hook onto a table. While some have trays, most do not, and that is probably their biggest disadvantage: baby eats (or spills and throws food) on your table instead of hers. At least they're cheap: about $25 to $40 at most stores. Best use: if your favorite restaurants don't have high chairs (or don't have safe ones) or if you plan to do some road trips with Junior.

Booster seats are more useful. With or without an attached tray, most strap to a chair or can be used on the floor. We use ours at Grandma's house, which spares us the chore of dragging along a high chair or hook-on chair. It's also convenient to do evening feedings in a booster seat in the baby's room, instead of dragging everyone to the kitchen. And you can't beat the price: $18 to $30 at most stores. One of the better brands is the Evenflo Snack and Play, which comes in two models (one with a cushion, one with out). Their theme is "the neat little eat seat" that turns most any chair into a high chair. The Snack and Play features an adjustable tray and seat—pretty neat.

## *Swings*

You can't talk to new parents without hearing the heated debate on swings, those battery-operated or wind-up surrogate parents. Some think they're a god-send, soothing a fussy baby when nothing else seems to work. Cynics refer to them as "neglect-o-matics," sinister devices that can become far too addictive for a society that thinks parenting is like microwaving—the quicker, the better.

Whatever side you come down on, we do have a few shopping tips. First, forget the wind-up models. Sure, you'll save about $20 and some batteries but don't believe those claims that they swing by themselves for 15 minutes. A basic battery operated swing runs about $70 to $90, and we found that Toys R Us has a pretty decent selection. You might be able to steal a deal on a swing at a second-hand baby store; we saw swings in decent shape for as little as $20 in such places.

Remember to observe safety warnings about swings, which are close to the top 10 most dangerous products as far as injuries go. You must always stay with your baby, use the safety belt, and stop using the swing once your baby reaches the weight limit (about 25 pounds in most cases). Always remember that a swing is not a baby-sitter.

The coolest swing we saw was the Graco Advantage. It does away with the overhead bar (which you always hit your baby's head on no matter how careful you are). Battery-operated, the swing has a flip-open tray, adjustable reclining seat, and thick padding. At $100 retail, it ain't cheap—but we've seen it for $85 in Toys R Us, $78.60 in the Baby Catalog of America (800-752-9736), and an unbelievable $69 at the Baby Superstore.

### *FACTOID*

SOME LAMPS ARE MORE
EQUAL THAN OTHERS

Looking for an unusual lamp for your baby's room? Animal Farm lamps by Form Farm offer a truly unique look. Made of recycled polyethylene, these whimsical opaque lamps give a gentle glow and include a stable of animal characters—the hot dog, cool cat, sleepy elephant, and more. The company even sells a couple of night lights, such as the Nighty Mouse and Owl Nightlighter. The retail price for the lamps is about $50; for a dealer near you, call 212-274-8592.

## *Pet Meets Baby*

If you already have a dog and you are now expecting a baby, you're probably wondering how your "best friend" is going to react to the new family addition. Doubtless you've heard stories about how a dog became so jealous of its new "sibling" that the dog had to be given away. How can you avoid this situation?

### *Here are seven tips on smoothing the transition.*

**1** IF THE DOG HASN'T BEEN OBEDIENCE TRAINED, DO IT NOW. Even if you feel confident that your dog is well trained, a refresher course can't hurt.

**2** DON'T OVERCOMPENSATE. You may start feeling guilty while you're pregnant because you won't be able to spend as much time with Fido after the baby comes. So what mistake do expectant parents make? They overcompensate and give the dog extra attention before the baby arrives. Big mistake. Do this and then the dog *really* misses you and resents the new baby. While it might seem counter-intuitive, gradually give your best friend *less* attention so he or she can adjust before baby comes.

**3** IF YOUR DOG HAS NEVER BEEN AROUND BABIES AND SMALL CHILDREN, NOW IS THE TIME TO INTRODUCE HIM—*BEFORE YOUR BABY IS BORN.*

**4** CONSIDER BUYING A BABY DOLL. Why? If you practice loving and attending to a baby doll for a few weeks prior to your baby's actual arrival, your dog can begin to get used to you paying attention to small bundles wrapped up in blankets. We did this, and our dog ZuZu got over her curiosity about it quickly. By the time the baby arrived, she didn't much care what we were carrying around (as long as it didn't smell like doggie biscuits!).

**5** BEFORE THE BABY COMES HOME FROM THE HOSPITAL, HAVE A FRIEND OR RELATIVE BRING HOME A BLANKET OR PIECE OF CLOTHING THE NEW BABY HAS SLEPT ON OR WORN IN THE HOSPITAL. This helps the dog get used to the smell of the new addition before you bring on the actual baby. We put a blanket the baby slept on in our dog's kennel, and we really think it helped smooth the transition.

**6** STRATEGIES FOR BRINGING BABY HOME. Make sure your dogs are under control when you first come home with your new baby (on a leash or under voice command). Greet your four-legged friend first, *without* the baby. This allows your dog to release some of his excitement and jumping (remember he hasn't seen you for a few days), without you worrying about the dog harming a baby in your arms. Next, Dad should hold the dog by the collar or leash while Mom shows Fido the baby. Give your dog time to sniff a little, but don't let the dog turn the situation into a lick-fest. If everything looks OK, you can release the dog.

7 NEVER LEAVE THE DOG ALONE WITH THE BABY—especially if the dog has shown any signs of jealousy toward your child. Don't allow the dog to sleep under the crib (there have been incidents of dogs standing up and pushing the mattress off its supports, causing the mattress to crash to the floor).

Always supervise how your baby plays with the dog. For example, now that our son is older (about eight months at the time of this writing), he finds our Dalmation very interesting. However, he tends to pull on her ears and tail whenever he gets a hold of them. So, we constantly encourage gentle petting and discourage grabbing. Ben is still very young, but in time he'll be able to terrorize our dog all by himself.

### What about cats?

C ats have recently surpassed dogs in popularity as America's favorite domestic pet. So as not to slight those cat lovers out there, here are three pieces of advice.

1 BEFORE YOU GET PREGNANT, HAVE YOUR CAT TESTED for toxoplasmosis, a disease that is caused by a parasitic organism that is transmitted to humans from cat feces. Toxoplasmosis is dangerous and may cause the fetus to become seriously ill or die.

If your cat is infected, have it boarded at a kennel or have someone take care of it for the period of infection (usually about six weeks). It's also best not to get pregnant during this time. You can avoid getting the infection yourself by having someone else clean out your cat's litter box. If you keep your cat indoors and he or she doesn't catch mice or birds outside, chances are the cat won't be infected (outdoor cats are more likely to be exposed to toxoplasmosis). Consult your doctor and your cat's veterinarian if you have any questions about this serious problem.

2 INTRODUCE YOUR CAT TO THE BABY SLOWLY. Similar to the way you would introduce a dog to your new baby, keep an eye on your cat's reactions. Don't leave your cat alone with the baby if you suspect any jealousy. Most cats will ignore the new addition with their usual aplomb.

3 CONSIDER USING A NET OVER YOUR BABY'S CRIB. Cats love to sleep in warm places and might decide to take up residence with your bundle of joy.

# THE BOTTOM LINE:

## A Wrap-Up of our Best Buy Picks

The best toys for infants include a basic set of stacking cups ($5), the Fisher Price Activity Center ($15), and the Gymfinity ($30). An activity seat with a toy bar (like the Playtime Bouncer Seat) is a good idea, with prices ranging from $30 to $50. Another good idea: buy a toy bar for your infant car seat ($12.95, see "What Are You Buying?" earlier in this chapter). Of course, our favorite stuffed animal/rattle is the Flatobearius line—at $9 to $12, they make affordable gifts.

In the nursery, we highly recommend the Diaper Genie "diaper disposal system" and the wipes by Baby Fresh and Suave. Don't forget a wipe warmer—this $20 to $25 device will make diaper changing a more pleasant experience for everyone. For monitors, we found the Fisher Price "Sound N Lights" to be the best deal at $40.

As far as where to shop, we found the prices at Toys R Us and in the Baby Catalog of America to be good deals. Consignment or second-stores are a fantastic source for bargains as well.

What about baby food? Forget Gerber and those other commercial baby food brands and head straight for Growing Healthy. This frozen baby food line looks and tastes like real food—what a concept. We also like the Earth's Best jarred baby food as a good, natural alternative.

The best high chairs are from Baby Trend (Home and Roam, $109) and Peg Perego (the Deluxe, $120). If you have a sense of humor, check out the funky high chairs from Peanut Butter & Jelly, which range from $159 to $199.

Questions or comments? What about day care? We'd like to do a section on day care bargains for the next edition of this book—call us with your suggestions at (303) 442-8792!

# Chapter 7

## Places to Go! Car Seats, Strollers, Carriers & More

How can you get a Century car seat at wholesale? You'll learn this and other tips on how to make your baby portable—from car seats to strollers, carriers to diaper bags. And what do you put in that diaper bag anyway? We've got nine suggestions, plus advice on dining out with baby. This chapter also features in-depth brand reviews of the best strollers, including which names are high-quality and which are hype.

Boy, we were surprised when we had dinner with another couple from our Lamaze class. Our babies were born about the same time, but this was the first time that the other couple had gone out to dinner in SIX MONTHS. Now, as first-time parents, we understand the urge to protect your baby when it's an infant. But, we took our baby on his first restaurant trip when he was one week old—are we nuts?

We don't think so. Part of this difference in eating-out habits may be explained by the fact we have a home office—we're stuck at home all day, and so we don't commute to work, we commute to play. Eating out is a way to stay sane. Also, we live in a rural area where there isn't any pizza delivery—or delivery of any kind for that matter.

So. . . if you live in a city and have access to Domino's, staying at home for a while after your baby is born won't be as much of a hardship. Nevertheless, at some point you'll have to crawl out of your cave and go somewhere with your baby. And that's what this chapter is about: the whole slew of products that make your baby portable.

### Getting Started: When Do You Need This?

As you can see from our example above, it's possible you could go six months or more without needing a stroller, diaper bag, or any of the other "places to go" gear. Possible, but unlikely. So, while you don't necessarily need a stroller (carrier, etc.) immediately, you might as well take care of this before the baby arrives.

Of course, there is one item you'll need before you can even leave the hospital: a car seat. By law, all states require children to be restrained in a car seat (although the laws vary as to which age groups are covered). Besides, you'll want to buy this item early (in your sixth to eighth month of pregnancy) so you can practice wedging it into the back seat.

## Car Seats

Since all states require children to be restrained by a child safety seat, this is one product that everyone must buy. Here's an overview of what to look for and how to save money.

## Smart Shopper Tips

### Smart Shopper Tip #1
ONE SIZE DOES NOT FIT ALL

*"My friend has as car seat that just doesn't fit very well into my car. Do car seat manufacturers put out any literature that tells you which car seat fits best in which cars?"*

Nope. You're basically on your own since car seat manufacturers take a "one-size-fits-all" attitude about their product. Since the backseats of cars can vary widely from model to model, you can bet that not every car seat will fit like a glove. The best advice: keep the receipt and check the store's return policy. Right after you buy the car seat, set it up in your backseat. If it doesn't fit, take it back. We'd never buy a car seat from a store that has a no-returns policy.

### Smart Shopper Tip #2
HOLDING YOUR BABY BACK: SAFETY HARNESS ADVICE

*"Which safety harness works best—the five-point, bar-shield, or T-shield?*

The consensus of the safety experts we consulted seems to be that the five-point harness is best, although this may be because there is more testing information available on this design than on the alternatives. The jury is still out on the bar-shield and T-shield designs (which lower over the baby's head). They may be more convenient since it's easier to remove Junior from the seat.

One important factor: see how easy it is to adjust the harness straps. Some models are more difficult than others. This factor is critical since as your baby grows, you'll have to monkey with these things.

### Smart Shopper Tip #3
INFANT CAR SEATS: ARE THEY WORTH IT?

*"Are infant car seats a waste of money? Since you can only use them until the baby reaches 20 pounds, it seems like a lot of money for such a short period of time."*

Wrong. Most babies don't reach the 20-pound mark until about six months—and that can be a very long six months if you don't have an infant car seat.

Why? First, it's helpful to understand that an infant car seat is more than just a car seat—it's also an infant carrier when detached from its base. Big deal, you might say? Well, since most infants spend the first few weeks sleeping, this is a big deal. By detaching the carrier from the base, you don't have to wake the baby when you move from the car to the house. Buy a regular car seat, and you'll have to unbuckle the baby and move her into another type of carrier (and most likely wake her in the process). Take it from us: let sleeping babies lie and spend the additional $35 to $45 for an infant carrier, even if you just use it for six months.

### Here are two more shopping tips for car seats:
♣ *How easy does it recline?* Some car seats have a lever in front that makes the seat recline (nice for a sleeping baby). Unfortunately, not all car seats recline equally—some levers are more difficult to work than others. Check it out in the store before you buy.
♣ *Most car seats are "convertible."* For small infants, you face it backward. Then, after your baby reaches about 20 pounds, it converts to a front-facing car seat (you do have to adjust the straps).

## The Name Game: Reviews of Selected Manufacturers

## The Ratings

★★★★ EXCELLENT—*our top pick!*
 ★★★ GOOD—*above average quality, prices, and creativity.*
  ★★ FAIR—*could stand some improvement.*
   ★ POOR—*yuck! could stand some major improvement.*

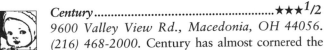

*Century* .........................................................★★★¹/₂
*9600 Valley View Rd., Macedonia, OH 44056. (216) 468-2000.* Century has almost cornered the market on affordable and easy to use infant car seats. We

liked the "position indicator," which shows you when the car seat is snapped correctly to its base. Basic models start at $35 to $40, while deluxe versions with canopies and thicker padding can cost $60 to $70. We weren't as impressed with Century's regular car seats ($60 to $100) because the styling and fabric choices lag behind the competition. The basic model (the 1000 STE) features a five-point harness, and deluxe models (the 3000 STE, 5000 STE or Nexus) feature bar shields, reclining seats, and "fancier" fabrics (although we thought the designs could have been better).

*Evenflo* ........................................................................★★★
*1801 Commerce Dr., Piqua, OH 45356. (800) 837-9201 or (513) 773-3971. In Canada, PO Box 1598, Brantford, Ontario, N3T 5V7. (519) 756-0210.* Evenflo markets a great line of car seats, with sturdy construction and a wide variety of stylish fabrics. The top of the line is the Ultara Premier seats, which come with either a five-point or shield restraint system. Pillow and cushions are removable, and the chair has a three-position recline. At $120 retail, it isn't cheap, but we have seen it for as low as $95 (for the Ultara V) in the Baby Catalog of America (800-752-9736) and even $79.99 (for the Ultara I) at Toys R Us. If that's too much, the Champion Car Seat sells for $60 to $70 and includes a "easy latch" belt system. Another interesting product: the "On My Way" infant car seat features a "smart handle" that "faces the right direction so carrying is easier than ever."

If we had to criticize Evenflo, it would have to be for their hard-to-follow instructions. At least they're available in English, French, and Spanish, so you can get confused in all three languages. Also, it's hard to thread the seat belt under some models (especially the Ultaras). Moreover, these seats are bulky and hard to switch from car to car. Despite these problems, we still like Evenflo—we've got one and have been happy.

*Fisher Price* ........................................................................★★¹/₂
*636 Girard Ave., East Aurora, NY 14052. (800) 828-4000 or (716) 687-3000.* Fisher Price sells a few car seat models, the most impressive of which is their Infant Car Seat. With nice, solid-colored padding, this T-shield style seat features an adjustable canopy—not a bad buy for $45 (available at Toys R Us).

*Kolcraft* ........................................................................★★
*3455 West 31st Pl., Chicago, IL 60623. (312) 247-4494.* The Deluxe Convertible Car Seat is a pretty good buy—its plush velour fabric is quite attractive, and the seat features a two-position recline and soft pillow. Not bad for $60 (at Toys R

Us). Of course, the company also makes less expensive models, including a five-point harness model for $50 that is similar to the Deluxe, but with lower-quality fabric. Kolcraft's Rock-N-Ride Infant Car Seat has a canopy and rocking base for $45.

*Travel Safety* ........................................................................★★
*1276 50th St., Brooklyn, NY 11219. (800) 637-7220 or (718) 438-6500.* New York-based Travel Safety has taken the concept of the air bag and applied it to child safety seats. The result is the "Air-Filled Car Seat." How does it work? Luckily, you don't have to inflate it manually—it comes with a pump that inflates (or deflates) the seat in 90 seconds (the pump shuts off automatically when the seat is full). Besides meeting all the federal safety requirements, the seat features extended side panels to support the baby's head and a five-point harness with front-adjusting straps. One advantage is its weight—just five pounds (contrast that with the 20 pounds traditional car seats can weigh). It even has a carrying bag with outside pockets to hold bottles, diapers, and toys!

So, is it worth the $100 retail price? Well, there are a couple of disadvantages: first, it can't be used for small infants (only for children 20 to 40 pounds). Because it's filled with air, you've got to be careful of pressure changes that could cause the seat to overfill. When you use it at high altitudes, on a plane or even on a hot day, you're supposed to fully inflate the seat and then let out 10 seconds of air. What a pain in the butt—especially for those of us in mountainous areas, where you might drive 20 minutes and change 1000 feet in altitude. And then there's that warning about hot days. Since most of the country experiences summer temperatures in the 90s, the Air-Filled Car Seat may not be as convenient as they promise during the warmer seasons. Nevertheless, this product might be just the ticket if you travel much and don't want to pay the $5 to $10 per day that car rental companies charge for car seats. (By the way, we've seen the Travel Safety Air-Filled Car Seat for as low as $85 at LiL' Things (817-649-6100).

## Safe & Sound

1 NEVER BUY A USED CAR SEAT. You don't know what happened to it—if the car it was in was in an accident (even a minor one), the car seat may be unsafe. What about a hand-me-down? Make sure it has never been in an accident—and confirm that the seat has not been recalled (see phone number below for the National Highway Traffic Safety Administration).

2   READ THE DIRECTIONS VERY CAREFULLY. Many car acci-
    dents end in tragedy because the car seat was used
improperly. If you have any questions about the directions,
call the company or return the car seat for a model that is easier to use.

3   USE YOUR CAR SEAT. Don't make the mistake of being in
    a hurry and forgetting to (or just not wanting to) attach
the restraints. Many parents merely put their child in the seat
without hooking up the harness. It is *more* dangerous to leave
your child in a car seat unrestrained by the safety harness than
it is to put him or her in the backseat.

4   CHILDREN UNDER 20 POUNDS MUST BE FACING BACKWARD.
    The best place is in the backseat. Another rule: don't put
the car seat in the frontseat (facing backward) when your car
is equipped with a passenger-side air bag. That's the latest
word from the safety experts, who are worried about possible
injuries if the air bag deploys and pushes the car seat back
into the seat.

### Recalls

National Highway Traffic Safety Administration has a toll-
free hot-line to check for recalls or to report a safety problem.
Call (800) 424-9393 or (202) 366-0123.

## Money-Saving Secrets

1   FORGET THE FANCY MODELS. We bought a $100
    car seat and another one that was just $50.
    Sure the $100 one had thicker padding and fancy
fabric, but surprisingly we found the cheaper model easier to
use—the seat belt slid easier under the base, it was less bulky,
and the straps were easier to adjust.

2   MIDAS MUFFLER AND BRAKE SHOPS OFFER A GREAT DEAL—
    A BASIC CENTURY CAR SEAT FOR $42 (model #STE-1000).
Midas says it's selling the seat at cost in order to get more
kids into safety seats. Call (800) 621-0144 or (312) 565-7500
to find the location nearest you. So how much would you
save? Well the Century STE-1000 (which features a five-point
harness and washable fabric pad) technically retails for $90,
although we have seen it for $57 in catalogs. And here's a
bonus: after your baby outgrows the seat, take it back to
Midas and they'll give you a $42 certificate for automotive
services. So, essentially, you get a car seat for free! Another
possibility: some health insurance companies (PCA in Texas,
for example) that offer parents-to-be a basic car seat at no

charge in exchange for their attendance at a parenting and safety seminar.

**3** CHECK OUT TOYS R US. Unlike other juvenile product categories, Toys R Us has all the premium brands (including Century and Evenflo) at prices that are hard to beat. Infant car seats start at $40, and regular car seats run $50 to $100—about 10% to 20% lower than the prices at baby specialty stores. Even better: wait for a sale. Toys R Us has a "Baby Month" sale in the spring when they knock even more off their prices. We just got a coupon book from the store offering another $7 off *any* car seat.

**4** IF THE BABY COMES EARLY, MANY HOSPITALS RENT CAR SEATS AT AFFORDABLE RATES. You can rent one for a few days until you get your own.

**5** VISIT THE "BABY ROOM" AT THE BURLINGTON COAT FACTORY (to find a store near you call 609-386-3314). They have incredible prices on car seats—for example, the Evenflo Ultara car seat was only $79.75 (retail is $100 or more). The Century "Party Time" car seat was $90.

Best of all, the Baby Room at the Burlington Coat Factory also carries high chairs, strollers, cribs, bedding and more. We saw such famous names as Peg Perego high chairs, Emmaljunga strollers and Dutalier glider-rockers! They even carry cribs by Child Craft and Simmons. Prices are 10% to 30% below retail.

## Strollers

### Sources to Find a Stroller

 ♣ *Mass merchandisers*. Chains like K-Mart and Target usually sell inexpensive, umbrella-type strollers. Toys R Us has a little wider selection, in the $20 to $100 price range.

♣ *Baby specialty stores*. You'll see all the upper-end brands here—at upper-end prices. We're always shocked to walk into a store and see strollers with $400 price tags.

♣ *Baby Mega-stores*. Chains like LiL' Things and Baby Superstore (see Chapter 2) combine the best of both worlds: high-quality brands at lower prices. The only drawback: some stores don't stock the entire line of popular brands. Instead, you may find just one or two models represented.

♣ *Mail order.* Yes, you can buy a stroller through the mail. We even found one catalog that offers significant discounts on premium brands like Peg Perego (see "Do It By Mail" later in this chapter). Other catalogs tend to sell strollers at full retail price. Add in the shipping (as much as $10 to $30 per stroller), and even the baby specialty stores might look like a good deal.

## What Are You Buying?

There are four types of strollers you can buy:

♣ *Umbrella stroller.* The name comes from the appearance of the stroller when it's folded up—you can carry it on your arm like an umbrella.
WHAT'S COOL: They're lightweight, and they're cheap—that is, low price (about $20 to $30).
WHAT'S NOT: They're cheap—that is, low quality. You don't get any fancy features like canopies, storage baskets, brakes, reclining seats, and so on.

♣ *Carriage/strollers.* A carriage is a basically a stroller in which the baby can travel lying down. Since this is only necessary when the baby is very young (under three months), pure carriages are a waste of money. Realizing this, companies make combination carriage/strollers.
WHAT'S COOL: If your baby is sleepy, she can lie down. Most combo carriage/strollers have lots of high-end features like reversible handles (so you can push the stroller and see your baby at the same time).
WHAT'S NOT: Hefty weight (not easy to transport or set up) and hefty price tags. Some carriage/stroller models can top $300 and $400.

♣ *Lightweight strollers.* These strollers are our top recommendation: they're basically souped-up umbrella strollers with lots of convenience features and not a lot of weight.
WHAT'S COOL: The ultimate in convenience, most have one-hand release for easy set-up and fold-down. An amazing number of features (canopies, storage baskets, high-quality wheels) at amazingly light weights (some as light as seven pounds).
WHAT'S NOT: Can be expensive—most models by high-quality brands run $200 to $300. Some models are so popular, you might have to wait for delivery.

♣ *Jogging strollers.* These are to strollers what mountain bikes are to ten-speeds. They feature three big wheels and lightweight frames—perfect for jogging or rough dirt roads.

WHAT'S COOL: How many other strollers can do 15 mph on a jogging trail? Some even have brakes (what a concept), and the best fold up for easy storage in the trunk.

WHAT'S NOT: While not as expensive as some lightweight strollers, they can still top $100, and some are close to $200. Consumer experts worry that jogging strollers have a tendency to tip over, and the brakes don't hold well on steep grades.

## Smart Shopper Tips

### Smart Shopper Tip #1
GIVE IT A TEST DRIVE

*"My friend was thinking of buying a stroller from a catalog. Should you really buy a stroller without seeing it first in a store?"*

Always try before you buy. Most stores have at least one stroller set up as a floor model. Give it a whirl, practice folding it up, and check the steering. Don't buy a stroller unless you can give it a thorough going over.

### Smart Shopper #2
THE CADILLAC EL DORADO OR FORD ESCORT DILEMMA

*"This is nuts! I see cheap umbrella strollers that sell for $30 on one hand and then fancy designer brands for $200 on the other. Is there anything in the middle?"*

Whether you drive a Cadillac El Dorado or Ford Escort, you'll still get to your destination. And that fact pretty much applies to strollers too—most function well enough to get you and baby from point A to B. The difference is the number of features.

Yes, there are options between the cheap and the top of the line. Toys R Us sells a wide variety of moderately priced strollers packed with convenience features. For $80 to $130, you can get strollers that recline, have storage baskets, reversible handles, comfy seat padding, and sun-blocking canopies. At the upper end of that price range, you can even get a combo carriage/stroller. While the brands Toys R Us stocks don't have the same durability or overall quality as their expensive specialty store counterparts, they do provide a nice compromise for parents on a budget.

Another option: get a premium brand stroller (Combi, Aprica, or Peg Perego) at a discount. As you'll learn later in this chapter, both the baby mega-stores and mail-order catalogs sell these brands at prices as low as $150.

## *Smart Shopper #3*
### WHAT FEATURES ARE REALLY IMPORTANT?

*"Let's cut through the clutter here. Do I really need a stroller that converts into a car seat? What features are really important?"*

A fair question. Let's take a look at what features really matter. First, we think the storage basket is a must. (And we're not talking about those itsy-bitsy storage baskets—go for one that is nice and deep.) We store the diaper bag and other miscellaneous items in it when we're at the mall. This also reduces the temptation to hang bags on the handle, a dangerous habit since it might tip over the stroller.

Other parents we interviewed really like strollers that recline, making it easy for their babies to sleep. Remember that all strollers don't recline equally—some just recline slightly while others go whole hog. If this feature is important to you, go for the most recline you can afford.

In a similar vein, another feature some parents love is the reversible handle trick (which lets you keep better tabs on a sleeping baby).

The wheels are an often-neglected aspect of stroller shopping. Bigger, knobby tires are better for rough surfaces but may be overkill if you're just going to the mall (perhaps they're better suited to unpaved walking trails, etc.). Some strollers even have mini-shock absorbers to give smoother rides. Be sure to check out the brakes.

If you're going to be taking any walks outside, a canopy is a must. Some cheaper strollers just have a sunshade, which doesn't block out the sun very well. A canopy that you can adjust to different positions is best—some canopies also have "peak-a-boo" windows that let you see the what the baby is doing (a nice plus).

We can't stress how much we love our seven-pound stroller—remember you're going to be hauling this thing around for quite a while (in and out of cars, folded up in airplanes, etc). Contrast that with bulky carriages that can weigh 28 pounds! Ouch! If your budget allows, we recommend you go for the seven-pound version over a heavier model any day. Another tip: check to see how easy it is to fold up the stroller—some models have a one-hand release, while others require six burly guys to get it in a trunk.

The bottom line: ask yourself how you're going to really use this thing. Short trips to the mall or major outdoor treks in the wilderness? Whether you plan to have more children in the future may also be a factor (go for a better brand that you can re-use). Finally, ask your friends and any other new parents about their experiences. See what features make sense and which brands hold up to the real-world abuse that strollers get.

## The Name Game: Reviews of Selected Manufacturers

 What is it about the Japanese and Europeans? Why is it they always whip our butts us when it comes to designing superior products with wheels—both cars and baby strollers? You'll notice that some of the best quality names in the stroller derby are Japanese (Aprica and Combi) or European (Emmaljunga and Peg Perego).

We evaluated strollers based on interviews with recent parents, as well as conversations with juvenile product retailers. For us, the most important attribute for strollers was convenience and durability (not to mention safety). Of course, price to value (as reflected in the number of features) was an important factor as well. From the over 30 companies who make strollers and carriages, we have picked these brands as the best of the best.

## The Ratings

★★★★ EXCELLENT—*our top pick!*
★★★ GOOD—*above average quality, prices, and creativity.*
★★ FAIR—*could stand some improvement.*
★ POOR—*yuck! could stand some major improvement.*

---

*Aprica* ........................................................................★★★★
*1200 Howell Ave., Anaheim, CA 92805. (310) 639-6387.*
Aprica (pronounced Ah-pree-cah) has been making strollers for 45 years—and has apparently figured out how to do it right. The Japanese brand has six different styles that are jam-packed with features like an "independent shock absorbing system" and tires with a lifetime guarantee (sorry, no air bags yet). Our favorite model is the CitiMini, which weighs just seven pounds but includes a storage basket, canopy, and more. Best of all, the CitiMini (like all Aprica strollers) features a release button on the handle that folds the stroller in one step—pretty cool. As you might expect, all this doesn't come cheap. The CitiMini retails for $200, although we've seen it as low as $179 in the Baby Superstore and $189 in LiL' Things. The only thing the CitiMini is missing is a fully reclineable seat and reversible handle. If you're looking for a combination carriage stroller, the Cabriolet EP has a reversible handle and weighs just 16 pounds (retail $249).

The fabric choices include a variety of colorful and contemporary prints (some pastels and florals are available as well). Overall, we like Aprica—their strollers are well designed and high quality; we only wish the prices weren't so high.

*Century* ...........................................................................★★
*9600 Valley View Rd., Macedonia, OH 44056. (216) 468-2000.* Century makes a wide variety of strollers, from the the E-Z Go Zoo Friends umbrella stroller ($19.99 at Toys R Us) to fancy combination carriage/strollers that cost $100. But the Century model that has everyone talking is their revolutionary 4-in-1 Car Seat Stroller. Yes, you read right—Century combines a infant car seat with a lightweight stroller. For infants up to 20 pounds, the carrier can be used in a car or it snaps to the stroller frame to create an infant stroller—no more lugging that heavy carrier everywhere you go. Later, it converts to a lightweight umbrella-type stroller. We have mixed feelings about this contraption. First, at $150 retail, it isn't cheap (although we've seen it on sale for $110 to $120). While it has some nice features (a storage basket and full canopy), all you're basically getting is an infant car seat (about $50 if bought separately) and a cheap umbrella stroller ($20 to $40). Add that up, and it makes you wonder how they came up with the $150 price tag. (We should note that JCPenney's catalog sells it for $119—a good deal). We might be more excited about the Century 4-in-1 if the stroller itself was of higher quality (better wheels, stronger construction, etc.).

*Combi* .........................................................................★★★★
*1471 N. Wood Dale Rd., Wood Dale, IL 60191. (800) 752-6624 or (800) 992-6624; (708) 350-0101.* Combi is our pick as one of the best strollers available today. And our favorite Combi model is the Travel Light Savvy-EX, which weighs a feather-light 7.7 pounds. The Savvy-EX includes a deep storage basket, a removable canopy, and a seat that reclines to 140 degrees. If we had to criticize anything about this Combi, it would have to be its folding operation—you must pull up on two releases that are on either side of the handle (not as convenient as the Aprica one-hand release). And the price isn't cheap either at a whopping $229 retail. We should mention that we saw this model for as low as $99 (on sale) at the Baby Superstore. LiL' Things has it for $159. (Sorry, the Baby Catalog of America doesn't sell Combi.) Of course, Combi also makes several other model strollers, including the 18-pound Avid stroller (about $170) with reversible handles and a fully reclining seat. Fabric choices are quite fashionable; our favorite is the leopard print.

*Emmaljunga* ....................................................................★★¹/₂
*Imported by Bandaks-Emmaljunga, 632 Aero Way, Escondido, CA 92029, (800) 232-4411 or (619) 739-8911.* Snob appeal, anyone? Made in Sweden, the Emmaljunga line (pronounced Em-ah-young-ah) features strollers that are built like a '57 Chevy—big, boxy, and lots of heavy metal. These are the strollers that you see nannies pushing on the Upper East Side of New York City—and at prices ranging from $250 to $450, you might have to fire the nanny in order to afford one. For all that money, you get a shock absorber system, chrome chassis, large wheels, and a five-point safety harness. What you don't get is much of a choice in fabrics—it's either navy or red. In order to compete with lightweight strollers, Emmaljunga recently rolled out the EmmaLite. While it has a nice canopy, the dinky metal storage basket is too small for any real use. And the weight is hardly what we'd term as "lite": 29 pounds. The EmmaLite costs about $260.

*Gerry* ............................................................................★★¹/₂
*(800) 525-2472 or (303) 457-0926.* The Roller Baby is Gerry's jogging stroller, which has a unique feature: it actually folds up and fits in a trunk (other jogging strollers require disassembly before you can fold them). With a weight of only 21 pounds, this stroller features 16-inch tires, brakes, and a tether strap. At $180 to $190 retail, it isn't cheap, but we've seen it as low as $139.55 (plus $16 shipping) in the Baby Catalog of America (800-752-9736). If you're looking for a jogging stroller, we think the Gerry Roller Baby is a best bet. For ages six months to six years.

*Graco* ..............................................................................★¹/₂
*Rt. 23, Main St., Elverson, PA 19520. (215) 286-5951.* Like Century and Kolcraft, Graco is a mass-market brand sold at outlets like Toys R Us. A typical offering: The Navy Geometric Travel Mate LX has a three-position reclining seat, large storage basket, and a one-hand/one-foot folding mechanism. Price: $70. If there is one aspect of Graco that differentiates it from other makers, it is probably their variety of fabric choices. From their Puppy Paws black and white pattern to the subdued navy striped design, the patterns are a cut above. We also noticed Graco makes several combination stroller/carriages in the $100 to $130 range. On the downside, we noticed several Graco strollers were involved in recalls in 1990 when the reclining seats caused several injuries.

*Inglesina Baby Ltd.* .......................................................★★¹/₂
*1190 Stirling Rd., Dania, FL 33004. (305) 987-6767.* Parents who are expecting twins (or more) should check out Inglesina,

an Italian-made line that has attracted notice for their multiple-baby strollers. The Biposto Piroet features a chrome chassis, a shallow metal storage basket, and an easy folding design. The price: $550. What if you're having triplets? Or quadruplets? Amazingly, Inglesina also makes strollers to hold three and even four babies, at prices that range from $700 to $840. Of course, Inglesina also makes strollers for parents with just one baby—the Rapido includes a full canopy, storage basket, and shock absorbers. Price: about $300 retail.

*Kolcraft* ...........................................................................★★
*3455 West 31st Pl., Chicago, IL 60623. (312) 247-4494.*
Kolcraft markets an interesting tandem (or two-child) stroller—their Side-by-Side Umbrella stroller fits through standard doorways and has sunshades. The price: $60. Of course, Kolcraft also makes a wide variety of other strollers (mostly for sale at discounters like Target and Toys R Us), including basic umbrella strollers for $30 and fancier models like the Royale for $75. The Royale includes a reversible handle and adjustable canopy. The fabric choices range from the basic (the primary color "Hopscotch") to the surreal ("French Pastel" is a hideous pattern).

*Peg Perego* ....................................................................★★★★
*3625 Independence Dr., Ft. Wayne, IN 46808. (219) 482-8191.* "Trouble-free" is how one veteran baby retailer describes this hot-selling, Italian-made line of strollers. Peg Perego makes strollers with names that sound like Pepperidge Farm cookies: the Domani, Amico, Puma, and the Classica. Perego's strollers have one-hand release and one unique safety feature: once there is weight in the seat, you can't collapse the stroller. Perhaps the best buy is the Domani, with its reversible handle, three-position backrest, and storage basket, for $199 retail (as low as $157 in the Baby Catalog of America; see review later in this chapter). The Amico is Perego's lightweight stroller, which includes a canopy, storage basket, and adjustable footrest. ($250 retail, $187 discount). If that's too much, we saw another Perego model (the Pilko) at the baby mega-stores for $130 to $180.

## Safe & Sound

 Next to walkers, the most dangerous juvenile products on the market today are strollers. That's according to the U.S. Consumer Product Safety Commission, which estimates that over 10,000 injuries a year occur from improper use or defects. The problems? Babies can slide out of the stroller, and small parts can be a choking hazard. Seat belts have broken in some models, while other babies are injured when a stroller's brakes fail on a slope. Here are some safety tips:

♣ *Never hang bags from the stroller handle*—it's a tipping hazard.

♣ *Don't leave your baby to sleep unattended in a stroller.* Many injuries happen when infants who are lying down in a stroller roll or creep and then manage to get their head stuck in the stroller's leg openings.

♣ *The brakes shouldn't be trusted.* The best stroller models have brakes on two wheels; cheaper ones just have one wheel that brakes. Even with the best brakes, don't leave the stroller alone on an incline.

♣ *Follow the weight limits.* Most strollers shouldn't be used for babies over 35 pounds.

♣ *Check for the JPMA certification.* The JPMA (the Juvenile Products Manufacturers Association) has a pretty good safety certification program. They require that strollers must have a locking device to prevent accidental folding and meet other safety standards, such as those for brakes. You can contact the JPMA for a list of certified strollers at (609) 985-2878.

### Recalls: Where to Find Information

The U.S. Consumer Product Safety Commission has a toll-free hotline at (800) 638-2772 for the latest recall information on strollers and other juvenile products. It's easy to use—the hotline is a series of recorded voice mail messages that you access by following the prompts. You can also report any potential hazard you've discovered or an injury to your child caused by a product. If you prefer, you can write to the U.S. Consumer Products Safety Commission, Washington, D.C. 20207.

## Money-Saving Tips

1 CHECK OUT THE DISCOUNTERS. Baby on a Budget (800-575-2224), the Texas-based mail-order discounter we profiled in Chapter 3, discounts certain premium brand strollers (call for the latest information). Later in this chapter, we'll spotlight the Baby Catalog of America, which offers great discounts on such well-known brands as Peg Perego. Finally, we'd be remiss to

not mention the baby mega-stores LiL' Things (for the store nearest you, call 817-649-6100) and Baby Superstore (803-675-0299). Both carry famous names like Combi and Aprica at rock-bottom prices.

2 WHY NOT A BASIC UMBRELLA STROLLER? If you only plan to use a stroller on infrequent trips to the mall, then a plain umbrella stroller for $20 to $30 will suffice. One caveat: make sure you get one that is JPMA certified (see above section for details). Some cheap umbrella strollers have been involved in safety recalls.

3 CONSIDER THE ALTERNATIVES. Some smart inventors have come up with alternatives to strollers. For example, the Snap 'n Go Stroller Frame from the Right Start catalog (1-800-LITTLE-1) turns major brands of infant car seats into a stroller—you just put the car seat in the frame. The cost: about $40.

4 CHECK FOR SALES. We're always amazed by the number of sales on strollers. Just the other week we received a coupon booklet from Toys R Us that featured a $10 off coupon on any Graco stroller over $70. That's nearly a 15% savings off the already low prices at Toys R Us. Another reason strollers go on sale: the manufacturers are constantly coming out with new models and have to clear out the old.

5 DON'T FALL VICTIM TO STROLLER OVERKILL. Seriously evaluate how you'll use the stroller and don't over buy. Strollers sometimes become status items among parents competing for the most attention.

## Wastes of Money

1 GIVE THE "BOOT" THE BOOT. Some expensive strollers offer a "boot" or apron that fits over the baby's feet. This padded cover is supposed to keep the baby's feet dry. We say save the $20 to $40 extra cost and buy a blanket instead.

2 SILLY ACCESSORIES. SOME STROLLER MAKERS OFFER EXTRA SEAT CUSHIONS OR HEAD SUPPORTS FOR SMALL INFANTS. While you get it in a matching fabric, you also spend twice as much as the same cushions cost at places like Toys R Us. Believe it or not, we've even seen stroller "snack trays" ($15) for babies who like to eat on the run. The only accessory in which you should invest is a toy bar (about $20), which attachs to the stroller. Why is this a good buy? If toys are not

attached, your baby will probably punt them out the stroller. Another affordable idea: Rinky Links ($9) from the Right Start Catalog (800-548-8531) enable you to snap toys to plastic rings that attach to the stroller.

## Do It By Mail

### The Baby Catalog of America

*To Order Call:* (800) PLAYPEN (1-800-752-9736) or
(203) 931-7760; Fax (203) 931-7764
*Or write to:* Baby Catalog of America 719-721 Campbell Ave.,
West Haven, CT 06516.
*Credit Cards Accepted:* MC, VISA, AMEX, Discover.

 If you're tired of high prices for strollers and carriages, you've got to get a copy of the Baby Catalog of America. Granted, the catalog itself is nothing fancy (just black and white pictures and line drawings of strollers), but the prices are fantastic. And, best of all, the Baby Catalog sells such premium brand names as Peg Perego, Aprica, Inglesina, and even Emmaljunga.

In fact, it's the sheer variety of different brand names available that really impressed us. From the basic (Century, Graco) to the super-expensive, the selection is expansive (including some of our top picks from Aprica and Combi). Unfortunately, the catalog doesn't list or show all the strollers available—you have to call for a quote on most brands. However, we did see quite a few of the Perego strollers listed, and the prices were discounted 10% to 30% off retail.

For example, the Colibri is Perego's lightweight (10 pounds) stroller with a reclining seat and shock-absorbing suspension. The retail is $140, but the Baby Catalog sells it for just $115.21 (nearly a 20% savings).

Of course, you have to pay shipping and handling. Thanks to the heavy package weight of some strollers (up to 35 pounds), this runs $10 to $20 extra. Yet, you do save the sales tax. Using the above stroller as an example, the cost at retail plus 8% sales tax would total $151.20. Even if you add in the $10 shipping from the Baby Catalog, you'd pay a total of $125 and still save $25. The savings are even more dramatic on the more expensive strollers, where you can shave $150 or more off the retail price.

The only exception to the sales tax/shipping cost trade-off is in Connecticut. Since the catalog is based there, they must collect 6% sales tax on all orders. On the upside, anyone (including those folks in Connecticut) can join the Baby Club of America (the Baby Catalog's parent company) for $25 per year. Members get an additional 10% off the catalog price and a special price sheet that "features baby care products not found in our catalog such as disposable diapers and formula."

## The Well-Stocked Diaper Bag

We consider ourselves experts at diaper bags—we got five them as gifts. While you don't need five, this important piece of luggage may feel like an extra appendage after your baby's first year. And diaper bags are for more than just holding diapers—many include compartments for baby bottles, clothes, and changing pads. With that in mind, let's take a look at what separates the great diaper bags from the rest of the pack. In addition, we'll give you our list of nine items for a well-stocked diaper bag.

## Smart Shopper Tip

DIAPER BAG SCIENCE

*"I was in a store the other day, and they had about one zillion different diaper bags. Some had cute prints and others were more plain. Should I buy the cheapest one or invest a little more money?"*

Here's our best piece of advice: buy a diaper bag that doesn't look like a diaper bag. Sure those bags with cute dinosaurs and pastel animal prints look cute now, but what are you going to do with it when your baby gets older? A well-made diaper bag that doesn't look like a diaper bag will make a great carry-on luggage piece later in life.

The best bet: Lands' End's high-quality diaper bag (see review later in the "Name Game"). Another option: the Designer Diaper bag from the Right Start Catalog (800-548-8531) is cleverly designed like a purse, complete with designer fabric. Inside you get a changing pad, storage pouch, bottle pockets, and a waterproof bag. Cost: $34.95.

The best diaper bags are made of tear-resistant fabric. Contrast that with low-quality brands that are made of cheap, thin vinyl—after a couple of uses, they start to split and crack. Yes, high-quality diaper bags will cost more ($30 to $40 versus $15 to $20), but you'll be much happier in the long run.

## Top Nine Items for a Well-Stocked Diaper Bag

After much scientific experimentation, we believe we have perfected the exact mix of ingredients for the best-equipped diaper bag. Here's our recipe:

1 GO FOR TWO DIAPER BAGS—one that is a full-size, all-option big hummer for longer trips and the other that is

a mini-bag for a short hop to dinner or shopping. Here's what each should have:

*The full-size bag*: This needs a waterproof changing pad that folds up, waterproof pouch or pocket for wet clothes, a couple compartments for diapers, blankets/clothes, etc. Super-deluxe brands have bottle compartments with Thinsulate (a type of insulation) to keep bottles warm or cold. Another plus are outside pockets for books and small toys. A zippered outside pocket is good for change or your wallet.

*The small bag:* This has enough room for a few diapers, travel wipe package, keys, wallet, and/or a checkbook.

2 STOCK EXTRA DIAPERS. Put a dozen in the big bag, two or three in the small one. Why so many? Babies can go through quite a few in a very short time.

3 A TRAVEL-SIZE WIPE PACKAGE. We find the best are the plastic cases that you can refill. Some wipe makers sell plastic packages that are allegedly "resealable"; we found that they aren't.

4 BLANKET AND CHANGE OF CLOTHES. Despite the reams of scientists who work on diapers, they still aren't leak-proof.

5 PAIR OF SUNGLASSES AND A HAT. We like the safari-type hats that have flaps to cover your baby's ears (about $10 to $20). Baby sunglasses serve two purposes: one, they shield your baby's eyes from damaging ultraviolet light; two, they look so darn cute in pictures.

6 A SMALL BOTTLE OF BABY SUNSCREEN. Babies can't take much direct exposure to sunlight. Besides sunscreen, other optional accessories include bottles of lotion and diaper rash creme. The best bet: buy these in small travel or trial sizes.

7 DON'T FORGET THE TOYS. We like compact rattles, board books, teethers, etc.

8 SNACKS. When your baby starts to eat solid foods, having a few snacks in the diaper bag (a bottle of juice, crackers, a small box of Cheerios®) is a smart move.

9 YOUR OWN PERSONAL STUFF. We put our wallet, check-book, and keys in the diaper bag. If we ever lose this thing, we're sunk.

## The Name Game: Reviews of Selected Manufacturers

***The Do-It-All Diaper Bag*** ........................★★★★
*Available from Lands' End, (800) 356-4444.*
Lands' End sells not one but four diaper bags: The Do-It-All Diaper bag ($29.50), the Deluxe ($45), the Little Tripper ($10), and the Backpack Diaper Bag ($29.50).

The Do-it-All is a best buy. Made of tough heavy-duty nylon fabric (the same as Lands' End's luggage), the diaper bag features a large main compartment for diapers and wipes, a clip for your keys, and a detachable waterproof pouch for wet clothes. Then there's another zippered compartment for a blanket or change of clothes, a waterproof changing pad and an expandable outside pocket for books and small toys. Outside, you'll find another zippered pocket and a small pouch with a Velcro closure. And, if that weren't enough, the bag also has two large pockets for bottles on each end of the bag.

Whew! That's a lot of stuff. But how does it work in the real world? Wonderful, as a matter of fact. We've hauled this thing on cross-country airline trips, on major treks to the mountains, and more. It still looks new. At $29.50, it isn't cheap, but considering the extra features and durability, we think it's worth the money.

How about those quick trips to the store? We bought the Little Tripper for this purpose and have been quite happy. With a strap that let's you wear it around your waist (like a fanny pack) or over your shoulder, the Little Tripper has a small main compartment that holds a few diapers and small case for wipes, as well as a clip for your keys. An outside zippered compartment holds a checkbook. For $10, it's a good value.

In case you need more room, the Deluxe ($45) is a bigger version of the Do-It-All (about 30% larger). It has a bigger changing pad, two zippered pouches for wet clothes and other items, a zippered compartment on the outside, and larger bottle pockets lined with Thinsulate to keep food cool or warm.

For outdoor enthusiasts, the Backpack Diaper Bag features a zip-closure bag (for wet diapers), a waterproof changing pad, two bottle pockets lined to keep drinks cool or warm and a see-through plastic pocket to hold toiletry items.

And here's the best feature: none of Lands' End's diaper bags look like diaper bags—no pink elephant prints or the words "BABY" plastered on the side. The solid red Do-It-All will easily segue into a carry-on after your baby is big enough to tote her own stuff (yes, that will happen some day). Four other colors are available, including purple, black, jade and royal navy.

## *Carriers*

Strollers are nice, but you'll soon discover that your baby doesn't want to sit in one for a long time. No, they really want to be with you. So, how do you cart around a baby for long distances without throwing out your back?

Several companies have come to the rescue with dozens of different carriers, all designed to make your little one more portable. One of the more famous is Nojo's Baby Sling (about $40; call 714-858-9496 for a dealer near you). The Sling enables you to hold your baby horizontally or upright. Babies seem to run hot or cold about the Baby Sling—we used one and found that our baby would go to sleep in it if he was really tired. However, he was less thrilled about the Sling when he was awake; he preferred to be looking out than being stuck in the thing. And that experience pretty much paralleled the experiences of the parents we interviewed—some had babies who loved the Sling and others were more indifferent.

Another alternative that we liked better was Kapoochi's Baby Carrier ($40, made by Medela, 800-435-8316 or 815-363-1246). You can carry the baby facing backward or forward—it's this flexibility that we found to be critical. Some babies like looking out, while others prefer the view of mom. Best of all, as your baby gets older, you can use the straps and pad of the carrier as seat restraints and extra padding in shopping carts, car seats, and so on. We liked the Kapoochi Carrier. It's easy to use and frees up mom's hands for other more important tasks—like picking up the phone and ordering pizza.

Snugli (available through the Natural Baby Catalog 609-771-9233 and other catalogs; see Chapter 11) markets an entire line of baby carriers. The Legacy, for example, retails for about $50 and converts from a front carrier to cradle-style design. We used a Snugli and found it to be easy and convenient.

Finally, serious outdoor enthusiasts go nuts over the Tough Traveler Back Pack ($79.95, available in stores or through One Step Ahead 800-274-8440). Adjustable for just the right fit, the Tough Traveler features cushioned pads, tough nylon cloth, and two-shoulder harnesses for baby. A comfortable seat provides head and neck protection for smaller children—you even get a zippered pouch for storage. For children through four years.

So, how do decide which carrier is best for you and your baby? Borrow different models from your friends and give them a test drive.

## *Restaurant Trips—*

We live in a town with wonderful restaurants—hence, when we became parents, we were loathe to forego this passion. Granted, some parents don't want to be bothered with eating out; one couple we interviewed didn't eat out with their baby until he was seven months old! However, it's not as difficult as you might think. Newborns and infants (up to a year old) can be surprisingly good dinner dates. After that point, things get a little trickier. Before you reach the "terrible twos," it is possible to eat out with your baby—if you master the "surgical strike." Here are our nine tips to eating out with baby:

♣ *Surprisingly, the easiest time to eat out with a baby is when he or she is a newborn.* Why? They tend to sleep all the time anyway. If your baby feeds every two hours, you can easily fit a nice meal (and even dessert) in the interval. Later, when the baby gets more active, is when the fun begins.

♣ *Before the baby is born, scout out restaurants that have booths and high chairs.* Also, check out delivery and take-out options. Let's be honest: some restaurants are more kid-friendly than others. The best have nice high chairs (not metal death traps), private booths (great for breastfeeding), diaper changing stations in the rest rooms (believe it or not, some places actually do have these), and waitpeople who are understanding. Create a mental "restaurant map" with spots that have all of the above amenities.

♣ *Make reservations.* Babies hate to wait for a table, or anything else. If you can't make reservations, call ahead to gauge the wait. Some restaurants have call-ahead seating, which puts you on a waiting list before you arrive. While you might have been willing to wait 30 minutes or more for a table when you were "without baby," the maximum now should be no more than 15 minutes. Think of this as a surgical strike—you want to get in, eat, and leave . . . not waste time waiting on a table.

## *Mastering the Surgical Strike*

♣ *Go for close parking.* We eliminate restaurants that don't have close, abundant parking. It's no fun searching for that elusive parking spot, dragging Junior three blocks, getting out a stroller, etc.

♣ *If you can't eat out, see if there is a restaurant delivery service in your area.* Not long ago, the only food you could get delivered was pizza. In our town, a new delivery service delivers food from 30 different restaurants. Now you can get your fix of Thai, Southwestern, French, or whatever for just a $3 delivery charge per order.

♣ *Go early.* We like to hit many restaurants in the 5:00 pm to 6:00 pm time range. It's less busy, the staff isn't harried, and the kitchen can get the meals out quicker.

♣ *You may have to forget dining out on the weekend.* The wait and crowds may make a home-cooked meal seem like a better deal on Saturday night.

♣ *Do the Cracker Dance.* Here's an all-purpose baby toy: the package of crackers. Not for eating, mind you, for playing. They're shiny, make neat noises, and are quite chewable—and restaurants tend to have them in stock. You'll enjoy this trick so much you'll probably start hauling around packages of crackers just in case your favorite cafe is out.

♣ *Walk your child around before the meal arrives.* Then, when the food hits the table, it's into the high chair (or carrier for young infants). That way you minimize the amount of time sitting in that high chair and the boredom your baby is bound to feel.

# THE BOTTOM LINE:
## A Wrap-Up of Our Best Buy Picks

 We strongly recommend buying an infant car seat/carrier—the sheer convenience makes it worth the $35 to $40 price tag. As far as "regular" car seats go, we liked the Evenflo and Century brands.

The best deals on car seats are at the Burlington Coat Factory, Toys R Us, LiL' Things, and the Baby Superstore. Basic models cost about $50, and plush models run $70 to $90. Another great deal: Midas Muffler Shops sell a basic Century car seat (STE-1000) for just $42—take it back to Midas after your baby outgrows it and they'll give you a $42 certificate for automotive services! It's a car seat for free.

Strollers are a world unto themselves, with prices ranging from $20 for a cheap umbrella style to $500 or more for a deluxe foreign model with all the bells and whistles.

What's our bottom line recommendation? We like the Combi Travel Light Savvy-EX ($159 at LiL' Things) and Aprica's CitiMini ($179 at the Baby Superstore). For urban warriors, these lightweight strollers can handle vigorous shopping trips to the mall or simple strolls in the park. Another brand that gets high marks: Peg Perego.

Like to jog? Gerry's Roller Baby jogging stroller ($139) features 16-inch tires and even folds up to fit in the trunk.

If all this sounds like overkill and all you plan is a few trips to the mall, a basic $20 umbrella stroller will probably do the trick. We also found a device that turns major brands of infant car seats into strollers (the Snap 'n Go, $40).

Now that you've got a car seat and diaper bag, don't forget the diapers. And the diaper bag. The best one we found was the Do-It-All Diaper Bag from Lands' End ($29.50). The Little Tripper ($10, also from Lands' End) is good bet as well.

The best carriers are Kapoochi's Baby Carrier ($40) and the Legacy by Snugli ($50). The famous Baby Sling ($40) gets mixed reviews from parents. Outdoor enthusiasts highly recommend the Tough Traveler Back Pack ($80).

If you buy the Century car seat from Midas, the Combi Savvy-EX Stroller, Lands' End Do-It-All Diaper Bag, and Kapoochi Baby Carrier at the discount sources we recommend, you'd spend about $275. At retail, these same items will set you back about $400.

 Questions or comments? Did you discover a car seat or stroller bargain you'd like to share with our readers? **Call the authors at (303) 442-8792!**

# Chapter 8

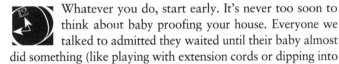

## Affordable Baby Proofing

I nside this chapter, you'll discover how to baby proof your home on a shoe-string budget. We've got room-by-room advice and several money-saving tips that might surprise you. Which devices work best? We'll give you the answers and share five mail-order catalogs that will save you time and money. Finally, learn what items should be in your baby's first aid kit.

### Getting Started: When do you need this stuff?

Whatever you do, start early. It's never too soon to think about baby proofing your house. Everyone we talked to admitted they waited until their baby almost did something (like playing with extension cords or dipping into the dog's dish) before they panicked and began childproofing.

Remember Murphy's Law of Baby Proofing: your baby will be instantly attracted to any object that can cause permanent harm. The more harm it will cause, the more attractive it will be to him or her. A word to the wise: start baby proofing as soon as your child begins to roll over.

### Smart Baby Proofing Tips

There is one basic truth about child safety: Safety devices are no substitute for adult supervision. While this chapter is packed with all kinds of gizmos and gadgets to keep baby out of harm's way, you still have to watch your baby at all times.

Where do you start? Get down on your hands and knees and look at the house from your baby's point of view. Be sure to go room by room throughout the entire house. As you take your tour, here are some points to keep in mind:

### General Tips

♣ *Throw away plastic bags and wrappings*—these are a suffocation hazard.

♣ *Put window guards on any windows you plan to open.* Otherwise, keep all windows locked.

♣ *Mini-blind cords can be a strangulation hazard.* Put them high off the floor or buy cord shorteners (available from many of the safety catalogs we review later in this chapter).

♣ *Always use gates at the TOP and BOTTOM of stairs.* Placing a gate two or three steps up from the bottom allows your child to practice climbing without extreme danger.

♣ *Keep your child out of garages and basements.* There are too many items stored in these areas that can be dangerous (like pesticides and gardening equipment).

♣ *Put the cat's litter box up off the floor.* Even better: install a cat-sized pet door in the laundry room, put the litter box in there, and keep the door closed.

♣ *Keep pet food dishes and water dishes out of baby's reach.* Besides eating dog or cat food (and maybe choking on it), some pets jealously guard their food and might snap at an eager toddler. Water dishes are a drowning hazard.

♣ *Fireplaces can be a major problem.* Never leave your child unattended around a fire. Even if there is no fire in the fireplace, the soot left behind is a toxic snack. Fireplace tools aren't good play toys either; put them away in a locked cabinet.

♣ *Cover outlets.* You can buy outlet covers from hardware stores or safety catalogs. Consider moving heavy furniture in front of some of your outlets as well.

## Bathrooms

♣ *Toilets make a convenient stepping stool and can be used to reach the bathroom countertop.* Take hair dryers and curling irons off the counter and put them in a locked cabinet.

♣ *Secure tub spouts or nozzles with protective covers.*

♣ *Set your hot water heater to a lower setting.* The best temperature for baby-friendly bathrooms is 120 degrees or less. As an alternative, you can purchase an anti-scalding device that attaches to showers or sink faucets. We saw one from the Perfectly Safe catalog (800-837-5437) called the ScaldSafe. The shower version sells for $16.95 and the sink model for $9.95. It shuts the water off immediately when it reaches 114 degrees.

♣ *Hide medication* (including vitamins), mouthwash, perfume, and anything else containing alcohol in a cabinet with a latch. Don't think that a childproof cap is really childproof. Junior is much smarter than those rocket scientists at the drug companies think he is. Keeping all items that pose a hazard out of reach is your best defense.

♣ *Get a toilet lock for all the toilets* (about $10 from hardware stores and safety catalogs). Toddlers are fascinated with the water in the bowl. If they fall in head first, they won't be able to get themselves out. Also, don't use those colored deodorant products in the toilet. Not only are they toxic and therefore inherently dangerous, but they also make the toilet water a more enticing blue color.

♣ *Check out those bath rugs and mats.* Get non-skid versions or buy rubber backing to keep baby from slipping when she starts walking.

♣ *Never leave buckets of water around,* in the bathroom or anywhere in the home. If your baby should fall in head first, the weight of his head makes it impossible for him to leverage himself out. The result could be a tragic drowning, even in just a few inches of water.

♣ *Separate your medicine and vitamins from the baby's.* You don't want to make any mistakes in the middle of the night, when you're sleepy and trying to get your baby's medication.

♣ *Don't store non-medicines in the medicine cabinet.* You might pick up a bottle of rubbing alcohol instead of cough syrup by accident.

## Kitchen

♣ *Remember the dishwasher is a fun toyland,* filled with all kinds of interesting objects. The best advice: keep it locked at all times. Lock the oven door as well.

♣ *Put all cleaning supplies and poisons into an upper, locked cabinet.*

♣ *Use safety latches on drawers with sharp cutlery and utensils.*

♣ *Latch any cabinets containing glassware.*

♣ *Lock up garbage in a place that's out of sight.*

♣ *Unplug those appliances*—you don't want Junior playing with the Cuisinart.

♣ *Protect your child from the stove.* We recommend purchasing a device that keeps hands away from the burners. One example is Shield-A-Burn from the One Step Ahead catalog (800-274-8440). This $20 plastic burn guard slides off the stove when not needed. Another option: the Stove Guard ($25 to $29, in different sizes) from the Perfectly Safe catalog (800-837-5437). These metal guards are four inches high, wrap around all four sides, and suction to the top of the stove. Of course, basic plastic knob covers are a good safety item as well (about $6 for a set of four).

♣ *Keep stools and chairs away from countertops, stoves, and sinks.*

♣ *Tablecloths can be yanked off your table* by an overzealous toddler, bringing dishes crashing down on her head. Use placemats instead when you're eating at the table; otherwise, the table should be cleared.

## Living Rooms

♣ *Forget using that coffee table for just about anything*—remove any small objects and potential missiles. If it's breakable, it should go up on a high shelf or in a locked cabinet.

♣ *Anchor bookcases to the wall with nails or brackets.* Shelves present a great challenge to budding rock climbers.

♣ *Inspect your houseplants and get rid of poisonous ones.* Which ones are poisonous, you ask? Check out the book *Baby Safe Houseplants and Cut Flowers*, which is reviewed in Chapter 10. This handy reference will give you the answers. Or ask your local nursery for a list of poisonous plants. Of course, even a "safe" plant should be placed out of reach. And don't forget to check silk plants and trees to make sure leaves cannot be detached and swallowed.

♣ *Pad that coffee table with bumpers*—especially if it's made of glass.

♣ *Extension cords are a notorious hazard.* Use as few cords as possible and hide them behind furniture.

♣ *Make sure the TV or stereo cart can't be pulled over.*

Babies also love to play disc jockey, so your stereo equipment should be moved far out of reach.

♣ *Consider buying a VCR lock to keep your little one from feeding the tape player her Cheerios®.*

## Bedrooms

♣ *Don't leave small objects like coins, jewelry, cosmetics, or medications on dressers or bureaus.*

♣ *Storing items under the bed is a no-no.* These are easy pickings for a baby.

♣ *Check how easily drawers in dressers can be pulled out.* Once babies can open the drawers, they may try using them as step ladders.

## Money-Saving Secrets

 **1** Woof! Go to the dogs for the Best Prices on Gates. Suspicious that many "baby" safety items would be cheaper if they didn't come from shops that sell baby items? We sure are. As evidence, check out the R.C. Steele Catalog (800-872-3773), a compendium of wholesale pet supplies. Inside, you'll find "pet gates" that are suspiciously similar to baby gates and are made by the same manufacturers. The only difference is the price.

For example, Pet Gate (made by General Cage) is a 29" high gate that adjusts from 26" to 46" wide. This gate can be pressure mounted or can be installed permanently with included hardware. The cost is only $25. The same type of gate from Hand in Hand Professional (800-872-3841), a children's toy and gadget catalog, was $35.

Here are a few other price comparisons of gates available from R.C. Steele:

♣ *A basic wooden pressure gate* (32" high and 30" to 50" wide) sells for $30 in the Safety Zone catalog but only $25 in R.C. Steele (or buy three for just $65).

♣ *A Gerry walk-through gate* (27" high and 28" to 39" wide) is $40 in the Perfectly Safe catalog and $38 in R.C. Steele.

♣ *An extra-wide wooden gate* from Nu-Line (24" high and 53"to 96" wide) opens on the side for walk-through convenience. Cost: $35 in R.C. Steele and $40 in Perfectly Safe.

The only disadvantage to ordering from R.C. Steele is that you must order a minimum of $50 worth of merchandise. However, if you plan to buy more than one gate (or you have a lovable pet in need of some new toys), you won't have any trouble meeting this minimum.

**2** OUTLET COVERS ARE EXPENSIVE. Only use them where you will be plugging in items. For unused outlets, buy cheap plate covers (these blank plates have no holes and are screwed into the wall over the plugs). Another option: put heavy furniture in front of unused outlets.

**3** MANY DISCOUNTERS LIKE TARGET, K-MART, AND WAL-MART SELL A LIMITED SELECTION OF BABY SAFETY ITEMS. We found products like gates, outlet plugs, and more at prices about 5% to 20% less than full-priced hardware stores.

**4** SOME OF THE MOST EFFECTIVE BABY PROOFING IS *FREE*. For example, moving items to top shelves, putting dangerous chemicals away, and other common sense ideas don't cost any money and are just as effective as high-tech gadgets.

## The Name Game

## The Ratings

★★★★  EXCELLENT—*our top pick!*
★★★  GOOD—*above average quality, prices, and creativity.*
★★  FAIR—*could stand some improvement.*
★  POOR—*yuck! could stand some major improvement.*

*Safety 1st*.................................................................★★
*210 Boylston St., Chestnut Hill, MA 02167. (800) 962-7233 or (617) 964-7744.* You can't walk into a baby store and not encounter Safety 1st. Usually you'll find an entire wall of Safety 1st products and accessories, such as outlet covers and cabinet latches. While they've been extremely successful, we can't help but think the company slaps its name on items without much forethought.

For example, we were very disappointed with Safety 1st's baby monitor, which didn't have continuous transmission (unlike nearly every other monitor out there). When the baby cried, it would flip on with a loud crackle. Although the company has since corrected this major flaw in its new monitors, we still have doubts about Safety 1st. How could the company market a product as essential as a baby monitor that was so useless in the real world?

So what's the bottom line? Safety 1st has a great selection of babyproofing items available but not necessarily the best quality. We suggest comparing different brands of safety items in your local hardware store, as well as considering some of the products available in mail-order catalogs reviewed in the next section.

## Do It By Mail

### Hand in Hand Professional.

*To Order Call:* (800) 872-3841; Fax (207) 539-4415.
*Shopping Hours:* Monday-Friday 8:00 am-5:00 pm Eastern Time.
Or write to: Hand in Hand Professional Catalogue Center, Route 26, R.R. 1 Box 1425, Oxford, ME 04270.
*Credit Cards Accepted:* MC, VISA, AMEX, Discover.

Hand in Hand is one of our favorite catalogs, probably because it carries such a nice variety of products at decent prices. The "Housewares" section contains mostly safety-related products. Here we found Escape Aid ladders for $50 to $65, Tot Loks for cabinets at $12.95 (set of two), and even Boo-Boo Bunny Ice Compresses for $15 (set of three). The selection isn't huge (it takes up only two pages), but we definitely recommend checking out Hand in Hand.

### One Step Ahead.

*To Order Call:* (800) 274-8440 or (800) 950-5120;
Fax (708) 615-2162.
*Shopping Hours:* 24 hours a day, seven days a week.
*Or write to:* One Step Ahead, 950 North Shore Dr.,
Lake Bluff, IL 60044.
*Credit Cards Accepted:* MC, VISA, AMEX, Discover, Optima.

One Step Ahead has a convenient index that lets you zero-in on any product. The catalog's three pages of babyproofing products include such items as gates (Supergate II, for example is $23.95), Safe Lok drawer latches ($6 for 6), and Toddler Shield coffee table bumpers ($30 to $60). They even offer the Coldfire 302 fire extinguisher ($20) and a lead detection kit ($30). While the catalog doesn't carry as many safety products as some competitors, the selection in One Step Ahead is decent, and the prices are worth comparing.

> "IT'S NEVER TOO SOON TO THINK ABOUT
> BABY-PROOFING YOUR HOUSE."

## Perfectly Safe.

*To Order Call:* (800) 837-5437; Fax (216) 494-0265.
*Shopping Hours:* Monday-Friday 7:30 am-10:00 pm;
Saturday 9:00 am-7:00 pm; Sunday 10:00 am-6:00 pm Eastern Time.
*Or write to:* The Perfectly Safe Catalog, 7245 Whipple Ave. NW,
North Canton, OH 44720.
*Credit Cards Accepted:* MC, VISA, AMEX.

This well-organized catalog says it's "the catalog for parents that care." It is an award-winning publication developed by the author of The Perfectly Safe Home book (available in the catalog as well, of course).

Perfectly Safe's latest catalog features over 70 products to "keep your children safe and healthy." A handy index spotlights such topics as the nursery, kitchen, bathroom, toys, windows and doors, and even educational software. We like the extensive kitchen safety section, which includes stove guards, appliance latches, and cabinet locks. There's even a device to check to see if your microwave leaks radiation ($7.95). Another interesting product: a "choke tester" for $2.50. This little gizmo enables you to test toys to see if they present a choking hazard.

Perfectly Safe's prices seem high—for example, the Thermoscan thermometer (which takes your baby's temperature instantly via the ear canal) was $119.95 (other catalogs sell it for about $100, and we've even seen it as low as $80 on sale). While most products are quite practical, others are somewhat silly. The "Baby Watch" is a "personal video observation system" with camera and 5-inch black and white monitor. Not cheap at $299.95.

Despite these transgressions, Perfectly Safe is the most comprehensive catalog of safety items available. It's not the cheapest, but the selection is hard to beat.

## Right Start Catalog.

*To Order Call:* (800) LITTLE-1 (800-548-8531);
Fax (800) 762-5501.
*Shopping Hours:* 24 hours a day, seven days a week.
*Or write to:* Right Start Inc., Right Start Plaza,
5334 Sterling Center Dr., Westlake Village, CA 91361.
*Credit Cards Accepted:* MC, VISA, AMEX, Discover.

Although the Right Start Catalog doesn't carry a huge selection of safety items, we found that the prices on what they do carry were very competitive. For example, Safe-Plate outlet covers with sliding socket guards were $15 for a set of four ($3.75 each). Safety Zone (see below) carries the same covers priced at two for $8 ($4 each). Although the savings don't seem like much, you may find yourself buying quite a few of these covers, and every little bit helps.

Right Start also sells stove knob covers ($7 for four), fireplace hearth cushions ($60 to $80), and a childproof medicine safe ($23). The products, which take up three pages of the catalog, are even more affordable if you are a Silver Rattle Club member. For $50 for the first year (and $25 per year thereafter), club members get an additional 20% savings, which makes baby proofing easier on the wallet.

## Safety Zone.

*To Order Call:* (800) 999-3030; Fax (800) 338-1635.
*Shopping Hours:* 24 hours a day, seven days a week.
*Or write to:* The Safety Zone, Hanover, PA 17333.
*Credit Cards Accepted:* MC, VISA, AMEX, Discover.

Finally a catalog for the hypochondriac in all of us. The Safety Zone is not just a catalog for kids' safety products. It also covers everything from travel safety (including a hotel door alarm), to personal health items (a monitor to test your fat), to car and home safety. Within its pages, however, there are quite a few items that may be useful for parents. For example, in the personal health section, Safety Zone offers the Thermoscan thermometer for only $89. Considering we've seen it in other catalogs for as much as $120, this is quite a good deal.

Other items we noted included wireless intercoms, portable safety vests, and traditional kidproofing products. For example, they carry four different kinds of safety gates, including the Safety 1st Safe Keeper Security Gate for $35. A neat item we hadn't noticed in any other catalog is a replacement high chair strap for $6.95. One caveat, however: some products available through the Safety Zone were less expensive elsewhere. For example, a set of two sliding outlet covers is $7.95 (or $4 each). In the Right Start, we priced them at $14.95 for four covers (or $3.75 each). And if you buy two or more sets from Right Start, the price decreases even more to $12.95 for four (or $3.24 each).

One of the best safety items we saw in the Safety Zone catalog are the magnetic "Tot Loks." These are cabinet locks that open with a magnetic key. They aren't cheap ($14.94 for three locks and one key), but they sure beat out the typical drawer safety latches on the market.

All in all, we strongly recommend the Safety Zone. While the prices aren't always the lowest, the sheer variety of safety products makes it a good read.

## *First Aid Friends*

Wonder what should be in your baby first aid kit? Honestly, as a childless couple, you were probably lucky to find a couple of plastic bandages and an ancient bottle of Bactine in your medicine cabinet. Now that you're Dr. Mom (or Nurse Dad) it's time to take a crash course on baby medicine etiquette. Here's a run-down of essentials.

♣ ACETAMINOPHEN (one brand name of this drug is Tylenol). If you suspect your child may have an allergy to dyes or flavorings, you can buy a version without all the additives. You may also want to keep acetaminophen infant suppositories in your medicine cabinet in case your infant persists in vomiting up his drops. Or refuses to take them at all. DO NOT keep baby aspirin in your house. Aspirin has been linked to Reyes Syndrome in children and is no longer recommended by the medical community.

♣ ANTIBIOTIC OINTMENT to help avoid bacterial infection from cuts and scrapes.

♣ BAKING SODA is great for rashes.

♣ A BULB SYRINGE to remove mucus from an infant's nose when she's all stuffed up. One of the top 15 fun parenting activities that no one tells you about.

♣ CALAMINE LOTION to relieve itching. (Caladryl is one brand name, and it now comes in a clear version, instead of that pink stuff.)

♣ A COUGH AND COLD REMEDY recommended by your pediatrician.

♣ A GOOD LOTION LIKE LUBRIDERM. Unscented and unmedicated brands are best. If your baby has very dry skin or eczema, buy a jar of Eucerin cream.

♣ MEASURING SPOON OR CUP for liquid medicine. For small infants, you may want a medicine dropper or syringe.

♣ PETROLEUM JELLY, which is used to lubricate rectal thermometers.

♣ PLASTIC BANDAGES like Band-Aids.

♣ SALINE NOSE DROPS for stuffy noses.

♣ SYRUP OF IPECAC to induce vomiting. DO NOT administer this stuff until told to do so by your physician or poison control center. Keep your local Poison Control Center's phone number handy. Syrup of ipecac is especially useful in cases of poisonings (although it may be contraindicated for small infants).

♣ THERMOMETER. Since rectal thermometers for infants have been an uncomfortable tradition for years, we like the new instant thermometers like Thermoscan, which gives you a temperature reading by inserting the unit into the ear canal. Earlier in this chapter we review several catalogs that sell this great device. You may want to avoid rectal thermometers if you're a little squeemish (although it's probably a good idea to have one as a backup, in case the batteries in your Thermoscan go dead).

♣ TWEEZERS. For all kinds of fun uses.

*(continued on next page. . . )*

After stocking up on all this stuff, you probably need a place to keep it all (and any other baby medication). We suggest a product in the Right Start Catalog called the Child Safe. This tamper-proof medicine chest will fit into closets or refrigerators. The cost is only $23 (or if you buy two or more, just $20 each). Even if you don't buy something like this, make sure your child cannot reach any medicines or vitamins in your house.

## Wastes of Money

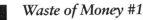

### Waste of Money #1

*"When I was visiting a friend's house, she had covered her outlets with special outlet plates instead of those inexpensive little plugs. Why would she go to the expense of plates?"*

Your friend's toddler probably discovered how to remove the plugs. It doesn't take an astrophysicist to figure out how to do this. While the sliding outlet covers are more pricey, they may be well worth the investment.

### Waste of Money #2

*"The other day I was looking through a safety catalog and saw some corner guards. It occured to me that they don't look a whole lot softer than the actual corner they cover. Are they worth buying?"*

You've hit (so to speak) on a problem we've noticed as well. Our advice: the plastic corner guards are a waste of money. They aren't very soft—and they don't have air bags that pop out when you hit them either. So what's the solution? If you're worried about Junior hitting the corner of your coffee table, you can either store it for a while or look into getting a soft bumper pad ($30 to $65 in catalogs). Similar bumpers are available for your fireplace as well. You may decide that blocking off certain rooms is another more affordable option.

### Waste of Money #3

*"I can't imagine that my daughter is going to be able to open the refrigerator any time soon. So why do they sell those appliance safety latches in safety catalogs, anyway?"*

There must be some super-strong kids out there who have enough torque to open a full-sized refrigerator. At this point, ours isn't one of them so a $6 refrigerator latch isn't on our shopping list. One point to remember: many appliances like stoves and dishwashers have locking mechanisms built in. And, keep all chairs and stools away from the laundry room to prevent your baby from opening the washing machine and dryer.

## Top Ten Safety Must Haves

 To sum up, here's our list of top safety items to have for your home (in no particular order).

♣ FIRE EXTINGUISHERS, RATED "ABC," which means they are appropriate for any type of fire.

♣ OUTLET COVERS.

♣ BABY MONITOR—unless your house or apartment is very small, and you don't think it will be useful.

♣ SMOKE ALARMS. Specifically, put one in your child's room and check the battery frequently. We replace our batteries twice a year, when we set the clocks forward and back.

♣ CABINET AND DRAWER LOCKS. For cabinets and drawers containing harmful cleaning supplies or utensils like knives, these are an essential investment. For fun, designate at least one unsecured cabinet or drawer as "safe" and stock it with pots and pans for baby.

♣ SPOUT COVER FOR TUB.

♣ BATH THERMOMETER OR ANTI-SCALD DEVICE.

♣ TOILET LOCKS—so your baby doesn't visit the Tidy Bowl Man.

♣ BABY GATES.

♣ FIRE FIGHTER DECALS. Often available from your local fire department or through Perfectly Safe catalog (800-837-5437), you place these decals on your children's room windows, as well as on the front door to notify fire fighters that there are children in the house.

## THE BOTTOM LINE:
### A Wrap-Up of Our Best Buy Picks

 Some of the most affordable baby-proofing tips are free—lowering the setting on your water heater to 120 degrees or lower, moving heavy furniture in front of outlets, not leaving plastic bags lying around, etc. Instead of buying expensive childproof outlet covers, just buy blank plates (less than $1) for unused outlets.

Baby gates are cheaper when the exact same product is called a pet gate. Order them at wholesale from R.C. Steele catalog. Sample savings if you buy three basic wooden pressure gates: $25.

Most of the brands of baby-proofing products were pretty similar. Safety 1st is probably the best known, although we have mixed feelings about their products. Mail-order catalogs are a good places to shop, with Perfectly Safe and the Safety Zone as two of the best. The Right Start catalog featured low prices on outlet covers and other safety items.

Questions or comments? Did you discover a bargain you'd like to share with our readers?
**Call the authors at (303) 442-8792!**

# Chapter 9

## The Best Gifts for Baby

What was the best baby gift you received? That was the question we posed to new parents across the U.S. In this chapter, we'll report on the results, some of which might surprise you. In addition to top gifts, we'll fill you in on "gift don'ts," advice on how to avoid wasting money. Finally, learn how to save money on baby announcements and which mail-order company discounts the best brands.

## Top Ten Best Gifts for Baby

1 ANYTHING HANDMADE. Moms universally praise gifts of quilts, blankets, embroidered pillows, cradles, or bassinets that were handmade by the gift-giver. There's something about handmade items, no matter how small, that's just more special than store-bought items. If you're handy with a needle and thread or hammer and nails, you know your gift will be loved and cherished. My dad made our son the most beautiful cherry cradle we've ever seen. You can bet it will become a cherished heirloom in our family.

2 *DUCKY MITTEN'S BOOK*. Designed by Judith Blau. Published by Random House. $5.95. This is a great cloth puppet/book made in the shape of a duck (a bunny version is available too). Designed for babies four months and older, these books combine reading together with a puppet that can (and will) be mouthed by your curious little one. You can have the puppet hop or wiggle, quack or flap along with the words to this simple story. It's an ingenious idea that introduces your baby to reading in a fun way.

Of course, any books you buy will be appreciated by new parents. Cloth books, board books, and bath books will get used the quickest, but children's classics in hardbound or soft cover are just as nice. Another idea: puppets in bright colors. We bought our son a dinosaur puppet, along with the mitten books mentioned above. They're great for interactive play.

3 FLATOBEARIUS FROM AMERICAN BEAR CO. These plush, stuffed-animal rattles will be your baby's first stuffed friend. For about $11, you can buy the golden bear version, the pink and white FlatJack (rabbit), or the black and white Flatopup. We've also seen giant versions of Flatopup and Flatofant (elephant) for $40 and smaller "Squishy Fish" (marlins, starfish, and sea horses) for $9. Call (800) 682-3427 or (312) 329-0020 for the store nearest you.

4 COMBI ULTRALITE SAVVY EX STROLLER. If you want to give a stroller as a gift, this is the one. The Savvy EX is a seven pound wonder, easy to operate, and it comes with a canopy and under-carriage basket. It's not cheap, but it is built to last. Available in a variety of colors, the stroller retails for $229. A best bargain: The LiL' Things baby mega-stores carry it for $159 and offer mail-order service (for the store nearest you, call 817-649-6100). For other Combi dealers, call (800) 992-6624.

5 HEAD SUPPORT INSERT FOR YOUR CAR SEAT. This is definitely a must-have for new parents. You shouldn't put your new (and tiny) baby in her car seat for the ride home from the hospital without a head support seat insert. What does a head support do? Since your little one doesn't have much neck control for the first few months, the baby's head may flop from one side to another when you take a curve (not fun for you or baby). Not to mention that some "convertible" car seats are very big for newborns, and a seat insert will help create a better, more comfortable fit. Several manufacturers make head supports, including NoJo (714-858-9717) and The Right Fit by Basic Comfort, Inc. (303-778-7535). Most cost $15 to $25.

6 FISHER PRICE BABY MONITOR. While a baby monitor is a popular gift, buying the wrong monitor can drive new parents crazy. We recommend the Fisher Price monitor from personal experience—it's one of the most sensitive monitors on the market. For $40, the Fisher Price features a sound-activated light display and a unique range-setting option. Say you live in an apartment building, and you don't want to broadcast your baby's noises to your neighbors' cordless phones. You can set the range setting to low and limit the broadcast area of the monitor. The result is greater privacy. Available at Toys R Us and other baby stores.

7 STACKING CUPS. *Parenting Magazine* lists stacking cups as one of the all-time great baby toys, and we have to agree. Our son started knocking over the brightly colored

stacked cups before he even learned to roll over. Later, he practiced drinking from one of the cups, and now he even takes them into the tub to play with. Someday, he'll probably use them to make sand castles at the beach. For $3 to $10, this is one toy your child will really use.

**8** DIAPER GENIE. I dream of the Diaper Genie. Okay, so we're a little obsessive about this innovative "diaper disposal system." If you had to change a hundred stinky diapers a week, you'd love it too. Of course, you don't have to buy this little miracle worker, but you will want to have some sort of diaper pail. The bottom line: we think the deodorized plastic that seals each diaper is safer than the usual charcoal filters used by conventional diaper pails. Cost ranges from $20 to $40, depending on the store you shop in (see Chapter 6 for price comparisons). Refill cartridges run $4 to $7—if you're giving the Diaper Genie as a gift, go ahead and get several refills too. Call (800) 843-6430 for a store near you.

**9** GRACO PAK' N' PLAY. What was life like before portable cribs? We know we couldn't be nearly as mobile without our Graco Pak' N' Play portable crib. We use it on visits to Grandma's house, or as a temporary playpen inside the house or out. Graco's version is so well designed that it sets up and breaks down in less than a minute. A bag is included to make travel easy. The Pak' N' Play retails for $90, but we've seen it on sale for $70 at discount stores like Target. Call Graco at (800) 345-4109 to find your nearest dealer.

**10** THERMOSCAN INSTANT THERMOMETER. What was life like before the fax machine? We'd put the Thermoscan Instant Thermometer in the same category of innovation—this wonderful device takes your baby's temperature by "measuring the infrared heat waves of the ear drum and surrounding tissue, converts it to an oral or anal equivalent and displays it on a screen." Wow! And it also makes toast. No more rectal thermometers—any parent who receives this as a gift will be eternally grateful. The Thermoscan retails for $100 to $120, but we've seen it for less in catalogs (the Safety Zone 1-800-999-3030 has it for $89).

## *Here are a few runners up for best baby gifts:*

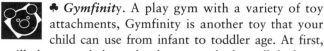 **♣ Gymfinity.** A play gym with a variety of toy attachments, Gymfinity is another toy that your child can use from infant to toddler age. At first, you'll place your baby under the gym to look at all the hanging toys. Later, you can take some of the pieces off, and he'll

play with them separately. Once he's standing and walking, you can adjust this activity gym so he can turn the gears and play with the toys from a standing position. We found this toy in the Baby Catalog of America (1-800-PLAY-PEN) for $38 and have even seen it at Toys R Us for as low as $29.99.

♣ *Baby Carrier.* Our favorite baby carrier is the Kapoochi by Medela. This brightly colored carrier can be used with the baby facing you in early months and then switched so that the baby faces outward as she gets older. This versatility is the Kapoochi's big plus. The cost: about $40. Call (800) 435-8316 or (815) 363-1246 for a store near you.

♣ *Baby Swing.* Love 'em or hate 'em, they get used. But, if you're buying this as a gift for someone else, check with the new parents to make sure they want one. Swings are available in a wide price range ($40 to $100; battery-powered models range from $70 to $100). You'll find them at most baby stores, Toys R Us, Target, and other discounters.

♣ *The Comfy Wipe Warmer.* We *highly* recommend this $25 gadget if you'd like to make changing Junior's diapers a more pleasant experience. Imagine using cold, wet toilet paper, and you'll understand the beauty of this little device! A wipe warmer keeps a box of wipes at a constant 98 degrees. The only negative: for some odd reason, we've had some AM radio interference when using our wipe warmer. But, hey, it's worth it.

## Top Five Gifts for New Moms & Dads

Let's not forget mom and dad, those tireless worker bees who are making all this baby stuff possible. We've got five gifts, from the practical to the whimsical, that would bring a smile to any parent.

1 A WATCH THAT'S ON BABY STANDARD TIME. Instead of numbers, this watch has "Nap, Eat, Poo" as the time keepers. Made by the Crazy Cat Lady Company, it can be ordered from the Celebration Fantastic catalog (800-527-6566, Item #2720, $49 plus shipping), which notes that this gift is "an adult size watch that features a drool and teething resistant band."

2 MOTHER'S LITTLE MIRACLE. Once you've had a baby, you can bet you'll be encountering some stains you've never seen before. We found this product seems to work wonders on anything that a baby can do. The cost: $9 per quart.

Once you use it, you'll be a believer. Call (310) 544-7125 or write to Mother's Little Miracle at 930 Indian Peak Rd., Suite 215, Rolling Hills Estates, CA 90274, to find a store near you.

3 BOOK LINKS MAGAZINE. There are a zillion children's books out there. How can a new parent tell what's worth the money? Book Links magazine is a bimonthly publication (published by the American Library Association) that reviews children's literature, from picture books on up. The cost is only $16.95 a year. To order, send a check for $16.95 to Book Links, 434 W. Downer St., Aurora, IL 60506.

4 HOW ABOUT A SUBSCRIPTION TO A PARENTING MAGAZINE? There are plenty of magazines out there to help new parents, including *Parenting*, *Child*, and *American Baby*. Check them out at your local newsstand or bookstore and send in one of the subscription cards for a gift the "keeps on giving."

5 HELP. But only when asked for. Yes, we think offering help before and after the baby is born is the best gift you can give new parents. Whether you put in for free baby-sitting time or simply stop by with a covered dish, new parents will be eternally grateful. But don't just assume they need you—always ask first!

## Gift Don'ts:

These are gifts you shouldn't buy unless parents specifically ask for them:

♣ *Diaper bags.* As far as gifts go, this one has "been there, done that." People have different ideas about what's useful, so ask before you buy. Better yet, buy something else and leave the choice up to the parents.

♣ *Baby bottle feeding system.* This may be offensive to a breastfeeding mom who might feel that her choice to breastfeed is being undermined (remember, new moms have very sensitive feelings!).

♣ *Gender specific clothes for girls.* Just because your friend is having a girl, don't rush out and buy lacy, frilly dresses in cotton-candy pink. Some moms prefer more toned down or less gender-cliche gifts.

♣ *Baby flatware.* A friend of ours received an Onieda Love Lasts baby flatware set that includes utensils for first-time eaters up to toddlers. This gift is useless until a baby is 4 to 6 months old, and even then we wonder about the practicality of baby flatware. Plastic spoons and forks are much more practical because they are gentler on the gums and will get tossed on the floor. In addition, expensive sterling silver spoons are really useless.

♣ *Walkers.* This product is an absolute no-no. There are too many injuries every year (over 21,000 just in 1989) involving walkers. A better bet is the Evenflo Exersaucer ($70 retail; as low as $55 in LiL' Things mega-stores—see the phone number earlier in this chapter for a store near you). The Exersaucer is a stationary toy that rocks, bounces, and approximates all the fun of walkers without the danger. Call Evenflo at (800) 837-9201 or (513) 773-3971 to find the store nearest you.

♣ *The right gift for the wrong season.* Your friend gives birth to a bouncing baby boy in August. Wouldn't a cute shorts and shirt outfit be a perfect gift? The answer is no, if you bought a six-month size. When the baby is the right size to fit into this outfit, it will be the dead of winter. Instead, buy the baby a summer outfit for next summer (in a 12 to 18 month size range).

♣ *Perhaps the silliest gift we ever heard about was a baby backpack.* Not a pack to carry the baby, mind you. No, this was a tiny backpack for the baby to carry. Perfect for those three-month-old nature hikers, we suppose.

What if you receive one of the "gift don'ts" for your baby? Don't despair. Consign it at a local thrift shop and buy something you really need. Make sure to keep all the packaging, instructions, tags and so on—it helps the consignment shop sell the item that much quicker.

## Announcements

### Getting Started

 Most printers take between five days and two weeks for delivery of standard announcements. You'll want to begin shopping for your design in advance, preferably when you're six or seven months pregnant. If you know the sex of your baby ahead of time, you can pick just one design. If it's going to be a surprise, however, you may want to either select two designs or one that is suitable for both sexes. When the baby is born, you phone in the vital statistics (length, weight, date, and time), and it's off to the printing presses.

## *Money Saving Secrets*

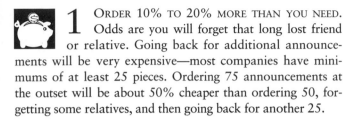

**1** ORDER 10% TO 20% MORE THAN YOU NEED. Odds are you will forget that long lost friend or relative. Going back for additional announcements will be very expensive—most companies have minimums of at least 25 pieces. Ordering 75 announcements at the outset will be about 50% cheaper than ordering 50, forgetting some relatives, and then going back for another 25.

**2** CHECK YOUR LOCAL NEWSPAPER FOR SALES. Many stationers have periodic sales when they discount 10% to 20% off announcements.

**3** COMPARE MAIL-ORDER PRICES. In Chapter 11, we list several catalogs that offer affordable options for baby announcements.

**4** CONSIDER ORDERING A BOX OF 100 SHEETS OF SPECIALTY LASER PAPER, DESIGNING THE ANNOUNCEMENT ON YOUR COMPUTER, AND THEN PRINTING IT OUT ON YOUR LASER PRINTER. Paper Direct catalog (800-272-7377) has a wonderful selection of appropriate stationery. We like the "New Arrival" (order #DT3041), with its stork and floral border. Price: $20 for a box of 100. Corresponding envelopes (order #RV4062 in Willow White) are $10.95 for 50. This requires a little more effort that the standard baby announcement but might be a fun project if you're so inclined.

**5** CHECK OUT THE PRICES FROM BABY ON A BUDGET. This mail-order company is featured in the following section as a best buy.

## *Best Buy*

### *Baby on a Budget*
(800) 575-2224

Looking for high-quality, name brand baby announcements at a discounted price? Baby on a Budget offers all the brands we review in the next section and more for 10% off the retail price. Not to mention the great service you get from owners and their staff. These guys really know baby announcements. Baby on a Budget can help you word announcements, find something unique for a special circumstance (twins, adoptions, etc.), or even help put together a custom announcement that you won't find anywhere else. Ask them about the "custom baby announcement" option—these announcements are personally drawn by an Austin, Texas, artist and feature your hobbies, interests, and more.

## Name Game

 While dozens of companies print baby announcements, we think the six companies reviewed and mentioned in this section are the best of the best. We should note that these printers do not sell directly to the public—you must place your order through one of their dealers (usually a retail stationary store). Call the phone numbers below to find the name of a dealer near you.

## The Ratings

★★★★ EXCELLENT—*our top pick!*
  ★★★ GOOD—*above average quality, prices, and creativity.*
    ★★ FAIR—*could stand some improvement.*
      ★ POOR—*yuck! could stand some major improvement.*

*Carlson Craft* ....................................................................★★★
*(800) 328-1782.* Carlson Craft can deliver your baby announcements in as little as seven days (although expect a 10-day wait for most orders). They cost on average $49 to $89 for 50 announcements. Carlson Craft has wonderful designs; we saw die-cut bunnies and border designs with cartoon baby clothes scattered about.

*Chase* ..........................................................................★★ ¹/2
*(508) 366-4441.* Chase's baby announcements include cute cartoons, twin announcements, and more—at very reasonable prices. Prices range from $42 to $92 for 50 announcements. The only negative: Chase takes a whopping three weeks for delivery.

*NRN Designs* ................................................................★★★
*(714) 898-6363.* California-based NRN Designs offers an unique option for baby announcements. While the printer doesn't have fancy die-cut designs, embossing or ribbons and bows, they do offer wonderful graphic designs. We were especially impressed with their Noah's Ark announcement—a hard to find design. Some of the envelopes even have coordinating graphics, creating a complete look from start to finish.

NRN's prices aren't cheap, but you can buy them in any increment so you don't have to waste money buying more than you need. You can purchase as few as 25 announcements with coordinating envelopes for $3 each. The price per announcement decreases as you buy more. For example, if you buy 125 or more, the price per announcement is only $2.

***William Arthur***................................................................★★★
*(800) 985-6581, (207) 985-6581.* No discussion of birth
announcements would be complete without the classical look
of William Arthur. These higher quality card stocks feature
cool type styles, linings, ink colors and bows. One particular
standout: a Beatrix Potter design in the palest of colors, suitable for boy or girl. Although 50 of these were $98, prices
start at $75. One note of caution: if you choose the pink par-
fait ink, select a heavier type style. This ink is a bit too pale
for delicate type styles.

## *If I had a million dollars . . .*

Looking for a unique announcement? Is money no object?
Consider checking out *Elite* (800-354-8321) and *Encore*
(800-526-0497). These printers have fabulous designs with
real ribbons and beautiful embossing—we even spotted a die-
cut baby shoe with real laces.

Encore's prices start at $73 and range up to $435 for 50
announcements. They require a minimum 50-piece purchase.
Elite's designs are priced from $74 to $389 for 50, with a
minimum order of 25.

Questions or comments? Did you receive an interesting gift that might make our list of all-time best or
worst baby gifts? **Call the authors at (303) 442-8792!**

# Chapter 10

## The Best Books for Baby & You

Each year some 40,000 new books are published. And if you stop by your local bookstore, you'll swear most of these are in the child care/parenting section. Which books are best? Which are a waste of time? We take a hard look at books for baby and you in this chapter.

First, however, a word on how to get any of these books. Unfortunately, most publishers don't have a toll-free order line. In most cases, you have to go to a bookstore or library. Remember that most bookstores and libraries can special order any book if they have the title, author, publisher, and ISBN (the International Standard Book Number). We've included this information in the reviews for your convenience.

If you're looking for a one-stop source for books and other educational materials, check out TeachSmart. With locations in Plantation, Florida and Dallas, Texas, TeachSmart is a superstore that has a wonderful selection of books, videos, educational toys, teaching supplies, and more. Most impressive is their software section, which includes several computers set up to demo the latest high-tech marvels. TeachSmart plans to expand nationwide; to find a store near you, call (817) 354-9960.

### Do You Need an "Anti-Hospital" Childbirth Book?

Depending on where you live, you might encounter hospitals that are not very "friendly" when it comes to natural childbirth. Several pregnancy books have been written with these hospitals in mind. Many have advice on how to deal with such hospitals—but do you need a book that takes such a hard-line when it comes to hospitals? Call or visit your hospital and ask some key questions:

? *Do you require enemas or shaving prior to delivery?*

? *Will you put an IV in as soon as I check into the hospital?*

? *Is 24-hour rooming with your newborn allowed or encouraged?*

? *Are on-demand feedings encouraged?*

? *What is the hospital's cesarean-section (c-section) rates?*

? *What childbirth preparatory classes are available and which method(s) are used?*

? *Are fathers allowed to attend births—what about other family members (children, including those under age 12) or friends?*

? *Are fathers allowed in the operating room for c-sections?*

? *Under what circumstances does the hospital use an electronic fetal monitor? Is it put on immediately upon arrival? Is it used only sporadically or constantly throughout labor?*

? *Does the hospital have special birthing rooms or just standard labor and delivery rooms? Will labor and delivery occur in the same room?*

? *Does the hospital have lactation specialists? Do they allow or encourage immediate breastfeeding after birth?*

? *Will I be allowed to eat or drink any light food or clear liquids while in labor?*

The response to these questions will help you determine how "user friendly" your hospital is. If any of their answers worry you, ask the hospital to explain the policy. Ask other couples who've given birth in that hospital for their impressions. Request a tour of the facilities with a maternity nurse or hospital administrator.

If it sounds like the hospital you intend to use for your birth is too controlling, you may want to shop for another hospital. If your doctor only has "privileges" at one hospital and you find that that hospital is unresponsive to your needs, consider reading one or more of the "anti-hospital" books we review in this section.

## *The Ratings*

★★★★  EXCELLENT—*our top pick!*
★★★  GOOD—*above average quality, prices, and creativity.*
★★  FAIR—*could stand some improvement.*
★  POOR—*yuck! could stand some major improvement.*

---

***Baby-Safe Houseplants & Cut Flowers*** ...................... ★★★★
By John & Delores Alber
*Published by:* Storey Communications, Inc., (800) 827-8673.
Also available through the Perfectly Safe mail-order catalog
(800) 837-5497.
*Copyright: 1993 • Cost: $12.95 • ISBN: 0-88266-869-2*

This is a great book for plant lovers with a baby on the
way. The first chapters detail important information on elimi-
nating poisoning risks and explain which poisons plants may
contain and their effects. The best part of this book is the
chapter titled "Buyer's Guide to Selecting Safe Houseplants,"
which includes a listing of all safe houseplants by categories
such as tall plants, plants suitable for hanging baskets, and
plants that do well in indirect light, among others. This list
should be carried with you when you shop for houseplants or
cut flowers.

The rest of the book catalogs common houseplants and cut
flowers and includes some drawings. We liked the comprehensive listings detailing each plant's Latin name, common
name, active toxins, and toxic plant parts. A description of
each plant is included as well as any data on its potential toxi-
city. The information is based on research from poison control centers and scientific studies. Finally, and most importantly, each listing contains the authors' recommendation for
displaying the plant or avoiding it entirely.

*Baby Safe Houseplants & Cut Flowers* also gives you
phone numbers and addresses for poison control centers
across the country. The index is wonderfully cross-referenced
by Latin name and by common name, so you can find the
plants you're looking for.

***The Best Toys, Books & Videos for Kids*** ...................★★★★
By Joanne Oppenheim and Stephanie Oppenheim
*Published by:* HarperCollins Publishers, Inc.,
10 E. 53rd St., New York, NY 10022
*Copyright: 1993 • Cost: $12.00 • ISBN: 0-06-273196-3*

As one of the most comprehensive review guides of its
kind, we highly recommend parents purchase a copy of *The*

*Best Toys, Books & Videos for Kids*. In addition to the products listed in the book's title, authors Joanne and Stephanie Oppenheim also cover audiotapes, software, and products for children with special needs.

Arranged by age, this 336-page guide includes a rating system, descriptions of products, line drawings, prices, and phone numbers for manufacturers. The no-nonsense reviews are clear and concise. We especially like the lists "Best Travel Toys for Infants," "Best First Birthday Gifts," and "Ten Blue-Chip Books Every Baby and Toddler Should Know."

The authors award four different ratings—platinum, gold seal, blue chip classic, and "Special Needs Adaptable Product" (SNAP). Our one complaint: the rating system is used only sporadically. Not every product is rated, making us wonder what the authors really think about it.

On the upside, the book provides safety tips throughout. For example, in the section on crib toys and mobiles, the authors advise that "mobiles should be removed by five months or whenever baby can reach out and touch them" to avoid strangulation.

*The Best Toys, Books & Videos for Kids* will grow with your child since products for kids up to age 10 are covered. In addition, the book has a section called "Using Ordinary Toys for Kids with Special Needs." To round out their commendable political correctness, they even give lists of "green" (ecologically minded) and multi-cultural products.

*Breastfeeding Secrets and Solutions* ........................★★★★
By Janice Graham
*Published by:* Pocket Books, 1230 Avenue of the Americas, New York, NY 10020
*Copyright:* 1993 • *Cost:* $10.00 • *ISBN:* 0-671-74963-3

Written by the author of *Your Pregnancy Companion*, I definitely looked forward to the release of this book, which came out near the end of my pregnancy.

This publication's biggest advantage is its very up-to-date information. Clearly written and based on excellent recent research, the book offered some new insights other books miss.

For example, *Breastfeeding Secrets and Solutions* has a chapter on the seven myths of breastfeeding. Myth number six is "Breastfeeding is an ineffective, unreliable method of birth control." The author asserts that breastfeeding for the first sixth months without any additional supplements to your baby's diet does indeed offer a reliable method of birth control. This runs contrary to the advice in many other breastfeeding books, whose overly-cautious authors tend to gloss over this topic.

I liked the illustrations of breast pumps and other visuals throughout the book. The best part of this book is its lack of preachiness. The author doesn't insist that you breastfeed your baby for years but offers gentle support for both extended breastfeeding and for women who must or want to end nursing earlier. Three cheers and four stars for this balanced approach.

### *Bringing Baby Home: An Owner's Manual for First-Time Parents* ..................................................★★★★

By Laura Zahn
*Published by:* Down to Earth Publications, 1426 Sheldon St., St. Paul, MN 55108 Distributed by and orders can be placed by calling: Voyageur Press
(800) 888-9653 or (612) 430-2210
*Cost: $8.95 • ISBN: 0-939301-91-1*

This is by far the *best* book we bought during our pregnancy. Being first-time parents, we were pretty clueless about what to expect or do when we brought our baby home. Bringing Baby Home offers real-life advice on what to expect, what to buy, and what the heck to do with our little bundle of joy.

*Bringing Baby Home* covers such deceptively simple topics as "how to pick up and hold a baby," "dipe 'n wipe," and, our favorite, "Pets—welcome to the family baby. . . maybe."

We especially liked the chapter about visitors ("or I'm coming to help"). Author Laura Zahn suggests that when you do have visitors, "don't offer refreshments and don't apologize for it." The book suggests you discourage friends and relatives from popping in to offer help, but if they do anyway, hand them a laundry list of things to do. "After all, if they really are there to help, they won't be offended by such a list."

Overall, Zahn's sense of humor and clear directions make this a simple, enjoyable book to read. Real advice for the real world—go buy it today.

### *The Complete Baby Checklist: A Total Organizing System for Parents* .......................................★★★

By Elyse Karline, Daisy Spier, and Mona Brody
*Published by:* Avon Books
1350 Avenue of the Americas, New York, NY 10019
*Copyright: 1992 • Cost: $10.00 • ISBN: 0-380-76347-8*

Yet another planner for new parents to keep track of all the various and sundry baby things, *The Complete Baby Checklist* is probably one of the best we've looked at.

Easy to read and use, the book starts with the preparations for baby's arrival and goes on to include mail-order sources, health records, even feeding tips and baby food recipes. I liked the total emphasis on the baby rather than on pregnancy. The result is a more compact planner that is easy to handle and use.

If you plan to borrow lots of things from friends and family, the "equipment/clothing loan record" will be invaluable. Other lists like the health records and baby-sitter instruction form are also extremely useful. On the downside, *The Complete Baby Checklist* does not have a "lay flat" binding, making it less convenient when you want to fill in the blanks. Despite this one flaw, the *Complete Baby Checklist* is a good attempt at organizing parents.

### *The Complete Book of Breastfeeding* .............................★★1/2
By Marvin Eiger, MD, and Sally Wendkos Olds
*Published by:* Workman Publishing Co.,
708 Broadway, New York, NY 10003
*Copyright: 1987 • Cost: $7.95 • ISBN: 0-89480-153-8*

*The Complete Book of Breastfeeding* lives up to its name, with coverage of just about every imaginable topic related to breastfeeding, from pregnancy through weaning. The authors include a discussion of the benefits of breastfeeding and a helpful chapter that addresses some of the questions and concerns women have.

The book is nicely organized, with charts, detailed drawings, and photos. Included are excellent discussions on subjects like "Ways to Build Up Your Milk Supply" and "Offering the Baby the Bottle" (which explores occasional supplemental bottles). The chapter on working moms is another plus: the authors are very supportive. We also agree with their criticism of hospitals that give new moms formula when they leave the hospital.

On the down side, *The Complete Book of Breastfeeding* is showing its stretch marks. Last revised in 1987, the book sadly has some advice that is out of date. For example, a whole section is devoted to advice on how to toughen the nipples during pregnancy in preparation for nursing. This is no longer recommended by the medical establishment, since the practice causes the release of the hormone oxytocin and may trigger early labor (not fun for anyone).

Not only does this book contain some outdated advice, it is also missing some of the most recent breastfeeding information. One study has shown that breastfeeding has been found to decrease the incidence of cancer in pre-menopausal women. This would be good for moms to know in case they need one more reason to breastfeed their babies.

We hope the authors update the book. In the meantime, we can only give it a lukewarm recommendation.

*Eating Expectantly: The Essential Eating Guide
and Cookbook for Pregnancy*.......................................★★★★
By Bridget Swinney, with Tracey Anderson
*Published by:* Fall River Press
PO Box 62578, Colorado Springs, CO 80962.
*Available by calling:* (800) 284-6667 or (719) 590-9464;
Fax (719) 594-6124. MC and VISA accepted.
*Copyright:* 1993 • *Cost:* $13.95 • *ISBN:* 0-9632917-3-4

One of the best nutrition books for pregnant women, *Eating Expectantly* offers common sense advice for real people. The author, a registered dietician, realizes that during your pregnancy you'll find it difficult to eat a completely perfect, well-balanced diet that doesn't contain some fat, chocolate, or fast food.

*Eating Expectantly* walks the reader through the three trimesters of pregnancy. Topics include what changes your body is going through, how the baby is growing, and which foods will help your pregnancy progress normally and result in a healthy new baby. We especially like Swinney's ten steps to a healthy diet, guidelines that thankfully don't come off as too preachy. In fact, the author asserts that you should "spare the extras" like fat and sugar but that "no food should be totally off limits." This certainly is quite a bit more realistic advice than we've read in other nutrition/diet books for pregnant women.

Another realistic aspect of *Eating Expectantly* is the author's unabashed realization that at some point you might visit a fast food restaurant (the horror!). Instead of slamming you for giving into your weakness for Big Macs and large fries, the book talks about which fast food options (as well as convenience foods and regular restaurant fare) are the most healthy. Author Swinney even has provided charts showing which fast foods are the highest in essential nutrients, such as calcium, vitamin C, zinc, etc. She even provides menu suggestions for many fast food restaurants.

Finally, the book ends with a collection of recipes for nutritious and delicious home-cooked meals, such as "Savory Oven Fried Chicken," "Colorado Stuffed Peppers," and "Chocolate Mocha Cake." Each recipe is accompanied by the dish's fat, calorie, carbohydrate, and protein content.

Overall, this is one of the best pregnancy nutrition books we've read. We like the common sense approach and the non-judgmental attitude. After all, pregnant women are only human, and an occasional piece of cake will probably pass your lips. This book helps you realize you can enjoy a little cheating now and then without harming your baby.

*Games Babies Play*.........................................................★★★
By Vicki Lanski
*Published by:* The Book Peddlers 18326 Minnetonka Blvd.,
Deephaven, MN 55391; (612) 475-3527
*Copyright: 1993 • Cost: $8.95 • ISBN: 0-916773-33-7*

*Games Babies Play* is a wonderful collection of entertaining games to play with babies, from birth to twelve months. This is the perfect book for the first-time parent who doesn't know or can't remember the words and games from their childhood, like "Eentsy-weensty Spider," "To Market, To Market," and more.

Vicki Lansky not only gives you the words to all the best rhymes but also offers instructions for games to develop verbal and physical skills. For example, she recommends helping your baby practice rolling over by laying her on one side of a blanket, picking up the blanket's edge, and then rolling your baby over.

All the games in the book are arranged by age and skill level. You'll find finger games and plenty of lullabies in the birth to three month section; more physical skills like knee rides and airplane rides in the three to six month section; independence-developing games like "kitchen patrol" (playing with pots and pans) and ball rolling in the six to nine month section; and small muscle control practice like spilling/pouring games and playing with tape recorders in the nine to twelve month chapter.

Each section begins with a little information on the developmental milestones to expect at each age. The author also includes cautions and safety tips into her game descriptions to help remind parents about what's safe. All in all, this is a great book that should be a part of your parental bookshelf.

*Mommy Made\* and Daddy Too: Home Cooking
for a Healthy Baby & Toddler* ....................................★★★★
By Martha and David Kimmel with Suzanne Goldenson
*Published by:* Bantam Books
666 Fifth Ave., New York, NY 10103
*Copyright: 1990 • Cost: $13.95 • ISBN: 0-553-34866-3*

As founders of the country's first commercial, fresh baby food business, the authors of *Mommy Made* offer their recipes and expertise to help other parents become baby food chefs. The book's premise is that you can make fresh, nutritious food for your child without a major investment of time and energy.

And that's just the beginning. The best part of the book is the hints and advice the authors give about the process of feeding your child solid foods. For example, they start out by stressing the importance of testing foods slowly to find out if your baby has any allergies or intolerances.

One reason I found this book indispensable is the removable chart in the back, which lists all the foods that you will be introducing to your child and when each food should be added to his or her diet. There is space on the chart to record the date the food was first introduced and to note any subsequent allergies or reactions. We found this chart an invaluable tool to keep such reactions straight.

Each recipe includes information on when to introduce the food, whether it's best for beginning eaters ("Primary Purees"), older babies ("Spoon and finger food for bigger babies"), or toddlers ("Table food for toddlers and grown-ups, too"). In fact, this cookbook isn't just for beginning eaters. Older children (as well as adults) will find recipes that appeal to a more sophisticated palate.

We also liked the other details covered in *Mommy Made*, such as food storage and transport and the "psychology of feeding the small." This section includes information about such cases as the toddler who insists on eating *only* peanut butter and jelly sandwiches six days a week and other interesting problems.

This is one of the best and most interesting baby food cookbooks we've come across. The authors' experience teaching seminars and making their own line of fresh, healthy baby food really makes it a sensible, useful guide for parents who want to get away from the grey matter in the commercial baby food jars.

*The New Child Health Encyclopedia* ...........................★★★
By Boston Children's Hospital
*Published by:* Dell Publishing
666 Fifth Ave., New York, NY 10103
*Copyright: 1987 • Cost: $19.95 • ISBN: 0-385-29541-3*

Boston Children's Hospital has complied a massive guide to child health and disease. This massive book weighs in at 721 pages! Wow! Over 100 different medical consultants contributed to the encyclopedia, including such heavy-hitters as T. Berry Brazelton.

So what do you get with this book, besides a handy paper weight? Just about everything you wanted to know about children's health, and probably a few things you didn't want to know.

The book starts out with some brief information on child development and accident prevention. The bulk of the *New Child* (over 600 pages) focuses on diseases and their symptoms. Each disease gets the star treatment—with detailed information on its cause, diagnosis, complications, treatment, and prevention. There is even information on obscure maladies such as hair loss and growing pains. We learned that the latter is not actually caused by growing, but by vigorous use of underdeveloped muscles and bones.

In some cases the advice seems a little unrealistic; the information on avoiding pet injuries includes advising your child to lie still on the ground when confronted with an aggressive animal. Sure. Despite these peculiarities, *New Child Health's Encyclopedia* is a helpful and comprehensive sourcebook. Even with its large size, we found it quite easy to use.

*Now That You're Pregnant* .........................................★★¹/2
By Louise Edeiken and Johanna Antar
*Published by:* Macmillan Publishing Co.
866 Third Ave., New York, NY 10022
*Copyright: 1992 • Cost: $12.00 • ISBN: 0-02-079031-7*

One of the first fill-in-the-blank pregnancy planners, *Now That You're Pregnant* provides an organizational format to plan for your pregnancy and the months following your baby's birth.

Beginning with a chapter on "Preparing to Get Pregnant," the book leads you through each month of pregnancy with checklists to help you decide where you want to deliver your baby, how to interview pediatricians, and how to research maternity leave policies at your office. The authors include useful appendices with space for personal information, "borrowed" lists for equipment and toys, and shopping lists. A layette checklist is included as well, plus some resources for magazines, books, and mail-order catalogs. Their list of support organizations is useful, too. For the budget-minded couple, the authors even include a spreadsheet on finances in the back.

Overall, we thought *Now That You're Pregnant* was a well thought out compendium of checklists and schedules to help expecting parents stay organized. Our only criticism: we thought there wasn't always enough room in each segment for notes.

*Take This Book to the Obstetrician With You*................★★★
By Karla Morales and Charles Inlander
*Published by:* Addison-Wesley Publishing Co., Reading, MA
*Copyright: 1991 • Cost: $9.95 • ISBN: 0-201-52380-9*

This book's subtitle is "A Consumer Guide to Pregnancy and Childbirth," and that's exactly what it is—an in-your-face, take-control-of-the-situation primer to navigating the medical establishment during your pregnancy and childbirth.

Authors Morales and Inlander are members of the People's Medical Society, a medical consumer group that advocates a much more proactive role for consumers in the childbirth process.

This book has one of the best chapters we've seen on choosing a birth practitioner (obstetrician, family practitioner, nurse, or lay midwife), as well an excellent discussion of birth settings (hospital, birth centers, or home births). Instead of merely explaining the differences between the options, Take This Book gives you questions to ask during the first visit and opinionated advice as to what is the best answer in each situation.

We really used this book. The chapter "The Birth" was particularly helpful, with detailed information on everything from episiotomies to induction of labor. The advice covers both vaginal births and cesarean sections.

*Take this Book* also includes several good appendices, including a pregnant patient's bill of rights and responsibilities. We liked the sample birth plan, as well as the listing of medical licensing boards in all 50 states (and their phone numbers). The glossary is excellent as well.

So, should you read it? Yes. The aggressive tone may turn off some readers—this is definitely an anti-hospital book dedicated to exposing common abuses and problems with childbirth in the U.S. Unlike books written by nurses and others who are part of the medical establishment, Take this Book's outsider mentality is a refreshing and needed approach.

*Welcome to Club Mom: The Adventure Begins* ............★★★
By Leslie Lehr Spirson
*Published by:* CompCare Publishers, 2415 Annapolis Ln., Minneapolis, MN 55441; (800) 328-3330
*Copyright:* 1991 • *Cost:* $9.95 • *ISBN:* 0-89638-255-9

The introduction to Club Mom claims the book is a humorous guide with an emphasis somewhere between the typical pregnancy book and the average parenting guide. With chapters like "Pit Stops," "Is There Sex After Childbirth?" and "Nap When the Baby Naps" (in the section called Membership Myths), author Spirson discusses at length the many hilarious truths about being pregnant, having a new baby, and (hopefully) having a life after it all. Amazingly, although you'd think Club Mom is merely a comic send-up of motherhood, Spirson does offer some real advice amidst the hilarity. For example, in the "Now What?" chapter, she addresses what to do once you get your bundle of joy home from the hospital:

> "*Even if you read every book, watch every video-tape, and spy on every mother you know, taking care of the baby will still be a huge and mysterious adjustment. Don't despair. Trust your instincts. All the baby wants now is to get back inside you. All you can do to help is hold the baby as much as possible, feed her whenever she's hungry and keep her warm and dry.*"

We highly recommend giving *Club Mom* as a gift to a pregnant friend or relative. Or read it yourself as a break from all the heavy reading you'll be doing about colic, episiotomies, and spider veins. A little levity is a must, and this book will help put things in perspective.

*What to Expect When You're Expecting* ...................★★★¹/2
By Arlene Eisenberg, Heidi Eisenberg Murkoff, and Sandee Eisenberg Hathaway, RN.
*Also from the same authors:*
*What to Eat When You're Expecting* ....................................★
*What to Expect the First Year* .....................................★★★★
*Published by:* Workman Publishing,
708 Broadway, New York, NY 10003

If you're pregnant, the odds are you won't be able to escape hearing about the "What to Expect" series, a trio of books that has reached legendary status. The guides have combined sales that have reached into the *millions* and a fanatical following of readers. Because of their influence, we wanted to do an extended review of each book.

*What to Expect When You're Expecting* (Copyright 1991; $10.95; ISBN ) was first published in 1984 and then revised with a second edition in 1991. The book's organization is excellent—the comprehensive month-by-month format makes the book easy to read. We liked the charts, illustrations, and absence of medical jargon. The beginning of each chapter covers such topics as "what you may look like" and "what you may be feeling."

But what about the advice? Well, it's hit or miss. Much of the information is good, but the book just isn't as comprehensive as we'd like. Several moms-to-be we interviewed also echoed this criticism. For example, there's no discussion of soreness in the abdomen late in pregnancy. *While What to Expect* omits this, other books like the *Pregnancy Companion* cover this subject.

The skimpy 10-page section in the back of the book titled "Fathers are Expectant Too" was pathetically short. We would have liked to see more info for fathers integrated into the book itself. Another gripe: the book starts out with a chapter entitled "Are You Pregnant?" and ends with "Preparing for the Next Baby." Information about preparing to get pregnant (getting a physical, improving your diet, etc.) should be at the front of the book, not the back.

The complaints above are minor compared to our biggest beef with *What to Expect When You're Expecting*—check out the authors' "Best Odds" diet (Chapter 4). They have crafted a diet plan that is similar to the regimen used by prisons in third world countries to torture inmates. Although the advice has merit (avoid high-fat foods, eat lots of vegetables), just take a look at this piece of advice: "The Best Odds diet recommends eating no refined sugars at all during pregnancy."

Excuse me? Are they kidding? While many expectant mothers aspire to cut back on sweets, going nine months without an ice-cream cone just doesn't happen in the real world. Their recommended fat intake is another shocker—the authors advise restricting this to two tablespoons of high fat a day. Basically, one bagel with cream cheese would shoot your fat allowance for the whole day.

To add insult to injury, the authors turned the "Best Odds Diet" into a separate book, entitled *What to Eat When You're Expecting* (Copyright 1986; $8.95; ISBN 0-89480-015-9). This flawed and useless guide to eating while you're pregnant really should be classified as fiction! In the section on dining out, the authors rule out Mexican restaurants but recommend French cuisine. At Mexican restaurants, the authors claim that "refried beans are laced with lard" and that "you're not likely to find fresh vegetables." Apparently, the authors haven't been to a Mexican restaurant lately—if they had, they'd note that many are replacing the lard in beans with olive oil and that salsas are brimming with fresh vegetables high in vitamin C. Instead of blanket admonitions to skip certain cuisines, we'd have much rather seen a dish-by-dish discussion of what's in and what's out.

Other books on this subject (most notably *Eating Expectantly*; see review earlier in this chapter) are more comprehensive and cover such real-world situations as eating at fast food restaurants.

Fortunately, the authors redeem themselves with *What to Expect the First Year*, a comprehensive reference book that weighs in at 671 pages. Divided into three sections, it gives a month-by-month look at what your baby is doing, what to expect during doctor visits, and so on. We liked the information on feeding your baby and on child development milestones. Another plus: detailed sections on illnesses (including a dosage chart for Tylenol based on your baby's weight) are great, as is a reference section with recipes, home remedies, and height/weight charts.

As with the other books in this series, the organization is good but has its drawbacks. The information on feeding your baby solids is scattered among several chapters, frustrating any attempt to get a comprehensive look at the advice. Another problem: this book (like the other two) goes far too long between revisions. At this writing, *What To Expect the First Year* has been five years without a revision—that means important medical developments, the latest diet advice and so on is missing.

So what's the bottom line on the "What to Expect" series? We recommend buying *What to Expect When You're Expecting* and *What to Expect the First Year*. Plan to augment these two books with a couple of other titles we recommend in this chapter, especially in the case of *What to Expect When You're Expecting*. Forget about the *What To Eat* book—check it out of the library if you're curious.

*The Womanly Art of Breastfeeding* ..............................★★★
By La Leche League International
*Published by:* Penguin, 375 Hudson St.,
New York, NY 10014. Available through the La Leche
League Catalog (708) 519-7730; Fax (708) 455-0125.
*Copyright:* 1991 • *Cost:* $11.00 • *ISBN:* 0-452-26623-8

*The Womanly Art of Breastfeeding* is probably the most widely read book on breastfeeding in the world, and with good reason. La Leche League was founded in 1956 by seven women who wanted to buck the bottlefeeding trend and return to breastfeeding their babies. The book is the result of their own experiences and the experiences of the many women whom they have counseled and interviewed. Now in its fifth edition, the book still offers tremendous support and information for today's breastfeeding moms.

We found the majority of the information in the book helpful. Especially nice were the quotes and personal experiences of the many moms interviewed by the writers. These women offer advice and creative solutions for the special problems and situations that arise with breastfeeding.

Nevertheless, there were several details in the book that could use improvement. For example, we found ourselves getting rather irritated with the constant plugs at the end of each chapter for La Leche League support groups and written materials (books, pamphlets, etc.). One listing at the end of the book would have been enough of a reminder for us. Moreover, we were uncomfortable with the pressure that this book places on mothers to stay home with their babies until they are three years old. Hello? Last we checked, it was the 1990s. For most moms, this is a worthy but often impossible goal. And the book's assertion that you will save enough money on your taxes and childcare costs to offset any lost income is just silly. As a result, this book treats the problems faced by working mothers in a cursory manner.

Our next beef: the roll of the father as a parental partner is missing-in-action in *The Womanly Art of Breastfeeding*. No wonder many men don't seem to want to be involved in the early raising of infants—the writers of the book seem to want to elevate mothers to the sole caregiver. The rare references to fathers makes you wonder if Murphy Brown was a contributing editor.

Despite all this, we still highly recommend *The Womanly Art of Breastfeeding*. The authors take their years of experience and combine it with wise words of encouragement to create a book that stands the test of time.

*Your Child's Health: The Parents' Guide to*
*Symptoms, Emergencies, Common Illnesses,*
*Behavior and School Problems* .....................................★★$^1$/2
   By Barton D. Schmitt, MD
   *Published by:* Bantam Books
   666 Fifth Ave., New York, NY 10103
   *Copyright: 1991 • Cost: $16.00 • ISBN: 0-553-35339-X*

This huge 600-page tome was given to us by our doctor. *Your Child's Health* covers everything you wanted to know about your baby's growth and development.

We liked the first section on emergencies and injuries, which includes tips and advice on dealing with both minor (insect bites) and major (electric shock) calamities. Another plus: the information on common illnesses includes such good advice as how to measure your baby's temperature.

This book's organization is just okay. Tips and subsections are bulleted for easy identification; however, in using the book, we found it took some effort to find the information we needed. For example, information on choosing good shoes was not provided in the section on feet in the chapter "Bones and Joints," but instead in the chapter "Growth, Development and Safety."

Nevertheless, we recommend *Your Child's Health*, which was awarded *Child Magazine's* Book Award. This expansive guide should be a part of your collection of reference books on your baby's health.

*Your Pregnancy Companion: A Month by Month
Guide to All You Need to Know Before,
During and After Pregnancy* ........................................★★★★
By Janis Graham
*Published by:* Pocket Books,
1230 Avenue of the Americas, New York, NY 10020
*Copyright:* 1991 • *Cost:* $9.00 • *ISBN:* 0-671-68557-0

This was one of my favorite books during my pregnancy simply because it was so clear and direct. There's no filler or pussy-footing around in this paperback book.

The book's month-by-month format helps you find your way easily. Each chapter tells you a little bit about what your growing baby is doing, as well as about the changes going on in your body. The author also covers your doctor's appointments, diet, exercise, feelings, and lifestyle changes. I really appreciated the consistency of each chapter.

Most of the information in the book mirrored what my doctor was telling me, as well as what other pregnancy books mentioned. In fact, when I couldn't find an answer to a question in one of the other books, *Your Pregnancy Companion* almost always filled in the gap. And with its forthright language, it gave me all the facts I needed about any situation.

For example, I found myself having pains in my groin area in my seventh month. This didn't seem to be addressed in other books, and I was rather concerned about it. *Your Pregnancy Companion* explained that this was a normal condition known as "round ligament pain." The ligaments supporting the uterus often get over-stretched, causing discomfort.

Overall, I highly recommend this book as an excellent addition to your pregnancy library.

Questions or comments? Did you discover a great book you'd like to share with our readers?
**Call the authors at (303) 442-8792!**

# Chapter 11

*Do it By Mail: Catalogs for Clothes, Baby Products & More*

Tired of the mall? Think those sky-high prices at specialty stores are highway robbery? Sit back in your favorite chair and do all your shopping for your baby by phone. With over 8000 mail-order catalogs out there, you can buy everything from bedding to furniture, clothes to safety items. We've rounded up the best 40 catalogs for baby and you—and they're all free for the asking!

Before we get to the reviews, a word on being a smart catalog shopper. Ordering from a mail-order company that's miles away from you can be a nerve-racking experience—we've all heard the stories of scamsters that bilk money from unsuspecting consumers. As a result, there are a few precautions any smart shopper should take:

**1** ALWAYS USE YOUR CREDIT CARD. Credit card purchases are covered by federal consumer protection laws. Basically, the law says if you don't get what you were promised, you must get a refund. Technically known as Federal Regulation C, the rule says you have 60 days to dispute the charge with the company that issued your credit card—but first you must try to work out the problem with the merchant directly. Call your credit card company to determine the exact procedures for disputing a charge.

What if you pay with cash or a check? If the company goes out of business, you're out of luck. We've interviewed some consumers who feel squeemish about giving out their credit card number over the phone. While you always have to be careful, ordering from a reputable mail-order company (like the ones below) with a credit card is very safe, in our opinon. And the consumer protection benefits of using a credit card far outweigh any risks.

**2** MOST COMPANIES HAVE RETURN POLICIES that enable you to get a refund or credit within a specified period of time. Make sure to confirm this before you order. Also ask who pays for the shipping on a returned item—some companies pay for this, while others don't.

**3** ALWAYS KEEP ALL INVOICES, RECEIPTS, AND ORDER CONFIRMATIONS. Inspect all packages thoroughly upon arrival and keep the original packing, just in case you decide to return the item.

**4** KEEP A LOG OF WHOM YOU SPOKE TO AT THE COMPANY. Get any names and order confirmation numbers and keep them in a safe place.

**5** CONFIRM DELIVERY METHODS. Some companies use United Parcel Service to deliver merchandise. The problem? UPS can't deliver to post office boxes and often requires you to be present when the package is delivered. If you're not at home, they leave a call slip, and you've got to go to the nearest UPS office (which could be a long drive) to pick up the item. A possible solution: give your work address and specify any floor, suite number, or building location for the delivery. Or you could request delivery by the U.S. Postal Service.

**6** THE TIME REQUIRED FOR SHIPPING WILL VARY WIDELY. Some companies offer two to three-day delivery, while others may take weeks. Customized items (like monogrammed bedding) take the longest. As for the cost, mail-order catalogs use a variety of methods to determine shipping charges. Some charge a flat fee, while others use a sliding scale based on the dollar amount of the order or the weight of the package. Please note that the prices we quote below do not include shipping.

**7** USE THAT 24-HOUR FAX NUMBER. Not all catalogs have operators standing by around the clock. However, many have fax numbers that you can use to place an order at any time.

**8** NEARLY ALL MAIL-ORDER CATALOGS ARE FREE FOR THE ASKING. Even though some have a price printed on the cover, we've never had to pay for one.

## *The Ratings*

★★★★ EXCELLENT—*our top pick!*
★★★ GOOD—*above average quality, prices, and creativity.*
★★ FAIR—*could stand some improvement.*
★ POOR—*yuck! could stand some major improvement.*

## National Parenting Center

Looking for more consumer information on the latest baby products? The National Parenting Center is a California-based group that produces a bi-annual "Seal of Approval" product report. The 10-page book reviews the latest toys, infant and music products, computer programs, and educational products. A one-year membership for $19.95 gets you this report, a monthly subscription to the "Parent Talk" newsletter, and various discounts on child-rearing products. For more information, call (818) 225-8990 or write to The National Parenting Center, 22801 Ventura Blvd., Suite 110, Woodland Hills, CA 91367.

## General Catalogs

*The Baby Catalog of America.* .....................................★★★ ¹/₂
    *To Order Call:* (800) PLAYPEN (1-800-752-9736) or
    (203) 931-7760; Fax (203) 931-7764
    *Or write to:* Baby Catalog of America, 719-721 Campbell Ave.,
    West Haven, CT 06516.
    *Credit Cards Accepted:* MC, VISA, AMEX, Discover.

 We just love this catalog. With super discounts on everything from baby products to toys, strollers to car seats, the Baby Catalog of America is a must.

Want a stroller by such premium names as Emmaljunga or Peg Perego but don't want to pay full retail? We found these and other strollers in the catalog. For example, Perego's Amico stroller is seen at up to $250 in retail stores, but you can get it for just $187.15 in the Baby Catalog (that's a savings of 25%!). They also carry such famous brands as Aprica, Inglesina, Century, and Graco.

The catalog carries a myriad of products, from nursery items like wipe warmers ($19) to the famous Diaper Genie ($26.44). Car seats? They got them, from such famous brands as Evenflo. We also saw toys, swings, books, tapes, portable cribs, baby monitors, and more.

The catalog itself isn't much to look at—most of the products are featured in murky black and white photos or illustrations. Another bummer: for some items, you must call to get a price quote. For example, the Baby Catalog of America carries "top brand crib bedding" from such makers as Lambs & Ivy, Nojo and Quiltex. However, you have to call for prices. We did just that for Lambs & Ivy's "Paradise" line and unfortunately found the prices to be disappointing. The comforter was $79.99, the dust ruffle $31.99, the headboard bumper $71.99, and a solid sheet $12.99. Other discount sources (see Chapter 3) have better prices on bedding and more top-quality brands.

Despite this letdown, we thought the Baby Catalog is worth checking out. We should note that the Baby Catalog is a division of the Baby Club of America—join the club ($25 annual membership) and you get an additional 10% discount off catalog prices (wow!) and a special price sheet that features baby care products not in the catalog (like disposable diapers and formula). You also get a newsletter, information on special closeouts, and exclusive sales for members. Another plus: you can sign up three "associate members" (family or friends) for free, and they get the same discounts.

*Exposures*................................................................★★ *1/2*

*To Order Call:* (800) 222-4947; Fax (414) 231-6942.
*Shopping Hours:* 8:00 am-Midnight, seven days a week.
*Or write to:* Exposures, 1 Memory Ln., P.O. Box 3615, Oshkosh, WI 54903.
*Credit Cards Accepted:* MC, VISA, AMEX, Discover.

If you're like us, you'll probably snap 10,000 pictures of your baby before she turns one. When our baby was born, the stock price of Kodak must have tripled overnight. But where to put all these wonderful snapshots? Call Exposures, a fantastic catalog that sells an amazing variety of picture frames and photo albums. You'll also find photo-related gifts, curio cabinets, and photograph storage systems.

Frame styles range from the basic (a 8" x 10" wood design for $19.95 in teak or rosewood) to the sophisticated (a gold, puffed-quilt frame with a diamond-shaped opening was a hefty $445). Some of the products geared for new parents include a nautilus frame with childlike fish and shells on a blue border ($15-$19). They also carry an "archival baby memories book" ($49), baby's first-year photo calendar ($15.95), and magnetic fridge frames. We love Exposure's photo albums, from the basic leather styles ($49,95) to a funky leather and wood option called the "Sola." The latter design has black leather cutouts on a natural wood cover for $44. Scrapbooks are also scattered throughout, including oversized options capable of storing 11" x 14" photos ($49.95).

Our only complaint: the service from Exposures can be inconsistent. The company had so many problems shipping orders last Christmas that they told us in early December that orders wouldn't arrive until January. Phone operators also tend to be a little gruff. Because the catalog's offerings are so unique, we hope they can iron out these wrinkles.

### J.C. Penney ........................................................★★★

*To Order Call*: (800) 222-6161. Ask for the following catalogs: Baby and You, For Baby, and Starting Small.
*Shopping Hours*: 24 hours a day, seven days a week.
*Credit Cards Accepted*: MC, VISA, JC Penney, AMEX, Discover.

J. C. Penney has been selling baby products for over 90 years. Their popular mail-order catalog has three free "mini-catalogs" that should be of particular interest to parents-to-be.

The 44-page "Baby and You" catalog features a wide variety of maternity clothes, plus a selection of cribs, linens, and furniture. Perhaps the best aspect of Penney's offerings is their collection of career maternity wear at affordable prices. For example, we saw a rayon/polyester pantsuit with cardigan jacket that had an attached laced vest for just $82.

Other "career essentials" include three-piece ensembles (jacket, pants, and skirt) for $69 to $72. As for more casual clothes, simple cotton/rayon chemise dresses in "spring prints" are just $39 to $42. A selection of nightgowns, swim suits, lingerie and hose round out the offerings in this catalog.

"For Baby" expands on the furniture offered in "Baby and You" with over 51 pages of cribs, linens, mattresses, safety items, car seats, strollers, swings, and even a few pages of baby clothes. The crib section features such famous brand names as Cosco, Bassett, and Child Craft. The best deal: a Child Craft "sculptured" crib in white maple with a single-drop side at $229. If you buy both the crib and mattress, Penney's offers discounts of $15 to $50 off the crib—a pretty good deal. Other choices range from a Cosco metal crib for $139 to a Bassett Shaker-style crib for $280.

The linen choices in "For Baby" include well-known brands such as Glenna Jean, Judi's Originals, NoJo, Lambs and Ivy, and Red Calliope. Prices are little high, but the package sets are good deals. For example, both Penney's and the Right Start Catalog sell the popular "Farm Animals" design from the Boynton for Babies line. The prices for the individual items (quilt, bumper, sheet, and dust ruffle) from Penney's were each $2 to $3 more expensive than the Right Start. (The sheet, for example, was $18 at Penney's while just $16 from the Right Start.) However, if you buy the three-piece linen set (quilt, bumper, and sheet) from Penney's, you get a better deal ($99 vs. $121 from the Right Start). Penney's also carries matching accessories for every line, such as mobiles, wall hangings, wallpaper, and curtain valences.

Car seats range from $40 to $110, including brands such as Evenflo, Century, and Cosco. A basic car seat runs $70—about the same price we saw it for at Toys R Us. The stroller selection is a little small but includes such good names as Aprica and Century. The "Landau" stroller from Aprica is

$160, and the popular Century 4-in-1 stroller is $119. Other miscellaneous items in the "For Baby" catalog include the Safety 1st baby monitor at $39, a diaper bag set for $30, and a diaper wipe warmer for $20.

Penney's third catalog "Starting Small" concentrates more on clothing, with sizes from infant to pre-school. Once again the selection of brand names is a mixed bag of some famous labels (Carter's and OshKosh) and some not-so-famous offerings (Oki-Dokie and Bright Future). We saw Carter's t-shirts, stretchies, receiving blankets, and layette gowns. One nice deal: Penney's offers discounts if you order two or more packages of certain items. For example, buy two packages of Carter's thermal blankets ($14 each) and you save $2 per package. A girl's cotton coverall with a bright floral pattern from OshKosh was $30 (buy two or more and they are $26 each).

So what's the bottom line? Penney's offers a good selection of maternity clothes, furniture, linens, and other baby products at decent (if not rock-bottom) prices. The best deals may be the maternity clothes and linens. On the downside, many of the furniture items come unassembled. We'd stick with the major name brands—some of the brands (such as the cribs imported from Indonesia) were a little too obscure for our taste. The catalogs could be organized better—the furniture catalog mixes prices for cribs, linens, and other accessories on the same page, making price comparisons difficult. Nevertheless, if you live in a remote area or in a town with sky-high prices, the Penney's catalog offers a good deal: name brands at decent prices.

### *Lands' End* ★★★★

*To Order Call:* (800) 356-4444; Fax (800) 332-0103.
*Shopping Hours:* 24 hours a day, seven days a week.
*Or write to:* Lands' End Inc., 1 Lands' End Ln.,
Dodgeville, WI 53595.
*Credit Cards Accepted:* MC, VISA, AMEX, Discover.
*Discount Outlets:* They also have 11 outlet stores in Iowa, Illinois and Wisconsin—call the number above for the location nearest to you.

Most people think of Lands' End as an affordable source for casual adult clothing. It might suprise you to learn the same catalog has a nice selection of kids clothing, outdoor wear, bedding, and even diaper bags.

While perusing their children's catalog (call the number above and request Lands' End's catalog for kids), we noted a selection of basics including their cotton knit coveralls and coordinating shirts. The coveralls come in six bright, solid colors, while the white cotton shirts have coordinating trim and are decorated with cute ducks, sailboats, balloons, and blocks. The whole outfit (shirt and coverall) is just $32.50. Considering we've seen coveralls alone that *start* at $30 in baby specialty stores, we think this is a great deal. Another outfit we liked was the rugby-striped playsuit. In fact, we wanted to buy this outfit even before we had a baby! This heavyweight cotton coverall is only $29.50 or if you buy two or more, a mere $25 each.

If the winters in your locale are long and cold, check out Lands' End's great winter clothes. They carry a wide selection of baby snowsuits and jackets, including one style that has white snowmen adorning a navy blue background ($59.50)— too cute. Polartec pants and hooded jackets are another option for your baby. Cost: only $47 for the set.

While the clothes are wonderful, our favorite Lands' End items are their diaper bags. The catalog sells not one but three diaper bags: The Do-It-All diaper bag ($29.50), the Deluxe ($45), and the Little Tripper ($10).

The Do-it-All is a best buy. Made of tough, heavy-duty nylon fabric (the same as Lands' End's luggage), it features a large main compartment for diapers and wipes, a clip for your keys, and a detachable waterproof pouch for wet clothes. Then there's another zippered compartment for a blanket or change of clothes, a waterproof changing pad, and an expandable pocket for books and small toys. Outside, you'll find another zippered pocket and a small pouch that has a Velcro close. And, if that weren't enough, the bag also has two large pockets for bottles at each end.

Whew! That's a lot of stuff. But how does it work in the real world? Wonderful, as a matter of fact. We've hauled this thing on cross-country airline trips, on major treks to the mountains, and more. It still looks new. At $29.50, it isn't cheap, but considering the extra features, durability, and versatility, we think it's worth the money.

How about those quick trips to the store? We bought the Little Tripper for this purpose and have been happy. With a strap that let's you wear it around your waist (like a fanny pack) or over your shoulder, the Little Tripper has a small main compartment that holds a few diapers and small case for wipes, as well as a clip for your keys. An outside zippered compartment holds a checkbook. For $10, it's a good value.

In case you need more room, the Deluxe ($45) is a bigger version of the Do-It-All (about 30% larger). It has a bigger changing pad, two zippered pouches for wet things, a zippered compartment on the outside, and larger bottle pockets lined with Thinsulate to keep food cool or warm.

And here's the best feature: Land's End's diaper bags don't look like diaper bags—no pink elephant prints or the words "BABY" plastered on the side. The solid red or blue Do-It-All will easily segue into a carry-on after your baby is big enough to tote her own stuff (yes, that will happen some day).

As if this weren't enough, Lands' End also has a catalog called "Coming Home With Lands' End," which features bedding and towels. Among the standouts in the bedding section: the Piglets "ensemble," which is covered with line drawings of little pigs, each with a different colored snout. The other more "feminine" bedding set featured pastel flowers. These mostly cotton, 200-thread-count bedding sets run $13 for the sheet, $36 for the comforter, $38 for the bumpers, and $18 for the dust ruffle—very affordable. Cotton blankets in pastel colors range from $16.50 to $18. Of course, the catalog's offerings change depending on the season. For example, we saw reasonably priced flannel sheets in the fall/winter catalog.

*Lilly's Kids (Lillian Vernon)* .........................................★★★
    *To Order Call:* (800) 285-5555, (804) 430-5555;
    Fax (804) 430-1010
    *Shopping Hours:* 24 hours a day, seven days a week.
    *Or write to:* Lillian Vernon, Virginia Beach, VA 23479.
    *Credit Cards Accepted:* MC, VISA, AMEX,
    Discover, Diner's Club.

An offshoot of the popular Lillian Vernon catalog, Lilly's Kids is a collection of gifts and toys just for kids. At 72 pages, Lilly's Kids is chock full of interesting items.

The catalog is well organized and provides information about age appropriateness with each toy's description. For example, a wooden snail pull toy ($9.98) with bright red and green accents is appropriate for ages 1 1/2 to 4. All the wooden toys throughout the catalog are stained or painted with nontoxic finishes.

For infants, a set of plastic pastel ducks ($9.98) that snap together would make for some fun baths. A great gift for a new baby might be the basket of toys with four velour animals (bear, lamb, rabbit, and duck, $14.98). Or consider the ABC soft blocks for only $14.98—we have a set and they're great!

Lilly's Kids even carries room accessories like clocks, peg racks, bedding, toy chests, and more—not to mention all the toys available for older kids. Many of the toys have an educational bent, while others have an emphasis on creativity. Overall, Lilly's Kids offers quite a wide selection of fun toys and gifts. Fortunately, most items are in the $5 to $20 range.

***Natural Baby: Alternative Products for
Children and Their Parents*** ...............................................★★
   *To Order Call:* (609) 771-9233; Fax (609) 771-9342
   (sorry, no toll free number is available).
   *Shopping Hours:* Monday-Friday 9:00 am-8:00 pm;
   Saturday 10:00 am-4:00 pm Eastern Time.
   *Or write to:* The Natural Baby Co. Inc., 816 Silvia St. 800 B-S,
   Trenton, NJ 08628.
   *Credit Cards Accepted:* MC, VISA, Discover.

The natural product craze has left no stone unturned. So, it shouldn't surprise you to find natural baby products and catalogs dedicated to environmentally-friendly babies. The Natural Baby catalog is trying to fill that niche, albeit at prices that may make the most ardent environmentalists shake their heads.

For example, you can find 100% cotton footed strechies in the Natural Baby catalog—an item we didn't see anywhere else. However, you'll pay $20 each. Perhaps this is a bargain for folks who don't want their child sleeping in polyester or nylon jammies (compare at about $12 to $15). In addition, Natural Baby also carries undyed, organic cotton children's clothes, unavailable elsewhere. Shoes, booties, socks, and 100% cotton tights round out their clothing selection. The catalog's biggest emphasis seems to be on cloth diapers and diaper covers. Diapers run $16.50 per dozen and Nikky brand diaper covers are $14.95 each. Their own brand of diaper cover sells for $3.95 each. If the thought of commercial diaper wipes is anathema to you, they offer packs of 12 washable cotton cloths for $8.95. Breastfeeding moms will find nursing gowns, bras, and reusable breast pads as well.

In addition to diapers and supplies, the catalog has car seats and covers, lambskins, toys, homeopathic medicines, and natural toiletries (shampoos, soaps, oils, etc.). We tried their remedy for cradle cap—the Natural Cradle Cap Ointment was a disappointment, however. It was expensive ($9.60 for one ounce), contained simple ingredients like vegetable and avocado oil, and, quite frankly, didn't work. Oh well, live and learn.

***One Step Ahead*** .............................................................★★★
   *To Order Call:* (800) 274-8440 or (800) 950-5120;
   Fax (708) 615-2162.
   *Shopping Hours:* 24 hours a day, seven days a week.
   *Or write to:* One Step Ahead, 950 North Shore Dr.,
   Lake Bluff, IL, 60044.
   *Credit Cards Accepted:* MC, VISA, AMEX, Discover, Optima.

Illinois-based One Step Ahead is a jack-of-all-trades catalog that covers everything from clothes to toys, car seats to organizational items. Similar to the Right Start catalog, One Step Ahead has a slightly heavier emphasis on clothing, shoes, and linens. For example, we thought their selection of shoes was excellent: suede moccasins were $14.95, and Cutiecakes brand shoes cost $7.95. For rainy climates, check out Puddleduckers vinyl boots for $14.95.

This catalog is easier to use than most because of its index, which is organized into sections such as mealtime, bath and health, auto safety, and "just for fun." Prices are very competitive compared to other catalogs (they also have a price gaurantee—One Step Ahead will match any price you see in another "children's direct mail catalog"). For example, we saw a Stroller Mate toy bar for the same price as the Right Start ($19.95). The only negative: One Step Ahead doesn't offer a frequent buyer club with additional discounts. Oh, well.

Nevertheless, One Step Ahead is a good all-around catalog. If you can't find it elsewhere, it's worth it to take a look in here. The prices are good, the selection changes frequently, and they do carry some unique items.

***Right Start Catalog*** ...................................................... ★★★★
*To Order Call:* (800) LITTLE-1 (800-548-8531);
Fax (800) 762-5501.
*Shopping Hours:* 24 hours a day, seven days a week.
*Or write to*: Right Start Inc., Right Start Plaza, 5334 Sterling Center Dr., Westlake Village, CA 91361.
*Credit Cards Accepted:* MC, VISA, AMEX, Discover.

One of our favorite catalogs, the Right Start is jam-packed with baby products—from changing tables to jogging strollers to safety products to toys. We found prices to be equal to or slightly less than regular retail stores.

One neat idea: If you think you'll be buying a lot of stuff from Right Start, consider joining their Silver Rattle Club for $50. This entitles you to a 10% discount off anything in the catalog (even during sales) for an entire year. We joined and saved $50 with our very first purchase (we bought a changing table, Thermoscan thermometer, bath products, jogging stroller, and more).

We liked their selection of strollers. They sell Aprica's CitiMini ($199) and the Century 4-in-1 carseat stroller ($149). Their section on bedding includes Lambs & Ivy's "Paradise" line ($179 for a four-piece set), as well as Beatrix Potter, Boynton for Babies, and more.

Another plus: the company's employees are amazingly helpful and friendly. The Right Start gets new items in all the time (you'll often see cutting-edge products before they hit the stores), and they have periodic sales that make the prices even more reasonable. Any new parent should be issued this catalog at the hospital—you won't be able to put it down.

## *Announcements Catalogs*

*H & F Announcements* ........................................................★★★
> *To Order Call:* (800) 964-4002; Fax (913) 752-1222.
> *Shopping Hours:* 24 hours a day, seven days a week.
> *Or write to:* H & F Announcements, 3734 W. 95th St.,
> Leawood, KS 66206.
> *Credit Cards Accepted:* MC, VISA, AMEX.

 H & F Announcements offers a mail-order birth announcement service that promises to ship within one to eight business days of receiving your order, depending on the style of invitation.

All announcements are printed on 4" x 6" or 5" x 7" cards, with your choice of pre-printed designs featuring bunnies, balloons, toys, sailboats, and more. Besides contemporary options, classic designs are also available with plain printing and no border. Another option: consider H & F's photo announcements (these take six to eight days from receipt of order). The catalog also features christening, shower, and birthday invitations.

All designs for invitations and announcements are priced the same. A minimum order of 15 is $19.75. Items are also sold in quantities of 25, 35, 50, 75, 100, and 125. An order of 50 announcements is $32.95. Prices include plain envelopes, colored ink, and 11 different type styles. Additional options are thank-you notes (50 for $18.75), your return address printed on the envelope (50 for $7.50), and ribbon tying (for some invitation styles—50 for $8.75).

If you're looking for basic and affordable baby announcements, H & F's catalog should be on your shopping list.

*Heart Thoughts* .................................................................★★
> *To Order Call:* (800) 524-2229; Fax (800) 526-2846.
> *Shopping Hours:* 24 hours. a day, seven days a week.
> *Or write to:* Heart Thoughts, 6200 E. Central #100,
> Wichita, KS 67208.
> *Credit Cards Accepted:* MC, VISA, Discover.

Heart Thoughts offers affordable baby announcements in over 100 different styles. Their recent catalog included "classic" birth announcements with black and white line drawings, formal cards with ribbon details, and the usual cutesy, cartooned designs. All are available with quick shipment—just one to two days, depending on the design (add an extra day if you want ribbons tied onto the cards).

Heart Thoughts' announcements are very affordable. At

the bottom of the price range are the "classic" designs ($22 for 50 announcements); at the top are the Royal Splendor folded cards (($115 per 50). Included in the price are colored inks and ribbons, as well as a choice of eight typefaces. For an additional $20, Heart Thoughts will even address them for you, plus print your return address on the back flap. Shipping prices are also reasonable: for example, it costs just $5.75 for second-day air shipping.

In addition to announcements, Heart Thoughts carries parenting and childbirth books, home exercise videos, and other gift items.

## Bedding Catalogs

**The Company Store** ...........................................................★★★
   *To Order Call:* (800) 285-3696 or (800) 289-8508;
   Fax (608) 784-2366.
   *Shopping Hours:* 24 hours a day, seven days a week.
   *Or write to:* The Company Store, 500 Company Store Rd.,
   La Crosse, WI 54601.
   *Credit Cards Accepted:* MC, VISA, AMEX, Discover.

 The Company Store made its reputation by producing high-quality down comforters and selling them at very reasonable prices. Although they've branched out into linens, the down comforters are still their most impressive product. Luckily, the Company Store also makes comforters for infants and children. The catalog offers four different styles, each in its own color pallette. Priced at $55 each, you can choose from pink with a teddy bear outline, white with scallops, blue with a square stitch, and yellow with a "karo step" stitch. Each design is made of 232-thread-count cotton fabric and filled with 8 ounce white down.

Other children's products offered by The Company Store include wool mattress pads and throws, crib blankets, comforter covers ($30), and sheets ($22).

We've ordered adult-size comforters and bedding from the Company Store and found the service to be very helpful. They even offer a custom-sewing service if you'd like a comforter made with your own fabric. Considering that basic comforters from traditional juvenile bedding companies can top $100, we think the Company Store offers a high-quality alternative at very affordable prices.

# Clothing Catalogs

**After the Stork** ................................................................★★★★
To Order Call: (800) 333-5437 or (505) 243-9100;
Fax (505) 243-6935.
*Shopping Hours:* 24 hours a day, seven days a week.
*Or write to:* After the Stork, 1501 12 St. NW PO Box 26200,
Albuquerque, NM 87125.
*Credit Cards Accepted:* MC, VISA, AMEX, Discover.

 After the Stork offers great prices on all-cotton children's clothing. While they may not be fancy, the clothes in here are good, well-made basics like the $18.50 Henley coverall in sizes 6 months to 4T. In three solids and one bright beach pattern, this is a perfect staple for your kids' closet. After the Stork also sells a wide assortment of socks, shoes, and hats for all the kids in the family. They even have nursing shirts, bras, and pads, as well as flannel crib sheets ($11.50).

The catalog offers a small discount on most items if you purchase two or more. For example, a basic cotton tank top is priced at $5.95, but if you buy two or more, the price drops to $4.95 each. Other clothes are discounted off "regular department store" prices. For example, we saw a sleeveless, empire-waist floral dress in sizes 2T to 6X. This dress was priced at only $12.50, compared to $22 in retail stores.

All in all, we highly recommend After the Stork. Besides being one of the few children's clothing catalogs offering discounts, the company also sizes their clothes to allow for shrinkage—a big plus. The designs may lack the pizazz of some of the other catalogs we researched, but considering how fast babies outgrow clothes, it's probably best to stick to affordable basics anyway.

**Biobottoms** ................................................................★★★★
To Order Call: (800) 766-1254; Fax (707) 778-0619.
*Shopping Hours:* Monday-Friday 5:00 am-9:00 pm;
Saturday 6:00 am-6:00 pm; Sunday 8:00 am-4:00 pm Pacific Time.
*Or write to:* Biobottoms, PO Box 6009, Petaluma, CA 94953.
*Credit Cards Accepted:* MC, VISA, AMEX, Discover.

Talk about cute! And whimsical. And 100% cotton. That's what Biobottoms is all about, with clothes for babies (newborn to 24 months), toddlers (2T to 4T), and older kids (to size 14). This California-based catalog started out selling "lamb-soft wool" diaper covers (called Biobottoms) for use with cloth diapers. Along the way, they branched into carrying colorful, 100% cotton clothing in bold patterns. The diaper covers come in two designs: the wool Biobottoms ($18 each) and their Cotton Bottoms ($14.50-$15), which combine a polyester inner layer surrounded by soft cotton. They also sell cloth diapers specifically made to fit their covers for $18-$25 per dozen and training pants for $18 per two-pack.

The bulk of the Biobottoms catalog showcases their bright, fun clothing. Check out the Cloud Coverall ($29) with matching socks ($5.50) or sunbonnet ($13) in pink or blue. Other whimsical designs included farm animal t-shirts ($15.50), gingham checked high-top tennies ($18), and plaid seersucker rompers ($26).

We purchased clothes for our son from this catalog and found them to be well made and long wearing. The items didn't shrink or fade after many washings, and our son found them very comfortable. The prices aren't a bargain, but the fun designs and high quality made them worth the purchase price.

**Brights Creek** ...............................................................★¹/₂
*To Order Call:* (800) 285-4300 or (804) 827-1850.
*Shopping Hours:* 24 hours a day, seven days a week.
*Or write to:* Brights Creek, Bay Point Place,
Hampton, VA 23653.
*Credit Cards Accepted:* MC, VISA, AMEX, Discover.

With an emphasis on good value, Brights Creek offers clothing for infants, children, and even a few items for adults. Despite the fact that their infant sizes start at size 12 months, we still think the catalog's affordable playclothes are worth a look. For example, a cotton jersey knit coverall for boys or girls was only $13.88. Brights Creek reports that the outfit retails for $20.99 (making their price a 33% discount off list). Other items offered include pull-on pants, shirts, cardigans, and dresses for as little as $3.88 (for a fleece coverall).

Unfortunately, you'll find few 100% cotton outfits. Most are polyester, acrylic, or blends.

**Children's Wear Digest**...............................................★★
*To Order Call:* (800) 242-5437; Fax (800) 762-5501.
*Shopping Hours:* 24 hours a day, seven days a week.
*Or write to:* Children's Wear Digest, 31333 Agoura Rd.,
Westlake Village, CA 91361.
*Credit Cards Accepted:* MC, VISA, AMEX, Discover.

If you're looking for name brands, check out Children's Wear Digest, a catalog that features clothes in sizes 12 months to size 14 for both boys and girls.

In a recent catalog, we saw clothes by Flapdoodles, EIEIO, Sarah's Prints, Guess, and Pattycakes. One neat design was an Earthling's "organically grown cotton romper" in a strawberry print for $34. Another interesting outfit, a striped chambray jumper with a cartoon goldfish, was $28.

Children's Wear Digest doesn't offer much of a discount off regular retail, but it does have a selection of sale clothes with savings of 15% to 25%. For example, a two-piece outfit with ruffled yellow top and plaid bloomer was $23, regularly priced at $30 (about a 20% savings).

One negative: the catalog's poor organization means you have search each page to find clothes for babies. Sections organized by age would be more helpful. Nevertheless, the majority of clothes are 100% cotton and many designs come with coordinating hats and socks for a complete look.

*Hanna Anderson* .......................................................★★★★
    *To Order Call:* (800) 222-0544; Fax (503) 222-0544.
    *Shopping Hours:* 5:00 am to 7:00 pm Pacific Time,
    seven days a week.
    *Or write to:* Hanna Anderson, 1010 NW Flanders,
    Portland, OR, 97209.
    *Credit Cards Accepted:* MC, VISA, AMEX, Discover.

There really is a Hanna. Her picture was featured in the company's recent catalog, touting their 20% credit for "Hannadowns." If your Hannas outlast your kids, you can send them back to Hanna Anderson for a 20% credit. The company donates the used items to charity.

Obviously, Hanna Anderson is not your typical catalog company. In fact, we think this is one of the best catalogs available for children's clothes. From basic layette to adult wear, they cover the gamut of clothing for your family. Their recent 76-page catalog features a mix of everyday basics and dress-up clothes, all in bright, cheerful colors. For babies, a special six-page layette section features detailed sizing information and a helpful "perfect gift" symbol to guide grandparents and friends in gift-giving. In the layette section, we liked the coordinated rosebud print pieces offered as a hooded coverup ($28), tie t-shirt ($15), and pilot cap ($8). The same pieces are also available in white at a lower price. The catalog has solid color onesies ($12.50) and "wiggle pants" for $17 to $19. What are those? These pants have extra room in the bottom for bulky cloth diapers (but unfortunately lack snaps at the crotch).

Hanna Anderson carries striped rompers and hooded coverups in addition to their unique zippered stretchie. The latter item has a zipper running the length of the outfit, from collar to ankle. For some reason, it is rare to find zippered stretchies at retail stores, so we were pleased to see Hanna carries them in three colors. Our favorite item has to be the "pilot cap" ($8). We bought a couple for our baby, and boy, are they cute! We also love all five of the bright colors, including spring green and Swedish blue.

Lest you think the catalog only carries layette garb for babies, let us reassure you that options for older children abound as well. Bright colored playclothes like plaid playsuits ($38), sweaters ($39), and even basic sweatpants ($19) make for fun shopping.

We can't say enough nice things about Hanna Anderson. You need to get this catalog!

*Maggie Moore* .....................................................................★★
To Order Call: (913) 865-0111 or (913) 865-0777; Fax ((913) 865-0999 (sorry, no toll free number is available).
*Shopping Hours:* 24 hours a day, seven days a week.
*Or write to:* Maggie Moore, 2901 Lakeview Rd., Suite C, Lawrence, KS 66049.
*Credit Cards Accepted:* MC, VISA, AMEX, Discover.

Kansas-based Maggie Moore sells attractive clothes that are in tune with the heartland. Designs are basic, with t-shirt and legging combinations, cardigans, jumpsuits, and sweats. Sizes range from 12 months up to adult.

We examined their holiday catalog and found an interesting velour dress with contrasting buttons for $45. To top it off, they show a plentiful number of hat designs including a velour "popover" with a contrasting bow. We especially liked the boy's fedora ($34). Maggie Moore excels at outdoor gear, featuring coveralls ($48), sledding suits ($35), cossack hats ($21), and winter mittens ($14) in strikingly bright colors.

Overall, the catalog showcases well-designed, traditional clothes that won't go out of style tomorrow. The majority are made of 100% cotton. Prices are in the moderate to expensive range.

*Olsen's Mill Direct* ...........................................................★★★
To Order Call: (800) 537-4979 or (800) 452-3699; Fax (414) 426-6369.
*Shopping Hours:* 7:00 am to 11:00 pm Central Time, seven days a week.
*Or write to:* Olsen's Mill Direct, 1641 S. Main St, Oshkosh, WI 54901.
*Credit Cards Accepted:* MC, VISA, Discover.

One of the best organized catalogs we've seen, Olsen's Mill Direct offers an attractive selection of such famous brands as Good Lad of Philadelphia, Hartstrings, Monster Wear, Sara's Prints, and Oshkosh. Another plus: the catalog has large photos of the clothes, so you can see what you're getting. For example, a beautiful set of matching outfits by Good Lad showed a girl's sailor dress and hat ($28-30), boy's suspendered sailor shorts ($30-32), and coordinating baby bubbles with cute hats for boys and girls ($26-30).

Although the prices seem to be about regular retail, each

catalog features several sale items. For example, a girl's OshKosh "busy body jumper" was $13 to $15 (regularly $18 to $20). One neat idea—consider coordinating overalls for grandpa and grandbaby. The catalog offers a small selection of matching overalls in adult sizes too ($31 to $40).

***Patagonia Kids***..........................................................★★*¹/₂*
    *To Order Call:* (800) 638-6464; Fax (406) 587-7078.
    *Shopping Hours:* Monday-Friday 7:00 am-7:00 pm;
    Saturday 9:00 am-5:00 pm Mountain Time.
    *Or write to:* Patagonia, Inc., 1609 Babcock St.,
    PO Box 8900, Bozeman, MT, 59715.
    *Credit Cards Accepted:* MC, VISA, AMEX, Discover.

Outdoor enthusiasts all over the country swear by Patagonia's scientifically engineered clothes and outerwear. They make clothing for skiing, mountain climbing, and kayaking—and for kids. That's right, Patagonia has a just-for-kids catalog of outdoor wear.

In their recent 40-page kids catalog, we found eight pages of clothes for what Patagonia calls "the little people." They offer synchilla (synthetic pile) clothes like cardigans ($42.50), coveralls ($40), and baby buntings ($54). We bought our baby a bunting from Patagonia and found that it had some cunning features. For example, with a flick of its zipper, it converts from a sack to an outfit with two leg openings, making it more convenient for use with a car seat. It also has a neck to knee zipper (speeding up diaper changes), flipper hands, and a hood with a drawstring. When your baby's bundled up in this, you can bet she won't get cold.

Other gear for tots includes two-piece sets of capilene long underwear ($29—flammable and not recommended as sleepwear!), flannel coveralls ($36), and fleece coveralls ($24). They even have a knit polo shirt for Junior for $22.

Although the selection of infant clothing from Patagonia is limited, the cold weather gear is unlike that from any other manufacturer.

***Playclothes*** ...................................................★★★
    *To Order Call:* (800) 362-7529 or (800) 222-7725; Fax (913)
    752-1095.
    *Shopping Hours:* 24 hours a day, seven days a week.
    *Or write to:* Playclothes, PO Box 29137, Overland Park, KS
    66201.
    *Credit Cards Accepted:* MC, VISA, AMEX, Discover.

As the name implies, Playclothes focuses on affordable, attractive, and comfortable clothing in bright, bold patterns and colors. For example, we saw an outrageously colorful coverall splashed with jungle animals for only $18. This

100% cotton outfit also had a matching baseball cap for $6. Sizes start at 12 months and go up to girls size 14 and boys size 16. Infant clothes were scattered throughout the catalog, rather than grouped into one section. Playclothes carries famous name brands, including Good Lad of Philadelphia.

Glancing through a recent catalog, we especially liked the bright animal prints and cheerful florals, such as the eye-catching giant strawberries and sunflowers on bubbles and dresses. The catalog even showcased licensed sports apparel like a Florida Marlins romper with matching hat for $25. Other teams included the Colorado Rockies, New York Yankees, and Atlanta Braves—what! No Mets?

*Storybook Heirlooms* ............................................................★
   *To Order Call:* (800) 825-6565; Fax (415) 525-2199
   *Shopping Hours:* Monday-Friday 4:00 am-9:00 pm;
   Saturday and Sunday 5:00 am-7:00 pm Pacific Time.
   *Or write to:* Storybook Heirlooms, 333 Hatch Dr.,
   Foster City, CA, 94404.
   *Credit Cards Accepted:* MC, VISA, AMEX, Discover.
   Discount Outlets: They also have two outlet stores in
   California and Nevada; call the above number for locations.

Storybook Heirlooms' theme is "timeless clothing for children." Unfortunately, you should interpret the word "timeless" to really mean "outrageously expensive." The catalog's specialty: bold floral prints with traditional styling.

For babies, we saw a boy's outfit with an argyle sweater, knit polo, knickers, and cap that priced out at an incredible $104. A baby dress embelished with crocheted lace and tiny pastel embroidery was $68. A less formal play outfit was $53—it reverses from floral to gingham check. The accompanying floppy hat ($20) was an adorable addition to the outfit.

The majority of outfits in the catalog are for older kids (toddler to girls size 14). They are also rather formal in design—not much here for the mud-puddle jumper. And if you happen to have a boy, don't count on much here for him; the focus is on girls apparel.

*Wooden Soldier* ...............................................................★
   *To Order Call:* (603) 356-7041 or (603) 356-6343;
   Fax (603) 356-3530 (sorry, no toll free number is available).
   *Shopping Hours:* Monday-Friday 8:30 am-9:00 pm;
   Saturday and Sunday 8:30 am-6:00 pm Eastern Time.
   *Or write to:* The Wooden Soldier, Kearsarge St.,
   North Conway, NH 03860.
   *Credit Cards Accepted:* MC, VISA, AMEX.

If you really need a formal outfit for your child, Wooden Soldier has the most expansive selection of children's formal-wear we've ever seen. Unfortunately, the prices are equally expansive. For example, we noted a girl's dress outfit of red velvet with plaid taffeta bows and flounce that cost a whopping $70. For the young man, a red velveteen shortall with ivory shirt was $68.

Wooden Soldier carries a few casual outfits, including an adorable Paddington Bear ensemble ($42) with corduroy shorts and a striped turtleneck. We even noticed Lanz sleepwear and an aviator's leather jacket, plus a few outfits for adults.

Overall, we were impressed with the designs in Wooden Soldier. It's fun to fantasize about outfitting your child in these gorgeous confections, but reality sets in when you note the prices and realize you're better off buying several play outfits for the cost of one of these.

## Maternity & Nursing Catalogs

**Bosom Buddies** ...............................................................★★
*To Order Call:* (914) 338-2038
*Or write to:* Bosom Buddies, PO Box 6138, Kingston, NY 12401.
*Credit Cards Accepted:* MC, VISA.

As you might have guessed from the name, this catalog features a wide selection of nursing bras and nursing gowns. For example, they have a 100% cotton underwire bra by Leading lady for $23. Another 100% cotton offering is the "pillow strap soft bra" in E to G cups ($29). The catalog also features accessories like bra pads, breast shields, and shells as well as books on childbirth, breastfeeding, and parenting. One of the more interesting offerings: Snibbs diaper covers imported from Sweden ($5.25 each).

Thumbs up for the detailed sizing information. Another plus: when we ordered from the company, we were pleased with the personal service and speedy shipping. Our only complaint: we wish they had a toll-free order number.

**Garnet Hill** ...............................................................★★
*To Order Call:* (800) 622-6216; Fax (603) 823-9578.
*Shopping Hours:* Monday-Friday 7:00 am-11:00 pm;
Saturday and Sunday 10:00 am-6:00 pm Eastern Time.
*Or write to:* Garnet Hill, 262 Main St., Franconia, NH 03580.
*Credit Cards Accepted:* MC, VISA, AMEX, Discover.

Let's be honest: Garnet Hill does not offer a lot of bargains, but they deserve mention for their line of maternity and nursing clothes, children's clothes, and children's bed linens.

This catalog's biggest selling point is that every product is made of "natural fibers," mostly cotton. Of course, the problem with Garnet Hill is you have to pay through the nose for that natural fiber content. For example, a denim maternity shirt was priced at $58 in a recent catalog. That's too much money for a shirt you're going to wear for just a few months. The rest of the maternity offerings are similarly expensive, such as leggings ($52), jumpers ($66), and knit dresses ($72).

The selection of nursing clothes is limited but includes a denim nursing shirt for $50, which I actually ordered (all in the name of research, of course). I liked the silver button detailing, and it's been fairly easy to use. Another plus: the shirt doesn't look like a nursing shirt.

The children's clothing is quite attractive, but similarly expensive. Most options are sized for toddlers and up, but a cotton flannel jumpsuit in beautiful bright checks ($33.50) was available in sizes 6 months and up. A few other outfits are sized for babies as well.

Garnet Hill also sells some infant bedding, including beautiful towels, sheets, blankets, and quilts. One standout: a set of flannel sheets with a cloud and stars motif was $44.

*Japanese Weekend*........................................................★★★★
   *To Order Call:* (415) 621-0555; Fax (415) 621-1198 (sorry, no
   toll free number is available). Ask for mail order.
   *Shopping Hours:* Monday-Friday, 9:00 am-5:00 pm Pacific Time.
   *Or write to:* Japanese Weekend, 22 Isis St.,
   San Francisco, CA 94103.
   *Credit Cards Accepted:* MC, VISA.

Japanese Weekend is a line of women's maternity clothing that emphasizes comfort. They are best known for their unusual "OK" belly-banded pants, which have a waistband that circles under your expanding tummy for support (rather than cutting across it).

In recent years, Japanese Weekend has expanded its line beyond the pants to include jumpers, tops, catsuits, nightgowns, and skirts. We really like the simple, comfortable style of the clothes and highly recommend them. The company should be commended for offering all-cotton clothing for moms-to-be and avoiding the all-too common polyester blends.

Japanese Weekend's catalog consists of spartan black and white pictures but does include detailed descriptions next to each outfit. As for prices, the OK pants are $37 (available in black, cream, navy, and red). The jumper is $65 and is available in black, navy, and red. One nice plus: Japanese Weekend will also send you a list of stores that carry their clothes (call the above number for more information). In addition, the designer has a company store in San Francisco (415-989-6667).

***La Leche League International Catalog*** ......................★★★
    *To Order Call:* (708) 519-7730; Fax (708) 455-0125.
    *Shopping Hours:* 8:00 am-3:00 pm Central Time,
    seven days a week.
    *Or write to:* La Leche League International Catalog, Order
    Department, LLLI, PO Box 1209, Franklin Park, IL 60131.
    *Credit Cards Accepted:* MC, VISA.

It ain't glossy, it ain't slick, but La Leche League
International's catalog is a treasure trove of information and
breastfeeding products. Dozens of books are featured, from
such notable authors as Dr. William Sears, Sheila Kitzinger,
and the La Leche League founders. La Leche Leagues' own
Womanly Art of Breastfeeding lists at $9.95. For dads, con-
sider Dr. William Sears' Becoming a Father: How to Nurture
and Enjoy Your Family for $8.95. Most products seem to be
reasonably priced, and if you're a La Leche League member,
they offer you a 10% discount on your orders.

Pithy, capsulated reviews make the catalog especially useful. We like the special sections highlighting childbirth, working mothers, parenting, and "food & fun." In addition to
books, the catalog features videos, tapes, gift items (such as
slings), and breastpumps.

In summary, this catalog is a great comprehensive resource
for breastfeeding families.

***Motherwear*** ...................................................................★★★
    *To Order:* (800) 633-0303, (413) 586-3488; Fax (413) 586-2712
    *Shopping Hours:* Monday-Thursday 9:00 am-8:00 pm;
    Friday and Saturday 9:00 am-5:00 pm.
    *Or write to:* Motherwear, Order Department, PO Box 114,
    Northampton, MA 01061.
    *Credit Cards Accepted:* MC, VISA, Discover.
    *Discount Outlet:* Northampton, MA (413) 586-2175.

The Motherwear catalog sells a wide selection of nursing
clothes, from dresses to casual wear. You can even find a few
matching baby outfits.

Motherwear is one of the few nursing clothing catalogs
that doesn't sacrifice style for convience. For example, we
saw a beautiful floral print dress in navy, red, green, and gold
($89) in a recent catalog. This dress had lace collar detailing
and drop-waist styling. The nursing openings are cleverly dis-
guised in a vertical panel with side access. The catalog also
contains a wide variety of casual tops, such as turtlenecks,
flannel shirts, and t-shirts. I purchased one of their flannel
shirts ($56) with a horizontal button placket across the front.
While the quality of the garment was excellent, I found it difficult to get the buttons undone quickly—especially with a
squirming, hungry child in my lap.

The most useful clothes in Motherwear are probably the tops that allow you to lift up a top panel to expose a slit down the front. This style seems speedier to open and makes it easier to position the baby. The side entry or the button placket designs don't seem to work as well.

Motherwear also carries various supplies, books, and videos on breastfeeding, as well as a few coordinating children's outfits. They even have Nikky diaper covers and Bumkins all-in-one diapers. Another nice plus: each catalog comes with a newsletter full of the most up-to-date information and resources on breastfeeding.

Overall, while we liked the catalog's emphasis on style, we were somewhat disappointed with the prices. The shirts especially seem out in the stratosphere—starting at $36 for a short-sleeve, jersey style with collar. Ouch! I'd rather spend less in a retail store for a top whose front I can just pull up or unbutton.

*Mother's Place* ...............................................................★★★
   *To Order Call:* (800) 829-0080 or (216) 826-1712.
   *Shopping Hours:* Monday-Friday 8:00 am-10:00 pm;
   Saturday 9:00 am-8:00 pm.
   *Or write to:* Mother's Place, 6836 Engle Rd., PO Box 94512,
   Cleveland, OH 44101.
   *Credit Cards Accepted:* MC, VISA, Discover.

Mother's Place maternity catalog claims to save mothers-to-be up to a whopping 50% off the cost of maternity clothes. Such a hefty discount commanded our attention.

At a slim 13 pages, the catalog is nevertheless crammed full of maternity outfits, most suited for career dressing. The cover featured a two-piece outfit with white collar and white accent buttons in a poly/rayon blend. Priced at only $35.99 (regularly $49.99), the outfit seemed like a great deal. Other designs ranged from smock tops and leggings, to jackets and pleated skirts. The standard drop-waisted jumpers (like a striped chambray number for $24.99) are there, as is the occasional party dress (a burgundy two-piece dress with white lace collar was a standout for only $34.99).

It's obvious that those prices are fantastic. Our only complaint is the heavy use of synthetic and blended fabrics—it would have been nice to see more cotton offerings.

me. Offerings include stretchies,
loor gear like hats, buntings, and
d stretchie with front snaps was
ble in any fabric, with or without
yles (as well as in gender-neutral
e available in either one, two, or
price from $7.95 to $19.95.
miewear? The discounts. For
multiple birth and "grandma"
5%. Also, several combination
sleepers with blankets for exam-
t 5%.
atalog only provides one small
making it difficult to see the col-
They do include line drawings of

with owner Sandi Howser and
d helpful. The catalog offers good
at preemies, including tips on how
ld be helpful for the uninitiated.

...........................................★★★
852 or (410) 876-9071.
a day, seven days a week.
ild Clothing Co., PO Box 245,

, VISA.

ning catalog was inspired by the
ter. Born prematurely at 24 weeks
ound, four ounces, their daughter
doll clothes. In an effort to improve
parents of preemies, they started

ce selection of clothes, from sleep-
essy christening outfits—all in pre-
r example, stretchies in several dif-
embroidery and lace accents, cost
o cotton rompers were priced at
e three-piece outfits of overalls, cap,
rand names include Little Me and

e available, such as Carter's t-shirts,
nnel pajamas just for preemies. That
a number of books on premature
infant massage. A neat book to con-
*ger Than My Teddy Bear* by Valerie

of options for preemies at h
bubbles, and dresses, plus out
jackets. For example, a foote
$14.95. The garment is availa
mittens, and in boy or girl s
prints). Receiving blankets a
three-layer fabric and range in

The best part about Pr
example, premiewear offer
discounts of about 5% to
packages of clothes (pairing
ple) are also discounted abo

The one negative: the
photo of the different styles
ors and patterns available.
each garment, however.

We spoke on the phon
found her to be friendly an
advice and information abo
to clothe babies, which sho

*That Lucky Child*...............
To Order Call: (800) 755-
Shopping Hours: 24 hours
Or write to: That Lucky C
Hunt Valley, MD 21030.
Credit Cards Accepted: M

That Lucky Child clot
birth of the owners' daugh
and weighing only one p
first wore Cabbage Patch
the options available for
That Lucky Child.

The catalog offers a n
wear to playclothes to dr
emie to newborn sizes. F
ferent prints, some with
$11.95 to $16.95. 100
$15.95 each, and adorab
and shirt were $21.95.
Something Precious.

Basic clothing items a
drawstring gowns, and fla
Lucky Child also carrie
babies, breastfeeding, and
sider for siblings is No B
Pankow for $4.95.

of options for preemies at home. Offerings include stretchies, bubbles, and dresses, plus outdoor gear like hats, buntings, and jackets. For example, a footed stretchie with front snaps was $14.95. The garment is available in any fabric, with or without mittens, and in boy or girl styles (as well as in gender-neutral prints). Receiving blankets are available in either one, two, or three-layer fabric and range in price from $7.95 to $19.95.

The best part about Premiewear? The discounts. For example, premiewear offers multiple birth and "grandma" discounts of about 5% to 15%. Also, several combination packages of clothes (pairing sleepers with blankets for example) are also discounted about 5%.

The one negative: the catalog only provides one small photo of the different styles, making it difficult to see the colors and patterns available. They do include line drawings of each garment, however.

We spoke on the phone with owner Sandi Howser and found her to be friendly and helpful. The catalog offers good advice and information about preemies, including tips on how to clothe babies, which should be helpful for the uninitiated.

*That Lucky Child*.............................................................★★★
   *To Order Call:* (800) 755-4852 or (410) 876-9071.
   *Shopping Hours:* 24 hours a day, seven days a week.
   *Or write to:* That Lucky Child Clothing Co., PO Box 245,
   Hunt Valley, MD 21030.
   *Credit Cards Accepted:* MC, VISA.

That Lucky Child clothing catalog was inspired by the birth of the owners' daughter. Born prematurely at 24 weeks and weighing only one pound, four ounces, their daughter first wore Cabbage Patch doll clothes. In an effort to improve the options available for parents of preemies, they started That Lucky Child.

The catalog offers a nice selection of clothes, from sleepwear to playclothes to dressy christening outfits—all in preemie to newborn sizes. For example, stretchies in several different prints, some with embroidery and lace accents, cost $11.95 to $16.95. 100% cotton rompers were priced at $15.95 each, and adorable three-piece outfits of overalls, cap, and shirt were $21.95. Brand names include Little Me and Something Precious.

Basic clothing items are available, such as Carter's t-shirts, drawstring gowns, and flannel pajamas just for preemies. That Lucky Child also carries a number of books on premature babies, breastfeeding, and infant massage. A neat book to consider for siblings is *No Bigger Than My Teddy Bear* by Valerie Pankow for $4.95.

**MothersWork** ................................................................★★
> *To Order Call:* (800) 825-2286 or (215) 625-9259;
> Fax (215) 440-9845.
> *Shopping Hours:* 24 hours a day, seven days a week.
> *Or write to:* MothersWork, 1309 Noble St., 6th Floor, Dept. PG,
> Philadelphia, PA 19123.
> *Credit Cards Accepted:* MC, VISA, AMEX.

You won't find any polyester pants in MothersWork, the catalog division of the upscale maternity chain. But, if it's style you want for maternity clothes (and price isn't much of an object), that's what you'll get.

For example, the catalog features the perfect career option for pregnant moms: three-piece suit and companion pieces. The three pieces include a 100% wool-crepe cardigan jacket ($148), a long-sleeve white blouse ($54), and a wool-crepe "adjuster" skirt ($88). Companion pieces ranged from a pleated slip skirt ($74) to maternity pants ($78). The catalog claims that some of the pieces can even be worn after pregnancy. At these prices, it sure would be nice—but don't bet on it.

MothersWork offers evening designs, like a red crepe evening dress with pearl-decorated neckline. As far as the casual clothes go, we liked the black knit jumpsuit with stirrups ($88) and a black and white checked swing top ($74).

These prices are steep, but if your career requires an investment in stylish maternity clothes and you don't have a decent maternity shop nearby, MothersWork's catalog might be the answer.

## Clothes for Premature Babies

**Premiewear** ................................................................★★★★
> *To Order Call:* (800) 992-8469 or (208) 733-0442.
> *Shopping Hours:* 24 hours a day, seven days a week.
> *Or write to:* Premiewear, 3258 E. Ridge Place,
> Twin Falls, ID 83301.
> *Credit Cards Accepted:* MC, VISA.

 For parents of premature babies, there just aren't a lot of clothing options. A typical department store usually has a very small selection of clothes for premies. But there is good news: we found a fantastic catalog for parents of preemies that offers great selection at reasonable prices.

Premiewear starts off the catalog with their Neonatal Intensive Care Unit line of clothes. These are for hospitalized babies weighing from 2 to 4.5 pounds. We saw t-shirts, gowns, sleepers, and caps that ranged from $3 for the caps to $16.25 for a sleeper. Next, Premiewear showcases a wide variety

# Safety Catalogs

*Perfectly Safe* .................................................★★★ *1/2*
To Order Call: (800) 837-5437; Fax (216) 494-0265.
*Shopping Hours:* Monday-Friday 7:30 am-10:00 pm;
Saturday 9:00 am-7:00 pm; Sunday 10:00 am-6:00 pm Eastern Time.
*Or write to:* The Perfectly Safe Catalog,
7245 Whipple Ave. NW, North Canton, OH, 44720.
*Credit Cards Accepted:* MC, VISA, AMEX.

 This catalog "for parents that care" is an award-winning publication developed by the author of *The Perfectly Safe Home* book (available in the catalog as well, of course).

Perfectly Safe's latest catalog features over 70 products to "keep your children safe and healthy." A handy index spotlights such topics as the nursery, kitchen, bathroom, toys, windows and doors, and even educational software. We like the extensive kitchen safety section, which includes stove guards, appliance latches, and cabinet locks. There's even a device to check to see if your microwave leaks radiation ($7.95). Another interesting product: a "choke tester" for $2.50. This gadget enables you to test toys to see if they present a choking hazard.

Prices may be a bit high—for example, the Thermoscan thermometer (which takes your baby's temperature instantly via the ear canal) was $119.95 (routinely sold for about $100, and if you're lucky, as low as $80 on sale). While most products are quite practical, others are somewhat frivolous. The "Baby Watch" is a "personal video observations system" with camera and 5-inch black and white monitor. Cost: $299.95.

Despite these transgressions, Perfectly Safe is the most comprehensive catalog of safety items available. It's not the cheapest, but the selection is hard to beat.

*R.C. Steele Wholesale Pet Equipment* ........................★★★★
To Order Call: (800) 872-3773 or (800) 872-4506.
*Shopping Hours:* Monday-Friday 8:00 am-8:00 pm;
Saturdays 8:30 am-5:00 pm; Sunday 10:00 am-
4:00 pm Eastern Time.
*Or write to:* R.C. Steele, 1989 Transit Way Box 910,
Brockport, NY 14420.
*Credit Cards Accepted:* MC, VISA.

R.C. Steele's pet supply catalog may seem like a strange addition to a book on baby products, but we've found they have some of the best catalog prices on safety gates. For example, the Gerry Walk-Thru gate was only $38.34 in R.C.

Steele—the regular retail price is $70. A General Cage Gate was only $24.87 in R.C. Steele, while the same type of gate from Hand in Hand Professional (800-872-3841) was $35. Looking for a basic, pressure-mounted gate? R.C. Steele has one for $14.37. We've seen the same gate in stores for $30 or more!

The only disadvantage to R. C. Steele is their policy requiring a minimum order of $50 worth of merchandise. If you need more than one gate or have a dog or cat friend who'd like some new toys, it shouldn't be too hard to meet this minimum!

*Safety Zone* ...................................................................★★★
> *To Order Call:* (800) 999-3030; Fax (800) 338-1635.
> *Shopping Hours:* 24 hours a day, seven days a week.
> *Or write to:* The Safety Zone, Hanover, PA 17333.
> *Credit Cards Accepted:* MC, VISA, AMEX, Discover.

Finally a catalog for the hypochondriac in all of us.

The Safety Zone is not just a catalog for kids' safety products but also covers everything from travel safety (including a hotel door alarm), to personal health items (a monitor to test your fat), to car and home safety. Within its pages, however, there are quite a few items that may be useful for parents. For example, in the personal health section, Safety Zone offers the Thermoscan thermometer for only $89. Considering we've seen it in other catalogs for as much as $120, this is quite a good deal.

Other items we noted included wireless intercoms, portable safety vests, and traditional kid-proofing products. For example, they carry four different kinds of safety gates, including the Safety 1st Safe Keeper Security Gate for $35. A neat item we hadn't noticed in any other catalog was a replacement high chair strap for $6.95. However, many products available through the Safety Zone were less expensive elsewhere. For example, a set of two sliding outlet covers was $7.95 (or $4 each). In the Right Start, we priced them at $14.95 for four covers (or $3.75 each). But, if you buy two or more sets from Right Start, the price decreases to $12.95 for four (or $3.24 each).

One of the best safety items we saw in the Safety Zone were the magnetic "Tot Loks." These are cabinet locks that open with a magnetic key. They aren't cheap ($14.94 for three locks and one key), but they sure beat out the typical drawer safety latches on the market.

All in all, we strongly recommend the Safety Zone. While the prices aren't always the lowest, the sheer variety of safety products makes it a good read.

## Toys and Entertainment Catalogs

***Constructive Playthings*** .......................................................★
   *To Order Call:* (800) 832-0572 or (816) 761-5900;
   Fax (816) 761-9295.
   *Shopping Hours:* 24 hours a day, seven days a week.
   *Or write to:* Constructive Playthings, 1227 E. 119th St.,
   Grandview, MO 64030.
   *Credit Cards Accepted:* MC, VISA, AMEX, Discover.
   Retail Outlets: They have six stores; call the phone
   number above for a location near you.

 Poor organization soured our opinion of the Constructive Playthings catalog. Although they do offer a selection of toys for infants and toddlers, it takes some looking to actually find them. The catalog is so cluttered that it takes the fun out of shopping.

In the baby section, we found the usual black and white rattles, crib toys, and musical products. More out of the ordinary was the Activity Bear, a plush polar bear with a variety of toys attached to "stimulate development" ($29.95). In addition, a musical jack-in-the-box ($14.95) and soft blocks ($12.75) were two infant toys that stood out. This catalog may be more useful for older children.

***Great Kids Company*** .......................................................★★★
   *To Order Call:* (800) 533-2166 or (800) 582-1493;
   Fax (919) 766-9782
   *Shopping Hours:* 24 hours a day, seven days a week.
   *Or write to:* The Great Kids Co., PO Box 609,
   Lewisville, NC, 27023.
   *Credit Cards Accepted:* MC, VISA, AMEX, Discover.

Great Kids Company is an educational toys catalog with the theme "quality products for educating today's kids." This 36-page publication focuses mostly on older children but does have a three-page spread called "Great Beginnings," which spotlights toys for younger children.

Toys are well priced. For example, the popular nine-piece My First Playset is $14.50—we saw it in another catalog for $15.95. Another toy we liked was the activity pots and pans set for $14.95. These six stackable pots and pans incorporate mirrors, rattles, and see-through bottoms. Toys range in age from three months to three years old.

The organization of Great Kids is excellent—the age appropriate listings make shopping easy. And the prices are very reasonable.

*Hand in Hand Professional* ......................................★★★★.
  *To Order Call:* (800) 872-3841; Fax (207) 539-4415.
  *Shopping Hours:* Monday-Friday 8:00 am-5:00 pm Eastern Time.
  *Or write to:* Hand in Hand Professional Catalogue Center,
  Route 26, R.R. 1 Box 1425, Oxford, ME 04270.
  *Credit Cards Accepted:* MC, VISA, AMEX, Discover.

Here's one of the best catalogs of toys for babies, infants, and toddlers. Maine-based Hand in Hand Professional features a wide variety of mainly educational products that you just can't find everywhere. For example, the Puzzle Path ($109.95) is a set of colored cushions that make into a three-foot circular jig-saw puzzle. The Penguin and Toucan Proppers ($29.95 each) are cute cushions that help prop up infants.

The catalog's organization is excellent—easy-to-find sections highlight such categories as art, music, bath toys, and the obligatory Barney products. The "All Through the Night" section features a selection of items such as a Moon Night Light ($14.95) and bedtime boardbooks. In "Places to Go," we saw strollers, toys, car seat boosters, and more. There are even safety items, organizational products, and a wide variety of books.

Perhaps the best thing about the Hand in Hand Professional catalog is their large selection of educational toys. For example, the "Puzzling Panda" ($19.95) is a rocking rattle toy and three dimensional puzzle for "laughter and learning." Age appropriate information is provided for each item.

The prices are moderate to high—in line with the Right Start catalog (whose prices are about the same as regular retail). All in all, we recommend Hand in Hand Professional as one of the best mail-order catalogs for moms and dads-to-be.

*Music For Little People* ...............................................★★★★
  *To Order Call:* (800) 727-2233; Fax (707) 923-3241.
  *Or Write to:* Music for Little People, PO Box 1460,
  Redway, CA 95560.
  *Credit Cards Accepted:* MC, VISA, AMEX, Discover.

Music for Little People is at the top of our list of children's catalogs. We love the huge selection of audiotapes, CDs, and videos, as well as the extensive collection of musical instruments—from electric guitars to harmonicas to autoharps.

One of our favorite sections is "Earth Beat," which "explores the music, legends, traditional instruments, games and wonders of this endlessly diverse planet." A sampling of the products in this section: a Taos hoop drum ($36 for unpainted, $60 for painted), the "Shake It to the One That You Love the Best" audiotape of songs and lullabies from

African musical traditions ($15.98 with songbook), and the Magical Marimbas ($118 to $230).

Music for Little People carries wonderful modern tape and CD standards by Peter, Paul and Mary, as well as classical selections by Beethoven, Tchaikovsky, and Mozart, to name a few. Even Joe Scruggs, one of our favorite children's artists, has a tape in this catalog ("Deep in the Jungle," $10). If you like this cassette, you'll love the rest of his tapes (available from Baby on a Budget, 800-575-2224).

Lest you think Music for Little People is exclusively about music, we also noted nature t-shirts, videotapes, puppets, books, and more.

The catalog is extremely well laid out and colorful, drawing you on to the next page with the promise of more unique products. We found ourselves immediately making lists of which tapes we wanted to order and which videos our child would be ready to watch in the near future. All the products have information on age appropriateness. As a side note, they also have a larger, more complete catalog of everything they carry. So if you don't see it in their regular catalog, call and ask.

Questions or comments? Did you discover a bargain you'd like to share with our readers? **Call the authors at (303) 442-8792!**

# Chapter 12

*Conclusion:*
*What Does it All Mean?*

**H**ow much money can you save if you follow all the tips and suggestions in this book? Let's take a look at the average cost of having a baby from the introduction and compare it with our "Baby Bargains" budget.

## Your Baby's First Year

|  | AVERAGE | BABY BARGAINS BUDGET |
|---|---|---|
| Crib, dresser, changing table, rocker | $1500 | $1100 |
| Bedding | $250 | $135 |
| Baby Clothes | $500 | $350 |
| Disposable Diapers | $800 | $300 |
| Maternity/Nursing Clothes | $1300 | $775 |
| Nursery items, high chair, toys | $400 | $225 |
| Baby Food/Formula | $300 | $250 |
| Stroller, Car Seat, Carrier | $200 | $140 |
| Miscellaneous | $500 | $500 |
| **TOTAL** | **$5750** | **$3775** |
| **TOTAL SAVINGS:** | **$1975** | |

**WOW! YOU CAN SAVE NEARLY $2000!**

We hope the savings makes it worth the price of this book. We'd love to hear from you on how much you saved with our book—feel free to write or call the authors at (303) 442-8792.

Of course, we should note a couple of points about the above list. In most cases, the Baby Bargains budget comes directly from the "Bottom Line" section of each chapter.

In some cases, we had to estimate the annual cost of the savings. For example, disposable diapers requires some math (sorry, we had no choice). We assumed you'll use 2000 diapers for the 1st six months (11 per day) and then 1080 for the last six months (6 diapers per day). The total is 3080 diapers for one year. (You use fewer diapers in the latter half of the first year since the baby's poops are more firm after six months of age.)

The "average" figure was estimated at 25¢ per diaper, which is the approximate price that disposable diapers cost at grocery stores. The "Baby Bargains" budget was 15¢ per diaper, about the cost of diapers through our discount sources.

Baby food is probably the trickiest item to figure the savings. We assumed you'd breastfeed the baby for six months (supplementing with a bottle from time to time, of course) and then feed him commercially-prepared solid foods until age one. Most of the "natural" baby food we recommend costs more than commercially prepared baby food. However, there would be some savings if you tried making your own baby food with the advice of some of the books we recommend.

Of course, one of the biggest bargains is deciding to nurse your baby, instead of using formula. We figure you'd save $400 in the first six months alone by breastfeeding!

## *What does it all mean?*

A funny thing happened today with our baby. For the last several weeks, he's been "talking" with a few cute syllables and words like "da-da." Well, yesterday he discovered the volume control. Now, instead of saying "Da-da, Ahhiee, Ba-Ba," he says "DA-DA, AHHIEE! BA-BAAA!" while thumping his fist on the table for added emphasis.

What's the lesson? We're not quite sure, but if we had to put into words, it would probably be something like "things change, sometimes overnight." Flexibility is the key to making this parenting thing work. The same applies to shopping for baby—be flexible and give some of the money-saving ideas a chance.

Certainly, you'll get endless words of advice from friends and relatives. They'll insist you only consider this brand or that product. Nod your head in agreement and then do what you think is best for you and your baby.

And remember the one universal truth about having a baby: "It'll change your life."

# About The Authors

# by Benjamin Fields

As the 9-month old son of the authors, I suppose I was the publisher's natural choice to write the "About the Authors" section. Who else spends more time with the writers than me? Well, I'd like to say that negotiations dragged on for days. The publisher was worried that no one would believe that a baby could actually string together six words in a sentence, much less compose a thoughtful and respectable biographical portrait of the authors (my parents). "Look, even great writers like Ernest Hemmingway and Dave Barry didn't write before they were five years old?" they said. And I replied, "Yeah, but they probably weren't breastfed."

Finally, we got to the the heart of the matter: compensation. The publisher offered me three book choices and a toy to be named later, before finally saying, "Do you want a cookie?" And I said, "Do fish swim?"

So here I am writing this thoughtful and respectable "About the Authors" section. Let's start with my mother, Denise Fields. She grew up in Loveland, Colorado, a town I have visited and have to say looks relatively normal on the surface. Denise (a.k.a. Mom) went to the University of Colorado and majored in Elizabethan English History, a fact I intend to remind her of when I announce my college major: Advanced Computer Game Theory.

While studying at dear old CU, my mom met my dad, Alan Fields. Alan is from Dallas, Texas, or so I'm told. I've only visited this place once and it was, to borrow a phrase from Neil Simon, hot. Africa hot. While we were there, we visited a Mexican restaurant called Zuzu's. That name struck a bell—I remembered that our dog is named Zuzu. This came as somewhat of a disappointment since I always thought our dog was named after the four-wheel drive sport utility vehicle.

Anyway, Mom and Dad got their start writing weddings guides in Austin, Texas, another place I don't care to visit in the summer. Apparently, my parents became quite the experts at weddings and went on to write a national best-selling book called Bridal Bargains. I should say it was first just a "book," with the prefix "best-selling" added one day in June 1991. That was the month a producer from the Oprah Winfrey Show called and invited Dad and Mom to be guests on the show. They tell me life improved dramatically after that.

Next, Mom and Dad wrote a book called Your New House: The Alert Consumer's Guide to Buying and Building a Quality Home. I took particular offense at the chapter that skewered real estate agents. "But I play with real estate agents every day in the backyard." I told Dad last week. "No, son," he said. "Those aren't real estate agents. They're just regular, garden-variety slugs." Just kidding.

Anyway, Mom and Dad moved back to Boulder in 1993. I was born shortly thereafter. End of story. Can I have my cookie now?

# Index

# Notes

# Notes

# Notes

# Bridal Bargains

# "Far & Away Weddings"

## Another book by the Fields!

*Want to get married on a tropical beach?*

*How about in an 800-year old castle?*

OR do you want to tie the knot back in a home-town that's across the country? How can you plan a wonderful wedding "long distance"? Find the answers in this new, paperback guide by the authors of "Bridal Bargains"! Inside this 225 page book, you'll learn:

- ♣ THE INSIDE SCOOP on over 25 exotic spots to tie the knot!

- ♣ SURPRISING STRATEGIES FOR FINDING WEDDING STORES and services "long distance."

- ♣ TRICKS FOR DEALING WITH "SURROGATE PLANNERS" (Mom and other well-meaning friends and relatives).

- ♣ WHAT YOU CAN DO IN YOUR "HOME CITY"—it's more than you think!

- ♣ IN-DEPTH "BATTLE PLANS" for those brief trips to the "wedding city"—suggested schedules for meeting with the most wedding merchants in the shortest period of time!

- ♣ CREATIVE IDEAS FOR COORDINATING far-flung bridesmaids and groomsmen!

- ♣ TIPS ON HIRING and working with wedding consultants and planners.

- ♣ INNOVATIVE WAYS TO USE TECHNOLOGY such as fax machines and video cameras to ease the planning process.

- ♣ And, of course, COST-CUTTING TIPS for holding down expenses!

$8.95

## Call (800) 888-0385 to Order!

First-class shipping is $3 extra—overnight service is available!
MasterCard, Visa, American Express and Discover Accepted!

# How to Reach Us

*Have a question about*
## Baby Bargains?

*Want to make a suggestion?*
*Discovered a great bargain you'd like to share?*

*Contact the Authors, Denise & Alan Fields*
*in one of four ways:*

*1. By phone*
*(303) 442-8792.*

*2. By mail*
*1223 Peakview Circle,*
*Suite 600,*
*Boulder, CO 80302*

*3. By fax*
*(303) 442-3744.*

*4. By e-mail*
*Our address is*
*adfields@aol.com.*

*Coming soon: our Web Home Page!*
*Call or e-mail us for the address!*

# Call for Updates!

C ALL 1-900-988-7295 TO GET THE LATEST UPDATES ON BABY BARGAINS. Things change quickly in the juvenile products business. By calling our special phone line (which is updated bi-monthly), you'll stay on top of any changes.

# 1-900-988-7295

## You'll hear about:

♣ New companies and services that were recommended by moms and dads.

♣ Hints and tips from our readers.

♣ Corrections and clarifications in our book (hey, we're only human!)

♣ The latest in baby news and trends.

♣ And much more!

### So, if you want the latest news on Baby Bargains, call 1-900-988-7295.

All this for just 75¢ per minute! The average message is four to eight minutes in length. Available 24 hours a day from any touch-tone phone, our Update Hotline will keep you current! *(This is a toll call that will be billed to your local phone bill. Using a touch-tone phone, you can easily access updates for any of our books)*. **Coming soon:** get updates via any fax machine or our home page on the Web. Call our office number on the previous page for more info!

# Join Our Preferred Reader List

*We've got lots of new books and special reports coming out over the next few years! Just jot down your name and address below, mail in the coupon and we'll keep you up-to-date!*

*Best of all, we have "early bird" DISCOUNTS especially for BABY BARGAINS preferred readers!*

------------------------------------------------------------------

Name _____

Address _____

City _____ State_____ Zip_____

Baby's Name & Birthdate _____

How did you hear about our book?_____

_____

What was your favorite section or tip? _____

_____

How can we improve this book? _____

_____

_____

_____

## Mail To:

### BABY BARGAINS
*1223 Peakview Circle*
*Boulder, CO 80302*

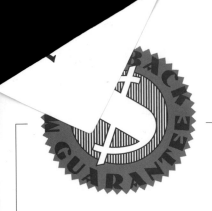

*MothersWork* ........................................................★★
*To Order Call:* (800) 825-2286 or (215) 625-9259;
Fax (215) 440-9845.
*Shopping Hours:* 24 hours a day, seven days a week.
*Or write to:* MothersWork, 1309 Noble St., 6th Floor, Dept. PG,
Philadelphia, PA 19123.
*Credit Cards Accepted:* MC, VISA, AMEX.

You won't find any polyester pants in MothersWork, the catalog division of the upscale maternity chain. But, if it's style you want for maternity clothes (and price isn't much of an object), that's what you'll get.

For example, the catalog features the perfect career option for pregnant moms: three-piece suit and companion pieces. The three pieces include a 100% wool-crepe cardigan jacket ($148), a long-sleeve white blouse ($54), and a wool-crepe "adjuster" skirt ($88). Companion pieces ranged from a pleated slip skirt ($74) to maternity pants ($78). The catalog claims that some of the pieces can even be worn after pregnancy. At these prices, it sure would be nice—but don't bet on it.

MothersWork offers evening designs, like a red crepe evening dress with pearl-decorated neckline. As far as the casual clothes go, we liked the black knit jumpsuit with stirrups ($88) and a black and white checked swing top ($74).

These prices are steep, but if your career requires an investment in stylish maternity clothes and you don't have a decent maternity shop nearby, MothersWork's catalog might be the answer.

## *Clothes for Premature Babies*

*Premiewear* ................................................★★★★
*To Order Call:* (800) 992-8469 or (208) 733-0442.
*Shopping Hours:* 24 hours a day, seven days a week.
*Or write to:* Premiewear, 3258 E. Ridge Place,
Twin Falls, ID 83301.
*Credit Cards Accepted:* MC, VISA.

 For parents of premature babies, there just aren't a lot of clothing options. A typical department store usually has a very small selection of clothes for premies. But there is good news: we found a fantastic catalog for parents of preemies that offers great selection at reasonable prices.

Premiewear starts off the catalog with their Neonatal Intensive Care Unit line of clothes. These are for hospitalized babies weighing from 2 to 4.5 pounds. We saw t-shirts, gowns, sleepers, and caps that ranged from $3 for the caps to $16.25 for a sleeper. Next, Premiewear showcases a wide variety of options for preemies at home. Offerings include stretchies, bubbles, and dresses, plus outdoor gear like hats, buntings, and jackets. For example, a footed stretchie with front snaps was $14.95. The garment is available in any fabric, with or without mittens, and in boy or girl styles (as well as in gender-neutral prints). Receiving blankets are available in either one, two, or three-layer fabric and range in price from $7.95 to $19.95.

The best part about Premiewear? The discounts. For example, premiewear offers multiple birth and "grandma" discounts of about 5% to 15%. Also, several combination packages of clothes (pairing sleepers with blankets for example) are also discounted about 5%.

The one negative: the catalog only provides one small photo of the different styles, making it difficult to see the colors and patterns available. They do include line drawings of each garment, however.

We spoke on the phone with owner Sandi Howser and found her to be friendly and helpful. The catalog offers good advice and information about preemies, including tips on how to clothe babies, which should be helpful for the uninitiated.

*That Lucky Child*.............................................................★★★
*To Order Call:* (800) 755-4852 or (410) 876-9071.
*Shopping Hours:* 24 hours a day, seven days a week.
*Or write to:* That Lucky Child Clothing Co., PO Box 245,
Hunt Valley, MD 21030.
*Credit Cards Accepted:* MC, VISA.

That Lucky Child clothing catalog was inspired by the birth of the owners' daughter. Born prematurely at 24 weeks and weighing only one pound, four ounces, their daughter first wore Cabbage Patch doll clothes. In an effort to improve the options available for parents of preemies, they started That Lucky Child.

The catalog offers a nice selection of clothes, from sleepwear to playclothes to dressy christening outfits—all in preemie to newborn sizes. For example, stretchies in several different prints, some with embroidery and lace accents, cost $11.95 to $16.95. 100% cotton rompers were priced at $15.95 each, and adorable three-piece outfits of overalls, cap, and shirt were $21.95. Brand names include Little Me and Something Precious.

Basic clothing items are available, such as Carter's t-shirts, drawstring gowns, and flannel pajamas just for preemies. That Lucky Child also carries a number of books on premature babies, breastfeeding, and infant massage. A neat book to consider for siblings is *No Bigger Than My Teddy Bear* by Valerie Pankow for $4.95.